Best Wishes!

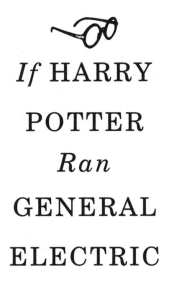

If HARRY

POTTER

Ran

GENERAL

ELECTRIC

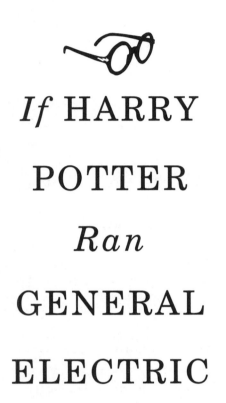

If HARRY POTTER *Ran* GENERAL ELECTRIC

LEADERSHIP WISDOM FROM THE WORLD OF THE WIZARDS

TOM MORRIS

CURRENCY

DOUBLEDAY

NEW YORK   LONDON   TORONTO   SYDNEY   AUCKLAND

A CURRENCY BOOK
PUBLISHED BY DOUBLEDAY

Copyright © 2006 by Tom Morris

All Rights Reserved

Published in the United States by Doubleday, an imprint of The Doubleday
Broadway Publishing Group, a division of Random House, Inc., New York.
www.currencybooks.com

CURRENCY is a trademark of Random House, Inc., and
DOUBLEDAY is a registered trademark of Random House, Inc.

All trademarks are the property of their respective companies.

Cataloging-in-Publication Data is on file with the Library of Congress

ISBN-13: 978-0-385-51754-6
ISBN-10: 0-385-51754-8

PRINTED IN THE UNITED STATES OF AMERICA

SPECIAL SALES
Currency Books are available at special discounts for bulk purchases for sales
promotions or premiums. Special editions, including personalized covers,
excerpts of existing books, and corporate imprints, can be created in large
quantities for special needs. For more information, write to Special Markets,
Currency Books, specialmarkets@randomhouse.com

3 5 7 9 10 8 6 4 2

"Are all your family wizards?" asked Harry, who found Ron just as interesting as Ron found him.

"Er—yes, I think so," said Ron. "I think Mom's got a second cousin who's an accountant, but we never talk about him."

CONTENTS

ACKNOWLEDGMENTS

I want to thank two fellow philosophers who first suggested that I should read Harry Potter: Professor David Baggett of Kings College and Dr. Jerry Walls, Senior Fellow in the Morris Institute for Human Values and Professor at Asbury Theological Seminary. They launched me into the adventure of great fun and insight that resulted in this book. Dave also provided extensive comments on my first draft and helped make it better. He has a great editor's eye for detail and a profound philosopher's sensibility, both of which are on display in his excellent book *Harry Potter and Philosophy*. Dr. Stephanie Richardson and Renee Vincent also helped me improve this book. I'm very grateful for their time and efforts. My new agent, Margret McBride, found this project the proper home. She and Donna DeGutis, along with their associates in the McBride Literary Agency, have been of tremendous help and encouragement. But it is Roger Scholl, chief wizard of editorial magic at Doubleday, who suggested the final form and precise focus of the book. To him I am very grateful.

I also want to thank all the kids, mothers, dads, teachers, and librarians who have encouraged other children, young people, and adults to read the Harry Potter stories. You're spreading enjoyment and wisdom through the world. Please visit my Web site, www. MorrisInstitute.com, and help me to do the same. I would love to hear from you.

Finally, I want to salute all the busy businesspeople I've seen on airplanes, throughout airports, and in hotel lobbies who are taking time to read all the Harry Potter books—on the way to your important meetings and at the ends of your long days. You are brave enough to seek enjoyment and wisdom wherever it is to be found. And you're showing the way to many of your colleagues.

Several of the ideas in two of my chapters were originally developed elsewhere but are augmented and significantly extended here. An earlier and much shorter version of Chapter 2 appeared in *Harry Potter and Philosophy*, edited by David Baggett and Shawn Klein (Chicago: Open Court, 2004). And a few of the paragraphs on ethics in Chapter 3 first appeared in *Realtor* magazine, May 2005, in the article "Take the High Road," as a part of their Excellence and Innovation Series. I thank them for permission to use some of that material in a new way here.

This book is dedicated to our newest family member, and a joyful little baby, my first granddaughter, Grayson Teague Morris, born May 27, 2004. May Gracie grow and flourish in wisdom and delight—perhaps one day in the imaginative company of Harry Potter and his friends. She has a lot to look forward to!

INTRODUCTION

Wouldn't it be more than a little strange if the best-selling children's books in modern times contained some of the deepest wisdom that contemporary businesspeople need for successful careers, great relationships, and flourishing lives? Many people might find it just exceedingly odd to hear that a series of wildly entertaining stories about wizards and witches conveys important insights on powerfully effective leadership. In this instance, truth is perhaps stranger than fiction—even wondrously strange fiction.

J. K. Rowling, the celebrated author of the Harry Potter stories, is a world-class business and life philosopher of the most practical sort. She can conjure deep and eye-opening wisdom from the lives of her wizards and witches, whether they are young people like Harry Potter and his friends or elder statesmen like Headmaster Albus Dumbledore. Her characters embody some of the most important insights of the ages about how to live and how not to live in this world. Her stories can instruct us in the most common adventures we all face. That's a big part of the reason she has touched so many lives with her books and has become nearly as popular among adults as with children. She's also a bit of a genius with quite a wit. And that doesn't hurt, either.

A few years ago, I wrote a book titled *If Aristotle Ran General Motors: The New Soul of Business*. It was a look at what many great philosophers throughout history have had to say about success, partnership, and the important connection between a sense of fulfillment in our work and sustainable excellence in what we do. It was also about the ultimate context and framework for business ethics. I explained carefully in the book's introduction that it wasn't really about either Aristotle or General Motors, but that I was just using these prominent names as emblematic of wisdom and work. Aristotle stood in for all the great thinkers through the ages that I consulted for advice, and General Motors represented the full range of organizations that could benefit from deeper philosophical insight about human nature and competitive excellence. I did, however, draw on Aristotle more than any other philosopher for the wisdom that modern business needs. He was in many ways my guiding light throughout the book.

In addition to being a great thinker of the highest stature, Aristotle is also known for having taught Alexander the Great—at a time when he was arguably no more than Alexander the Average, a callow youth in need of wisdom and guidance. But association with greatness can breed greatness. After studying with the great philosopher, this talented young man managed to go on to attain a distinctive greatness and world stature of his own. I have come to believe that the immensely popular Harry Potter novels show a similar process at work. The Hogwarts School headmaster, Albus Dumbledore, is an impressive thinker and exemplary leader who by force of character, personal prowess, and strength of conviction organizes and leads an ongoing fight against evil that spans all the stories. He also in many ways mentors the precocious Harry Potter. Under his influence, Harry has already developed into what's called, in the world of business, a "star performer," as well as into a very effective young leader himself. It's hard not to suspect that Harry is being groomed to become the next Dumbledore in their world of witchcraft and wizardry. What the beloved headmaster displays, and what Harry experiences, can teach all of us some very important lessons in business and life, and can do so in an extraordinarily engaging way.

For years, I've traveled the country as a public philosopher, bringing ancient wisdom and new ideas to the good people of corporate America. And throughout these journeys, I've often seen more adults than children sitting on airplanes and in airports reading the various Harry Potter books. I soon found myself asking a question. Why is there all this adult interest in these children's books? In part, I'm sure it starts with curiosity. We want to know what our children are reading, and especially what they are devouring so avidly. We are interested in why these books are so incredibly popular, to the extent of pulling kids away from television and the computer and back to the printed page. Some parents tell me they started on the books by just reading aloud to a child and soon got hooked. When we do sample them, these books then go on to keep our interest because we see truths in the young lives being portrayed, and in the actions of the adults in their world, that can help us all refocus and sharpen our own perspectives on the meaning of our often complex and stressful experience as older people making our way in an uncertain world. The wisdom of the wizards can enlighten us all. We sense it and we appreciate it.

When I first started reading the Potter stories and became totally immersed in their magic, I found myself one day addressing hundreds of marketing professionals on the topic of success. In the middle of the presentation, I spontaneously diverged from my planned remarks and began talking about how Harry Potter deals with situations of great challenge and tremendous danger. The response from this room of high achievers was instant and phenomenal. These young professionals had nearly all read Harry Potter to their kids, and they suddenly came alive in a wave of real enthusiasm as I pointed out in a crisp and applicable way the wisdom in the stories that applies to our own business challenges. They got a huge kick out of the fact that we were talking seriously about Harry, and they all scribbled more notes on the wise ways of this wizard than they had been taking down on Plato and Aristotle's best advice. That's when I first knew there was something in the Potter stories that would resonate deeply with all of us throughout the grown-up world of business.

This book takes for its title the whimsical-sounding speculation of what would happen if our popular young wizard were, at a later age, to be put in charge of a major global corporation. I have decided here to use symbolically the name of a company that seems to have been endowed with magic from its early beginnings in the work of Thomas Edison through its phenomenal development into the creative international powerhouse it is today. Most business commentators for many years have considered the former head of General Electric, Jack Welch, to be a major wizard of organizational leadership and financial growth. His successor, Jeffrey Immelt, now seems intent on bringing an even broader range of magic back into this vast corporation, focusing it on the sort of research, discovery, and invention that can change all our lives for the better, exploring new forms of clean energy, seeking cures for debilitating diseases, and plunging into the nearly magical realm of advanced nanotechnology, in an effort to harness the incredibly small for the sake of very big human needs.

My choice of General Electric as emblematic for business in this book is with a wink and a nod toward their great history, their exciting present, and the amazing potential they have for the future. It's also more than a happy accident that a main GE research facility bears the name "The House of Magic." Having said all this, however, I should clarify that it's not my intention in this book to comment on any particular aspect of this specific organization, but rather to examine some of the most important wisdom that underlies success in any organization, any business career, and any life. If Harry Potter became the reigning wizard of GE at some point in the future, he might end up being a lot like Jeff Immelt. He would employ the deep truths he has been learning in all his adventures, and all his relationships, in an effort to create a measure of real good for the world. It's some of the most important of those truths that we're going to explore together in this book.

WHAT THE HARRY POTTER STORIES OFFER US

J. K. Rowling is a master storyteller. Almost everyone knows that. She clearly understands that in any great story the details are as important as the destination. In each of her books, she takes us on an amazing voyage of the heart and mind. She grips our imagination while holding us in suspense. She entertains and teaches us. She builds up a fascinating alternate world, intersecting with our own, where magic is all around and the battle between good and evil is vivid. She is a wonderful writer. Readers of all ages recognize this and applaud her for it. But what not nearly as many people realize is that, through her stories, Rowling is also serving the world as a nearly magical sage in her own right. She is an amazingly deep and reliable guide to the daunting complexities and essential simplicities of life that we all experience.

Not enough of us these days read the great wisdom guides of the past, like Plato or Aristotle, Seneca or Emerson. Few people even pick up the fables of Aesop, the plays of Sophocles, or—apart from the urging of Oprah—the classic novels of the last two hundred years, with their sharp, insightful explorations of the human condition. But when we do come across a book or even a film that, beneath its surface entertainment values, whispers a deeper meaning, we respond. And we do so with enthusiasm.

Great stories can provide insights into the narratives of our lives.

The Harry Potter books are chock-full of insights about things that really matter to each of us. They can teach us about life and work and provide us with important lessons we all can use, whatever our stage in the journey might be. There is real wisdom to be found in each of these books about friendship, adversity, success, leadership, honesty, courage, loyalty, love, and ethics that can help anyone live a better and more accomplished life.

MAGIC, VIRTUE, AND MEANING

The most distinctive feature of the novels about Harry Potter may well be their engaging portrayal of a world of magic existing distinct from, yet intermingled with, our regular, nonmagical—or Muggle—world. It's a feature of the books that has drawn the ire of critics and the praise of fans. But, however important the magic of wands, brooms, cauldrons, potions, and spells might be to the vivid storytelling of these books, it is merely incidental to their philosophy of life.

Consider for a moment what may be among the most common uses of the words "magic" and "magician" in modern American English. I can't count the number of times in my life I've heard someone in a business context say something like "I wish I could just magically solve all these problems" or "I'll try my best to deal with this situation, but remember, I'm no magician." By looking at Hogwarts and its world, we can see that these common sentiments reflect a fundamental misunderstanding.

Harry's daily reality is a world full of magic, and yet the people within it have loads of challenging problems, just like us—except, perhaps, they may have to put up with even more. At least we don't have dangerous magical creatures lurking about and dark wizards running around threatening us with frightening spells and powerful blasts from their wands. What is particularly interesting is that the most difficult problems that the people in Harry's world face are rarely solved with just magic, but rather by the use of intelligence, reasoning, planning, courage, determination, persistence, resourcefulness, creativity, fidelity, friendship, and many other qualities traditionally known by the philosophers in our world as virtues. Magic for the wizards and others in Harry's reality is a tool, among many other problem-solving tools. But tools have to be used by people, and it's ultimately the skill and character of the person using such a tool that determine how effectively it can be employed to deal with any serious situation or difficulty.

I think Rowling's aim in the Harry Potter books is not at all to convey to children, and to her many other readers, the importance of wand-and-spell magic in the lives of her characters, but rather to display the magical importance of the classic virtues in their lives and, by implication, in ours as well. This in turn can give us all a clue about the nature and meaning of a successful life. The meaning of life is not to be found in elixirs or incantations, secret words, or exotic objects with esoteric powers, but in real moral virtue and the magic of what it can help us do. In conveying such a philosophy of life, Rowling is at one with the greatest philosophers who have gone before her.

All the parents and other adults who buy these Harry Potter books for the children in their lives, or who just read them for their own entertainment, need to understand the wealth of wisdom they contain. I am writing this little book for them, as well as for all those younger people who love Harry and want to see some of the real story behind the stories, the deeper ideas breaking out at the surface and those that are just percolating underneath. I'm writing for those avid readers and real-life friends of Harry who want to learn from him all they can. And I've conjured this book especially for anyone who wants to find a little more of the real magic in business and life. To each and every one of you, I offer this look at the wisdom of the wizards. Using its ideas, you can read about Harry and his cohorts with more understanding, you can use the best of what you learn, and you might even be able to enlighten some of the worst Muggles you find around you.

I'll be referencing and quoting throughout from *The Sorcerer's Stone* (SS)—which Rowling herself titled and published originally as *Harry Potter and the Philosopher's Stone*, mentioning the great elusive quarry of alchemy, but which she couldn't offer in America under that title because some marketing gurus here were sure that few people in the

United States would know what a philosopher is and that, certainly, no one would buy a book with that word in its title—*The Chamber of Secrets* (CS), *The Prisoner of Azkaban* (PA), *The Goblet of Fire* (GF), *The Order of the Phoenix* (OP), and *The Half-Blood Prince* (HB). I'll draw all quotations and other references, along with their page numbers, from the American editions of the books, published by Scholastic Press.

If Harry Potter ran GE, some surprising things might happen. Let's explore together what the real magic behind it all could be.

1

ALBUS DUMBLEDORE, CEO

They're only truly great who are truly good.
—George Chapman (1559–1634)

There are two main heroic characters in the Harry Potter stories: Harry, of course, but also Professor Albus Dumbledore, the great wizard and headmaster of Harry's school. The *Oxford English Dictionary* defines a "hero" as a "man of super-human qualities, favored by the gods," an "illustrious warrior," and as a "man admired for achievements and noble qualities." In different ways, Harry and his impressive headmaster are all these things. The principal difference is that Harry is just starting to find his footing on the high road of heroism. When we first meet him, Professor Dumbledore is already far along the path. He is in many ways a paradigmatic leader.

Dumbledore is like a light on a hill, the North Star, an ancient beacon that keeps voyagers from crashing in the fog. He is a natural leader for all the forces of good in Harry's world. He is the embodiment of nobility, goodness, prowess, wisdom, intelligence, and sound perspective. He is also a kind of old-fashioned surrogate father figure to Harry: close, yet in some ways distant; always concerned, despite sometimes appearing aloof; deeply involved, and yet still separate and a bit mysterious. He tells Harry whatever he believes the young man needs to know, when he's sure he's prepared to hear it, and offers him help at just those times when he needs it most. He is also a powerful protector and a vigilant guardian for all those around him.

To fill out the picture further, this masterful leader is also something of a Renaissance man, having a diversity of personal interests and accomplishments outside the realm of his primary responsibilities. As in the case of the Management Guru and CEO trading cards that gained some humorous attention in the real world of business a few years ago, the top performers in the world of the wizards are also featured and briefly profiled on trading cards that the younger wizards-in-training collect and swap. The biggest difference is that the featured wizards can move around in the photos reproduced on their cards and wave or wink at anyone looking at them. The card in honor of Dumbledore states that he is widely considered to be the greatest wizard of the modern age and mentions, among his many achievements, his renowned defeat of a well-known dark wizard, as well as his important discoveries in the fields of chemistry and alchemy, along with his love of chamber music and bowling.

Dumbledore isn't just a man of science, a top educator, and a master of his craft. We learn at the beginning of book six that his interests range as far as to include a love for knitting patterns. With his well-rounded life, personality, and character, the headmaster is simply what all adults ought to be. He also displays, in a great many ways, the essence of leadership excellence. In each of these respects, he is an ideal role model for the young Harry as he grows and develops.

Because the great Dumbledore is so important in all the books, and in Harry's life, our journey will start with a close look at him. He is a one-man study of wisdom at work in the world. He embodies the virtues essential to leadership excellence and guides his own path forward with a profound philosophy of life. He sets the standard high for what all wizards—and the rest of us, too—should aspire to become. Because of this, we need to take a bit of time to see exactly what he is like.

LEADER, TEACHER, PHILOSOPHER

Years ago, when I wrote the book *If Aristotle Ran General Motors*, the title came from a simple thought experiment. I had been wondering: If one of the greatest thinkers in all of human history—the ancient Greek philosopher Aristotle—could magically be put in charge of a major modern corporation—like the huge automaker General Motors—what would happen? How might things be different? Which aspects of a deeper wisdom about life would he bring into people's daily experience there? What would be important to a great thinker like Aristotle in this sort of context? How would he lead others to a more sustainable excellence and a more satisfying form of success? As I worked on the answers to these questions, I discovered more than I ever could have imagined.

When I first read the original few volumes of the Harry Potter stories, and then couldn't stop myself from reading them over and over, a similar question gradually came to mind. Most of the important action in these books centers around the Hogwarts School of Witchcraft and Wizardry, where Harry and his friends are students. Hogwarts isn't just the dramatic stage for Harry's schoolboy adventures, it's usually the setting for his toughest problems and somehow also the source of his ultimate solutions. It's certainly a school of magic, but it's also a school of life. I realized quickly that I couldn't help but ask my old philosophical question, but with a new twist here.

What if Aristotle ran Hogwarts? What would this amazing school be like with the great philosopher of the ages as its headmaster? What wisdom would he put into action? How would things be done? What would a sage like Aristotle do to inspire his staff and students to success? But as soon as I began to ask this question, or cluster of questions, it struck me that there is one simple, surprising answer.

If the ancient philosopher Aristotle could be transported magically through time and across the firm yet translucent barrier between reality and fiction to run Hogwarts, he might well be nearly indistinguishable from the actual headmaster, the wise and good Dumbledore. In fact, I've come to think of Headmaster Dumbledore as something like a nearly ideal Aristotelian figure. He embodies a philosophy of life and leadership very similar to Aristotle's conception of what it takes to live the good life together with other people in any setting. Professor Dumbledore's student Harry is, by contrast, more like a work in progress—a young man in a state of ongoing Aristotelian becoming. He's a great lump of fine clay in the process of being formed into a wonderful and useful pot under the skilled hand of a master potter. It's difficult not to suspect that, at some point, he himself will become Master Potter in more than one sense of the phrase. Just as Aristotle's prize student Alexander of Macedonia went on to incredible accomplishments of his own after having come under the insightful philosopher's influence, Dumbledore's prize student at Hogwarts is clearly also a young man capable of growing into greatness under the influence of a master.

If anyone were to object that Dumbledore isn't literally Harry's teacher, but rather the principal or headmaster of the very private school in which the boy actually is taught by many other instructors who fall along the whole human spectrum of wisdom and goodness, as well as their opposites, I would reply that this distinction gets the situation completely wrong. Dumbledore is Harry's most important teacher by the example he sets, as well as by the many interactions he has outside the classroom with this young wizard in training. Harry's other instructors provide him with many magical tools, but Dumbledore gives him the life instruction, guidance, and ongoing encouragement he needs for a proper use of those tools. The headmaster is clearly Harry's major mentor.

Dumbledore is a master in something resembling the traditional technical sense, and Harry is his chief apprentice. The two of them together display some of the central elements of this classic form of education. The greatest teachers are always masters of their subjects who lead, train, guide, and inspire their student apprentices to their own forms of excellence. They never just pass on information. The master is a model, coach, helper, and motivator as well as a teacher and trainer. Watching what a master does and how he does it is every bit as important for an apprentice as hearing what he says and how he says it. In fact, as the influential British scientist and philosopher Michael Polanyi explained in his classic 1958 book *Personal Knowledge*, some of the most important insights and skills embodied by a true master can never fully be put into words and can only be shown, not said. The classroom for this sort of teacher always extends beyond the walls of any schoolroom or office and encompasses much more of life. Harry learns from his headmaster in all sorts of settings and in all sorts of ways. What he is learning, in bits and pieces and in fits and starts, is the way of true greatness.

The best leaders teach by example and guide with encouragement.

We all need to remember that people are watching us and learning from us by seeing what we do as well as hearing what we say. In fact, it's always our behavior much more than our speech that ultimately communicates to other people. If we comport ourselves like Dumbledore, and thereby show the people around us the proper way forward, we have the ability to communicate and convey true greatness to others. But, typically, like young Harry, we first need to get our own model of greatness in some older figure like Dumbledore. If it's not obvious who our headmaster should be, we need to seek out such a person—in our own neighborhoods, in our industry, across town, down the hall, or wherever we can find such a wizard of wisdom. What we haven't ourselves received, we can't pass on to others. The insights that come from experience can help us along like nothing else. But learning just from our own experience is the hardest approach to life. A great mentor is a person who has filtered his or her own prior personal experience, along with the experience of many others, analyzed it fully, and extracted from it the wisdom it contains. Why shouldn't we all seek to learn from the experience of older and wiser people we trust? We all need masterful moral mentors to show us the way forward, so that then we can go on to point others in the right direction as well.

The strongest business organizations believe in developing leaders. And the wisest leaders themselves take their mentoring responsibilities seriously. No amount of succession planning can take the place of an ongoing culture of mentoring, which then ends up being a part of the best succession planning there can be. Our emblematic corporate touchstone, General Electric, has always been known for its strength of leadership training. Its top leaders are especially noteworthy, within the context of modern business, for being largely homegrown and internally groomed for greatness. They develop a distinctive form of leadership excellence, serve their company well, and then many eventually go on to take the helm at other major corporations, continuing to lead, and to develop leaders, in those new contexts.

Philosophers have long understood that, in many ways, we become like the people we're around. Corrupt leaders tend to hire corruptible people and then mold them into their image, to the long-term mutual detriment of all. Fortunately, good leaders know to hire the best people they can find, then ground them in the most effective and ethical practices of business leadership that will elevate their game to everything it's capable of being. The best leaders understand that greatness gives rise to greatness like nothing else can.

ARISTOTELIAN GREATNESS

Dumbledore is in many ways an Aristotelian figure, embodying, about as fully as any person might, the individual virtues this insightful philosopher identified as the ingredients of a good, effective, and happy life. Aristotle, as well as most other ancient philosophers, thought of a "virtue" as an individual human excellence—a personal characteristic that can facilitate the living of a worthwhile and successful life. Here is a quick list of the virtues according to Aristotle, and a very brief understanding of each:

Courage—a commitment to do what's right despite the threat of danger

Temperance—a rational moderation and proper self-restraint in our pleasures

Liberality—a freedom in giving to others what can be of help to them

Magnificence—a capacity for acting on a grand scale

Pride—a true sense of honor and worthiness

Good Temper—an inner calm manifested by appropriate outward behavior

Friendliness—the demeanor of treating others convivially and sociably

Truthfulness—a strong disposition toward honesty in all things

Wittiness—the ability to see and express humor appropriately

Justice—the fundamental disposition of treating others well and fairly

Clearly, in light of the range of what he includes, Aristotle was concerned about what it takes to live the best and fullest life.

Leadership excellence arises from personal excellence.

Dumbledore displays all these virtues, and in that way serves as a great role model for all his students and fellow faculty members. This is a large part of what makes it possible for him to be such an exemplary leader. It's also very important to who he is as a person. Aristotle believed that a happy life is one lived in accordance with virtue—a life of excellence. This is exactly the sort of life Dumbledore lives every day. And it's deeply relevant to leadership. A truly great leader must first be a truly great person. Exemplary leadership over the long run, and across all dimensions of its results, is always the expression of a full and excellent life. Otherwise, what too often presents itself to the world as being real, solid, results-oriented leadership is just empty posturing that's more about appearance than reality. Authentic leadership is the sort of outer function that can spring only from the inner person. The great philosophers have always seen this. Building the inner person is vital to creating a great organization, strong community, or excellent business. Leadership is never just a set of actions or habits that can be equally effective regardless of the character and personal qualities of the leader.

Aristotle believed that we are always in a process of becoming what we are capable of being. Life itself is a dynamic process. Whenever we make a decision, whenever we act or react, we are never just doing, we are always becoming. We can see Harry Potter, like almost any person at his stage of life, go through a lot of turmoil as he grows in the direction of what he's capable of being. It's often a bumpy road. He sometimes disappoints us, but occasionally he amazes us. Under the example and tutelage of Dumbledore, he has an opportunity to develop into something great. But, in order to appreciate that exciting fact more fully, we have to learn a bit more about who Dumbledore really is.

Headmaster Dumbledore is presented to us as the ideal of a good wizard. He is often characterized as a great wizard, the greatest of the age. But even more important is the fact that he is described by many of those who know him well as, simply, a "great man" (GF 455). My single favorite account of him comes in book three, *The Prisoner of Azkaban*:

> Professor Dumbledore, though very old, always gave an impression of great energy. He had several feet of long silver hair and beard, half-moon spectacles, and an extremely crooked nose. He was often described as the greatest wizard of the age, but that wasn't why Harry respected him. You couldn't help trusting Albus Dumbledore, and as Harry watched him beaming around at the students, he felt really calm for the first time. . . . (PA 91)

Dumbledore has developed his skills as a wizard to the very highest level, and, like many great leaders, he is a person with tremendous energy. Because of this, he is an unparalleled top performer in his area of expertise. He knows his stuff. He's a star. But that isn't the most salient feature of the man. Ultimately, he is a great leader because he's a wise man who knows human nature, and who acts in everything he does with great character. At one point in *The Order of the Phoenix*, Harry's reliably levelheaded friend Hermione is defending the trustworthiness of a man Harry and his buddy Ron are otherwise inclined to be very suspicious of, and she makes a decisive point:

> "Dumbledore trusts him," Hermione repeated. "And if we can't trust Dumbledore, we can't trust anyone." (OP 555)

This was not an argument the boys were even tempted to resist.

Dumbledore inspires trust and is genuinely trustworthy. He knows the power and importance of truth, which is always the foundation for trust. He lives the truth and brings it into his dealings with others. But he also understands that not everyone is equally well prepared to grasp and deal properly with every possible truth. In response to a question that the very young, preteen Harry once asks him about the real truth concerning his own life story, Dumbledore makes a very important statement about how he views truth and how he handles it:

> "The truth." Dumbledore sighed. "It is a beautiful and terrible thing, and should therefore be treated with great caution. However, I shall answer your questions unless I have a very good reason not to, in which case I beg you'll forgive me. I shall not, of course, lie." (SS 298)

Dumbledore understands that access to truth should be appropriate, must sometimes be earned, and should always be deserved. He also makes a strong commitment here to Harry: He will never lie to him. This is a very important statement made late in the first book, *The Sorcerer's Stone*. We've already seen by then that the students of Hogwarts tell lies quite casually and often, just like too many young people their age, and far too many adults, in the real world. They lie to protect themselves and their friends from censure, reprimand, embarrassment, worry, and danger. They sometimes deceive for purposes of self-advancement and petty gain. They fib out of convenience or from sheer laziness. The worst among them prevaricate to cause trouble. And some of the adults around them are no better. But the man most of the students admire beyond all others, their revered headmaster, takes a strongly principled stand on the issue of truth and honesty in all his dealings with Harry. We'll more fully appreciate the nature of this stand when we come to a closer examination of related issues in our chapter devoted to truth and lies.

Business, like life, demands truth and trust. Without truth, people can't work effectively. Without trust, people can't work efficiently. We have seen amply displayed over the last few years what results when truth is in short supply in any business context. Disaster most often ensues. Dumbledore models for us in this regard one of the most important qualities for great leadership. His character is impeccable. His commitment to truth is strong, and his capacity to inspire and elicit both truth and trust from his colleagues is unrivaled. As the contemporary business author Jim Collins demonstrates in his widely acclaimed book *Good to Great*, despite many dominant mass media images to the contrary, the best leaders aren't necessarily flashy, flamboyant, larger than life, inflated-ego media hounds who posture as icons of greatness and pontificate as oracles of organizational excellence. The best leaders in most circumstances tend to be just completely committed people with keen intelligence, great skill, focused energy, a clear vision, the courage of their convictions, a passion for what they're doing, strong character, and a robust sense of concern for others. They tend to be like Dumbledore.

The twin pillars of effective leadership are truth and trust.

Throughout the Harry Potter stories, Professor Dumbledore shows us how good character inspires trust, respect, and loyalty. A great leader doesn't literally have to command respect or demand the loyalty of his associates. His example evokes and naturally draws forth these responses. In order to motivate people, he doesn't seek to create a climate of fear and punishment, but he is, by contrast, able to deal with others in kindness and gentle regard for their interests as well as his own.

Harry's terrible uncle, Vernon Dursley, shows us the polar opposite of this. In the first chapter of the first book, we are told that, during what was a "perfectly normal" morning for him at work,

He yelled at five different people. He made several important phone calls and shouted a bit more. (SS 4)

Mr. Dursley is a really miserable man who inflicts his unhappiness on others without either realizing or caring that this is what he's doing. He's thoroughly self-absorbed, ambitious in the pettiest of ways, and basically serves the world as a cautionary tale to anyone who does not recognize the proper path to excellence and honor. Dumbledore doesn't need to yell and shout at his coworkers. He doesn't have to and wouldn't in any case. He has the utmost respect for those with whom he works, he displays this in all his actions toward them, and they naturally tend to reciprocate when dealing with him.

We live in an age when some very talented and ambitious people have drifted so far away from a proper perspective on business excellence that they praise paranoia, cynicism, and skepticism above all other qualities as essential ingredients for business success. Of course, in any business, as well as in life more broadly, there are times for belief and times for doubt. There are certainly circumstances where caution is vital and we ought to be very slow to trust. But nothing of importance ultimately can be built without trust between people. Most of the time, it's better to venture a risk and believe in other people than to adopt a stance of thoroughly skeptical suspicion toward them. In part because Dumbledore is so trustworthy himself, and in part because he always hopes the best of others, so long as they allow him that indulgence, the headmaster tends to be a trusting soul, firmly believing in the people around him. He would not have allowed them into his circle in the first place if he had not thought this trust appropriate. Of course, it's possible to be mistaken in trusting another person, and even tragically wrong about someone. But a great person tends to venture the risk of trust in order to make impor-

tant things happen, unless he has what he considers to be a good reason not to do so on a particular occasion. In *The Goblet of Fire*, one of
the teachers at Hogwarts, addressing a fellow instructor with a trou-
bled past, characterizes their mutual boss as exactly the sort of person
who is strongly inclined to trust others, and who even believes in second chances for individuals who might not have been wholly trustworthy at some point in the past (GF 472).

Dumbledore does believe in second chances. He understands that
someone can make a mistake—even a serious mistake of moral judgment in the past—and still recover from it. People can learn from
their mistakes and change for the better. It's far too rare, but it happens. Wizards and ordinary human beings can fall from grace and be
redeemed. We can mess up, and then clean up, and end up better than
we started. The adventure of life is often just like that. The great
leader doesn't expect his people always to have been perfect, but he
does expect them to be learners who always seek to improve.

There is a generosity of spirit in Dumbledore. He sees beyond the
categories that too often define people and is capable of giving the
downtrodden and despised an opportunity when no one else will. He
seems typically to be able to see into the soul of a person and not let
the weight of popular opinion sway him from what he discerns. That
is how Hagrid, the beloved groundskeeper at Hogwarts, originally got
his job, despite being of greatly feared giant parentage and having
long ago been dismissed from Hogwarts when he was a student, on
what turned out to be false charges. Dumbledore from the beginning
trusted him, and continues to do so, without qualification:

"I would trust Hagrid with my life," said Dumbledore. (SS 14)

The headmaster also gave the good Professor Remus Lupin a
chance to teach at Hogwarts, despite his being a member of the
widely hated, feared, and distrusted category of werewolves. This
leader appraises people as individuals and doesn't pay much attention
to the labels often put on them. Because of this, he is never much

impressed by general categories of negative judgment and the prejudices they evoke, especially when they relate to where, or from what group, a person was born. Addressing a colleague of his with a very different perspective, Dumbledore explains his view like this:

"You fail to recognize that it matters not what someone is born, but what they grow to be!" (GF 708)

This philosophical wizard is wise enough to recognize that we're all in a state of growth and becoming. Neither our birth nor our current status, or place in life, necessarily defines our intrinsic value or ultimate destiny. People of any background, and with nearly any history, can grow to be good, useful, and even great. Just as a lofty birth is no guarantee of personal accomplishment and excellence, humble beginnings do not prevent noble achievements. Indeed, they can even enhance the overall status of the end attained. It has often been said that we are not to be judged just by the place in life at which we have arrived but also by the distance we have traveled to get there. This is a sentiment with which Dumbledore would heartily agree.

Although Professor Dumbledore is a tremendously accomplished and revered adult of great stature in the community and is in a position of authority over all the students and faculty of Hogwarts, he is fair-minded, kind, and always grateful for the good contributions of others. He entertains no unseemly sense of self-importance, but rather seeks to define himself in service to others. He genuinely cares about people and appreciates them. When Harry regains consciousness in the school hospital after a frightening confrontation with evil, the first sight that greets him is especially reassuring:

The smiling face of Albus Dumbledore swam into view above him. (SS 295)

The headmaster is a person who shows kindness to everyone around him, and his efforts have tremendous results. He even describes to Harry at one point an occasion when he counseled another wizard that we should treat others "with kindness and respect" even when we suspect that they may be potential enemies (OP 832). Dumbledore's ethics create a high standard for those around him in every way. He treats other people the way he himself would want to be treated if he were in their place, and the proper results of this high moral stance show. In fact, Dumbledore seems to live the advice of the great writer Johann Wolfgang von Goethe, who once advised, "Treat others as if they were what they ought to be and you will help them to become what they are capable of being." Taking the moral high ground and always showing others an appropriate form of respect can be transformative in helping them to see the proper path forward themselves and grow in the direction of their own best future.

The most easily forgotten leadership virtue is kindness.

THE VIRTUES OF GOOD HUMOR
AND GREAT FEELING

Dumbledore is at once, in many ways, a serious man, possessed of tremendous nobility and great dignity, and yet also very comfortable having fun. He is often seen with a twinkle in his eye. He seems genuinely amused in circumstances whose humor can be appreciated only by someone with a very cool head and an extraordinarily keen wit. And he occasionally uses small and subtle forms of humor to help take the edge off a difficult situation.

On the night that little Harry Potter's parents have just been murdered by the powerful, evil wizard Voldemort, Dumbledore and his most trusted colleague, Minerva McGonagall, are keeping watch outside the home of Harry's aunt and uncle, waiting for the baby boy to be brought there for safe refuge. Voldemort had tried to kill tiny Harry as well, and yet for some reason the spell had rebounded on him and apparently stripped him of power. But nothing is certain at the moment. As they are speaking quietly about the terrible events that have just transpired, Professor McGonagall displays a common reticence even to pronounce Voldemort's name, calling him "You-Know-Who" instead. Dumbledore politely corrects her on the circumlocution, this small bit of linguistic evasiveness, and adds that he's been trying for years to get people to call the wicked man by his proper name. He explains that there is no need to be afraid of identifying him properly. McGonagall replies that it's easy for Dumbledore to say this because it's widely known that he is the only person whom Voldemort fears. As they continue the conversation in such difficult circumstances, and it's clear that McGonagall is quite on edge over it all, Dumbledore makes a small joke about himself that seems to ease the tension and subtly alter the mood (SS 11). We soon come to learn that this is just a typical display of his ongoing tendency to make a very casual remark, or even a little joke, in even the most highly charged of circumstances, when doing so might help others to settle their emotions and think more clearly. He often uses a spark of wit to defuse a tense situation or to put things into a better perspective. By doing so, he displays his own inner peace, changes the emotional tone of the circumstances, and helps to calm the other people around him. A good leader needs to know when to excite people and when to calm them down. Appropriate humor, used well, can accomplish much.

This great man is even capable, on occasion, of genuine silliness. In the context of one official school celebration, we see him seated at the head table, wearing a flowered bonnet, and laughing away at a colleague's joke. On another occasion, Dumbledore stands up at the opening-of-school banquet when Harry first arrives, announces to the assembled school that he intends to say just a few words, utters several nonsense syllables, and sits back down. Harry turns to an upperclassman and asks whether the headmaster is a bit cracked. He's told quite straightforwardly that, yes, perhaps Dumbledore is a bit mad, but that he is also a true genius and the best wizard in the world.

Dumbledore's acknowledged eccentricity and his ability to have fun to the point of silliness never detract in the least from his elevated image in the eyes of those who know him. This is the mark of a genuinely remarkable individual. It's easy for people who know recent business history to be reminded here of the famous antics of those rare few business leaders like Herb Kelleher, the flamboyant head of Southwest Airlines. His notorious love of silly fun and dramatic stunts just further endeared him to the people who benefited in so many other ways from his sound leadership over the one airline that has remained safe and profitable for many years in the most uncertain of times and most volatile of industries. His spirit of fun was infectious and quickly spread through not only the employees of Southwest, but to their many customers as well.

Leo Wells isn't a household name. But I think he should be. He is the founder and chairman of Wells Real Estate Funds, one of the largest real estate investment funds in America, and one of the biggest owners of commercial real estate in the nation. Leo is a great businessman. He is a thinker and a man of action. And he certainly has a serious side, a gravitas redolent of noble commitments and high aspirations. He wants the best for all his associates and insists on excellence and superior customer service in all things. He can be a demanding boss, expecting as much of others as he does of himself. But I've also seen him crooning out Elvis tunes to an audience of associates with a strong, clear warble reminiscent of Roy Orbison and belting out high-spirited gospel songs late into the night during a companywide retreat. He has fun and, like Dumbledore, can even be a little silly at times. When he takes the stage in front of hundreds of Wells associates, or just as many sophisticated financial clients, he can tell stories like nobody else and spontaneously fire off one-liners as funny as any comedian could hope to attain. I've seen elegant, buttoned-down crowds double over in laughter at his down-home southern-boy antics. And they typically go away with a renewed and deepened respect for the many dimensions of this visionary leader. The positive power of humor and good fun is certainly not limited to fiction. Every noble leader can use it and every person in business can benefit from it.

Like many great leaders, Albus Dumbledore can be quite provocative, but he is not himself easily provoked. The sort of baseless criticisms, groundless charges, and offensive insults that would send most people into a state of high agitation, and many into a rage, seem not to touch him at all. When he once comes upon Rita Skeeter, a thoroughly unprincipled journalist who has just written and published a completely unjustified, scandalously negative characterization of him in a widely read newspaper, he politely refers to her piece as "enchantingly nasty" and adds:

> "I particularly enjoyed your description of me as an obsolete dingbat." (GF 307)

As she tries to explain and justify herself, detaining him from pressing business, he replies with customary good humor, a smile, and a courteous bow, saying that he will be delighted to hear all her explanations when there is more time. A former Secretary General of the United Nations, Dag Hammarskjöld, once said, "The only kind of dignity which is genuine is that which is not diminished by the indifference of others." We could substitute "hostility" or "ridicule" for the word "indifference" in this wise remark and have at least a hint of an explanation for Dumbledore's remarkable steadiness in the face of opposition or ill will.

This great man who can joke and laugh can also cry. The spirit that can discern and enjoy a full range of humor can also experience and savor other aspects of the ethical and aesthetic side of existence. Dumbledore is a sensitive soul who appreciates the finer things in life. That's why the school is always decorated so beautifully for holidays and celebrations. Every significant event is marked with a feast, and every feast is itself a significant event. The headmaster understands ritual and really relishes the overall pageantry of life. He is also deeply moved by the mystical power of music, which, even if being performed quite poorly by a chaotic chorus of students, can bring tears to his eyes.

At the end of *The Order of the Phoenix*, after Dumbledore has just informed Harry of the deepest and most difficult truth about his destiny that he will ever have to face, we are told that Harry saw "a tear trickling down Dumbledore's face" (OP 844). A great man or woman has great feelings, natural emotions that respond to the world both appropriately and deeply. And he or she is not afraid to show them. But the truly great person does not let his emotions unhinge him. He remains in control of them and governs them in accordance with what he knows to be best. The deepest emotions are compatible with the highest rationality in any life that is in full control of all its faculties. But without proper self-control, no amount of passion or intellect can guarantee either great leadership or even long-lasting personal success. Understanding this more fully will help us grasp another side of the great Dumbledore.

How we govern and express our emotions can deepen or destroy our connections with others.

EMOTIONAL SELF-CONTROL

Dumbledore keeps his head when all around him seem to be losing theirs. He rises above the petty emotions of irritation, anxiety, and frustration that overcome so many people in difficult circumstances. He is not buffeted about by feelings or emotions he can't control. In one particularly difficult and extremely tense situation, where tremendous power has been arrayed against both him and Harry and numerous adversaries physically surround the two of them, preparing to take them forcibly into custody, we read that Dumbledore remained sitting at his desk in a remarkable pose of utmost calm, with a completely peaceful expression on his face (OP 610).

Dumbledore manifests inner serenity to an almost supernatural degree, in even the most dangerous of circumstances. When finally confronting the evil Voldemort in person, a man widely believed to be the most powerful of wizards, in what appears to be a culminating battle of mortal combat promising imminent death for at least one of them, Dumbledore displays the same utter calm. And he surprises Voldemort tremendously by not attempting to kill him when he has the chance. The two wizards are at some distance from each other, and Voldemort has just tried twice to slay his nemesis with fatal spells projected from his wand. Dumbledore defends himself but doesn't move in for a kill. We can't help but notice his total composure in the face of the dire threat he continues to confront as events develop. He even calls Voldemort by his birth name and in this subtle way refuses to accept or even acknowledge the evil persona he has so assiduously cultivated. Rowling tells us that he speaks calmly, and even conversationally, to this dangerous dark wizard as he walks in his direction (OP 814). His powerful and measured actions in the rest of this confrontation finally cause a confused and shaken Voldemort to flee. In the course of the fight, the great Dumbledore never shows any emotions of fear for his own safety, or even anger at his opponent, only the complete focus of a man who knows what he is doing.

There is just one moment when a fleeting emotion of concern shows through. Young Harry, thinking that the fight he has been watching is over before it actually is, prematurely moves out from behind a protective obstacle that has been shielding him from harm. Dumbledore sees this and shouts for Harry to stay where he is. Rowling says that Harry heard in his voice for the first time ever a tone that sounded like fear (OP 815). This is very telling. The first and only display of anything like fear on the part of this courageous and admirable man is not fear for himself or his own safety, but for his student, Harry. Yet Dumbledore nonetheless maintains his focus and wins the day. He does not allow any emotion to overwhelm him or detract from his purposeful action in even the most dangerous of circumstances.

Professor Dumbledore experiences a powerful emotion like anger only when he catches real evil at work and when immediate harm threatens his students or other innocent people. And in the life of this great wizard, anger is always channeled into appropriate action. At one point, the greatly feared "dementors," the mysterious, nonhuman guards of Azkaban, the terrible wizard prison, come onto the Hogwarts campus against Dumbledore's direct orders. They do something during a sporting event, the school Quidditch match, to make Harry fall off his flying broomstick and plummet through the air. The head-master takes action immediately.

> "Dumbledore was really angry," Hermione said in a quaking voice. "I've never seen him like that before. He ran onto the field as you fell, waved his wand, and you sort of slowed down before you hit the ground. Then he whirled his wand at the dementors. Shot sil-ver stuff at them. They left the stadium right away. He was furious they'd come onto the grounds." (PA 181)

In *The Order of the Phoenix*, when the headmaster discovers that a man he trusted and whom he had ordered to guard Harry had left his post for frivolous reasons and rendered Harry vulnerable to an attack, which then happened, he reacts again with justified anger. Hermione later describes the headmaster on this occasion, with astonishment and marvel in her voice, as simply scary (OP 64).

This is not a sight the students often see. And because of that, it can be shocking and even frightening for them to witness. It is not that Dumbledore ever loses control of himself—he doesn't—but just that the students were so accustomed to seeing his kindness and gen-tleness, his good humor and calm benevolence, they were simply sur-prised by the force and power of his reaction to grossly dangerous irresponsibility or any form of complicity in the face of evil.

As the philosopher Aristotle realized, anger itself is no vice, but rather can be a proper and praiseworthy response to a situation and also a strong stimulus to action. In his famous essay on virtue and excellence, *The Nichomachean Ethics*, he says, "The man who is angry at the right things and with the right people, and, further, as he ought, when he ought, and as long as he ought, is praised" (Bk. IV, Ch. 5). This seems to describe Dumbledore quite well. On those rare occasions when he experiences the emotion of anger, it is always appropriate, well directed, effective, and limited.

In the very rare circumstances when the headmaster is confronted with pure evil, he reacts with tremendous force of personality and power, as in one situation where he comes upon a thoroughly wicked imposter who has taken the physical form of his old friend, Alastor Moody, in an effort to accomplish real evil. When Dumbledore confronts the wicked man, Harry sees a "terrible" expression on his face that strikes him as conveying a "cold fury." The sense of power emanating from the great wizard is clear and palpable (GF 679). But neither anger nor even that unique experience of "cold fury" can cause Dumbledore to act unwisely or inappropriately. He always focuses on what needs to be done, and he then does only what is right. And in so doing, he shows Harry Potter, as well as all the others who witness his actions, how a person of wisdom and virtue ought to live.

DUMBLEDORE'S PHILOSOPHY OF PROPER LIVING

Dumbledore's philosophy of life seems simple and powerful. On the one hand, he upholds the value of sensible rules at school and in life. But he is also able to see how certain situations can escape the grip of particular predetermined rules. When he first speaks to Harry and his friend Ron, after learning how they prevented a young girl's murder and stopped other heinous deeds planned by the evil Voldemort (but only by engaging in actions that violated a number of school rules), he begins by recalling that he had previously warned them both that any further violations of rules on their part would have to result in their immediate expulsion from the school. Ron is stunned at the prospect of what the headmaster is about to say and do next. But Dumbledore merely remarks that this just shows how anyone can be wrong on occasion and that, instead of being expelled, they'll both be given special awards for their extraordinary service to the school (CS 331).

It seems that for Dumbledore the ethics of proper living is not ultimately based on mere rules. But it's also not a matter of simply doing without rules and operating on a case-by-case basis in life, either. We can't just stumble forward without any general rules or principles to guide us and rely on nothing more than choosing the actions that we predict will have the most desired consequences. Dumbledore once says to Harry:

> "The consequences of our actions are always so complicated, so diverse, that predicting the future is a very difficult business indeed." (PA 426)

Some people think that the demands of ethics are satisfied by good intentions alone. They believe that good actions are just those actions that are intended to have good consequences. This is an approach and attitude that has gotten many modern corporate executives into serious trouble. Intending to save the company, or to make it more profitable, can certainly be a good thing, but ethics is all about what you do, and what you refrain from doing, to realize your purposes, however good those purposes might be in themselves. Dumbledore realizes the danger of just focusing on intentions and anticipated results. He knows that the world is too complex to allow us to predict accurately the full range of consequences that any of our actions may have. Good intentions can indeed produce good actions, but they can also inadvertently produce bad actions as well as unintended bad consequences. Ethical conduct requires scrupulously obeying some rules, but it also requires something beyond rules and far beyond merely good intentions. Dumbledore, like Aristotle before him, understands that genuinely ethical action arises out of virtue, and it comes out of the choices we make that are rooted in virtue. This is a theme that we'll explore more fully in a later chapter.

We live in a time when most people seem to believe that ethics is all about staying out of trouble. That's why discussions of business ethics so often focus on matters involving rules, compliance, and legal consequences. Dumbledore's view appears to be rather that of the ancient Greek philosophers and the most profound thinkers in other cultures throughout history: Ethics is really about creating strength. It is a matter of making choices that preserve those values and qualities most deserving of preservation. It's about doing what's right in any given circumstances, regardless of the consequences we might happen to predict, and it's about becoming a properly formed, strongly virtuous person as a result.

All of ethics comes down to the choices we make every day. And who we become is a result of those choices. Our exemplary leader says, quite succinctly:

> "It is our choices, Harry, that show what we truly are, far more than our abilities." (CS 333)

This is one of the most important philosophical insights in the Harry Potter books. It could actually be the underlying theme of all the books. It's also one of the most important realizations that any leader, and any person in business generally, can have. And it's a truth that this great wizard's life displays. In the end, it is perhaps not Dumbledore's own abilities that inspire such awe and respect among his peers and students, great as they may be, but rather his choices. His example helps others to see what in this life is truly choice-worthy—to use an important category bequeathed to us by Aristotle. And, as we shall soon see, young Harry increasingly gets the point. If more leaders in our world did, too, there would be far fewer scandals in business life today.

The insightful journalist and bestselling author Malcolm Gladwell has traced the moral disaster of Enron to a very simple and misguided human resources strategy—"Hire the smartest people in the room." Intellect and ability are without doubt of vital importance in the world of business, as they are in almost any other domain of modern life. But they aren't the only important things in the world. Finding the right people is always in part about finding people with the strongest character, people who reliably make the best choices and are worthy of the highest trust. Smart people who make bad choices can be very dangerous to be around, as Harry's world amply demonstrates.

There are many aspects to strength of character. An ability to make the right choices hinges on all of them. Honesty is important, as is a proper sense of loyalty, an empathetic appreciation for the needs of others, moderated desires, and a grounded, appropriate personal sense of self-worth and dignity. Any leader should seek to surround himself with people who have such qualities. All of us should of course also strive to embody them in our own lives, as well as one more crucial aspect of character that is especially important to mention: A courageous ability to stand firm on the right values, regardless of the pressures and threats posed by a particular situation, is vital for strong character. Because of the fundamental role of courage in the moral life, and in the life of sustainable business excellence, this important virtue will be the next topic that we explore. But first, a quick final word on what we can learn from our headmaster.

THE LESSONS OF THE HEADMASTER

If you want to be a great leader, be a great person. Work on embodying and living the classic virtues. Broaden and deepen yourself as a human being. Seek to govern everything you feel and whatever you do in accordance with your most fundamental beliefs and values. Believe in other people. Show that you care about them. Never forget the power of apprenticeship. Make it a habit to exercise appropriate control over all your emotions and actions. And remember to have fun whenever it's at all possible.

We learn from Dumbledore that not even the best of us is perfect. He makes mistakes, just as we all do. But by basing his life on wisdom and virtue, by developing and living out of the resources of an exemplary character, he guarantees that the impact he will leave on his world is a legacy of great good. We can go and do likewise.

2

THE COURAGEOUS
HARRY POTTER

Be courageous!
—*Thomas Edison, Founding GEnius at GE*

From the perspective of many ancient thinkers, the single most important human virtue is courage. Interestingly, it's a virtue just as crucially needed in the modern world of business. A leader without courage will inevitably fail. Jack Welch, the legendary former chairman and CEO of GE, often cited as the most admired manager of modern times, has repeatedly stressed that a leader needs the courage to make an unpopular decision when he instinctively feels that it's the way to go. A manager without courage can't confront difficult challenges in a high-pressure situation and still do the right thing. Even frontline workers all clearly need the courage of their convictions to resist temptation and do what's best in any situation, whether anyone's watching or not.

The fundamental virtue in business and life is courage.

The courage to take risks, to tell the truth, and to act on principle regardless of what others around you are doing is of unmatched importance for sustainable success in any legitimate business context. Many business and leadership books acknowledge this in some way, but few offer any concrete guidance about how we can develop this fundamental virtue in our lives and then actually muster the courage that's necessary at those times when it's needed the most.

In this chapter, I want to consider the one thing out of all his many positive characteristics that may be Harry Potter's single most striking quality, other than his basic goodness—his personal courage. We can learn a great deal about this important virtue and its cultivation in our own lives by examining some of Harry's exploits during his first six years at the Hogwarts School of Witchcraft and Wizardry. But before we get into the details, let me fill in a little background. It will be useful for us to consider this particular virtue initially in the context of other virtues recognized and encouraged at Hogwarts. No great virtue ever stands alone. But each of us may embody one virtue to a greater degree than others.

THE VIRTUES AT HOGWARTS

Hogwarts is a residential school. The faculty, staff, and students live on the grounds, in different areas of the large castle that are spoken of as houses. We're told that the original founders of the four student houses at Hogwarts valued different qualities in people above all other attributes and created their respective residence halls to celebrate and encourage their favorite virtue. Gryffindor House was founded for "the bravest," Ravenclaw for "the cleverest," Hufflepuff for "hard workers," and Slytherin for those with "great ambition" (GF 17). A student can, of course, be well endowed with more than one of these qualities—Hermione Granger, for example, is very brave, exceptionally clever, and extremely hardworking—but it was the intent of the founders of these different houses to give each student a place for the development of whatever might be his or her greatest strength or most distinctive quality out of these four.

At the Hogwarts opening-of-school ceremony and dinner in the Great Hall each fall, first-year students are called forward, one at a time, to sit on a stool in front of the assembled school and be "sorted" into the different houses where they will find their new home. A bewitched old wizard's hat known as "the sorting hat" is put on the head of each of the new students to look into their souls, discern their distinctive potential, and assign them to the house that will best cultivate that particular strength. When Harry Potter, Ron Weasley, and Hermione Granger arrive for their first day at school, the sorting hat assigns all three of them to Gryffindor—the home of the brave. But when it's slipped onto Harry's head, the old hat at first seems puzzled. It sees in him too many talents and distinctive abilities to allow for an easy assignment. It begins to reflect on what it sees, and Harry can hear its ruminations. The hat mentions his courage first, then his intellect, and finally his strong desire to prove himself that it also discerns in his heart. It then asks itself, or perhaps Harry, where he should be put. Harry instantly and very strongly rejects in his mind the possibility of Slytherin, because he's already met some of the boys headed there and doesn't at all like what he's seen. The hat picks up his thoughts and tells him that Slytherin house could help him on to greatness, but that if he's sure he doesn't want it, then the choice should be Gryffindor (SS 121).

What the hat says to Harry is very interesting. Slytherin House encourages the virtue of ambition. Notice that ambition is a virtue and not a vice. It's the desire to excel and do great things. But many students in Slytherin show that their concern for greatness far outstrips any interest they might have had in goodness. So they often pursue their ambitions without the "hindrance" of ethical considerations. The sorting hat expresses the belief that an association with people focused on greatness could help Harry along to that goal. But Harry seems to sense the price that many of them pay, and he's not interested. He wants anything other than to be stuck in Slytherin. And his talents would prepare him to be a contributing member to any of the houses. That's what makes the decision of where to put Harry initially so difficult for the hat.

Harry seems to have it all. But the sorting hat finally responds to the full range of everything it senses by sending him to the one residential house founded to support and develop the quality of courage. And that's very interesting indeed, since the young Harry Potter is a boy who experiences about as much fear and anxiety as it's possible for someone his age to feel. In fact, Rowling goes out of her way to represent, in as vivid a manner as she can, Harry's visceral experience of the negative emotions and sensations centering on fear.

FEELINGS OF FEAR

Throughout the first six books, Rowling describes any experiences of fear that are had by all her main characters other than Harry, from the outside, in terms of their overt behavior and visible body movements. Whenever she wants to convey that one of them is feeling afraid, she'll tell us that his knees gave way, that he was shaking, that he had terror in his eyes, or that he opened his mouth with a look of horror on his face. All these descriptions are given from an onlooker's point of view. Only Harry's negative emotions are characterized from the inside, as if the author wants us to appreciate as vividly as possible what he goes through whenever he is confronted with great danger or even tremendous uncertainty. It's as though she wants to put us into a position to feel Harry's emotions with him, in order to help us understand the magnitude of what he's experiencing. Rowling knows that we'll understand the nature of his courage only if we really grasp what he has to overcome in order to attain that courage. And then, of course, we'll also understand that no matter how afraid or even terrified we ourselves might be in some circumstances we have to confront, we can do like Harry and move forward with courage. If he can do it, we can do it, too.

Courage does not mean fearlessness, but a determination to do what's right even in the face of fear.

Let me give a few examples of this. When Harry is at the train station attempting to push through what appears to be a solid wall between platform nine and platform ten, in order to find platform nine and three-quarters and catch the train to Hogwarts for his second year at school, the wall won't yield as it's supposed to, and he can't get through, while time is running out. We're told that he looked at the clock with a sick feeling deep in his stomach (CS 68). Like the rest of us, Harry often feels fear in his midsection. In various passages, we read that his stomach lurched, clenched, turned over, grew icy cold, churned, squirmed, felt hollowed out, or seemed to contain a lead weight. At other times, Harry experiences fear a bit higher up, in his chest and heart. It's revealed at different times that his heart gave a terrible jolt, or that it jumped into his throat, banged hard against his rib cage, or tied itself into a knot. The descriptions are so visceral and vivid as to give us all a sympathetic quiver of inner recognition.

Occasionally, Harry faces danger beset with a sensation of numbness or paralysis in his legs, or even throughout his whole body. He tries to scream, but no sound comes out. His mouth is so dry, he can barely talk. His brain jams up momentarily, frozen with horror. His head swims with a dizziness of fear. He reels with an icy numbness in his brain. And these things happen quite often in the stories. At a certain point, it can seem as if we're dealing here with an unusually skittish and extraordinarily fearful young man. He is certainly not someone insensible to danger. He recognizes it wherever it is and in fact feels it deeply. And yet he somehow always manages to overcome these visceral sensations, however strong they might be, and goes on to embody the virtue of courage to the point of standing up to his most feared adversary, saving the day, and earning high praise from all people of goodwill. He is seen and acclaimed by others as noble, valiant, and bold. He is clearly willing to risk his life for his friends.

At a climactic point in the story of *The Sorcerer's Stone*, in front of the entire student body, Headmaster Dumbledore decides to award extra points for the yearly interhouse competition in recognition of Ron and Hermione's brave deeds during the school year, and then in reference to Harry's extraordinary courage he gives out the most points:

"Third—to Mr. Harry Potter . . ." said Dumbledore, ". . . for pure nerve and outstanding courage, I award Gryffindor house sixty points." (SS 306)

The awarded points allow Gryffindor to tie their chief rival for the overall yearly school championship. And then, when Dumbledore awards a few more points to the same house for another student's courage, Gryffindor emerges victorious.

At the end of book four, Dumbledore commends Harry and says to him simply this:

"You have shown bravery beyond anything I could have expected of you." (GF 695)

From a man of great wisdom and discernment, who customarily expects the best of nearly everyone, this is high praise indeed.

HARRY'S RECIPE FOR COURAGE

What allows a quivering, fear-prone, and often quite terrified boy to face up to some of the greatest dangers of his time and prevail? It will be interesting to reflect for a moment on what courage is, then look at how such a sensitive soul as Harry can attain it when he needs it. The results of this examination will benefit us all.

Courage is doing what's right, not what's easy. It's doing what seems morally required in a specific situation, rather than what seems physically safe or socially expected. It's doing what's best, overall, rather than necessarily what's best for you. A courageous person properly perceives danger, takes it very seriously, and understands when important values are at stake that require facing that danger— and then he or she somehow manages to overcome the natural urge for self-preservation, self-protection, comfort, personal gain, or even an altruistic concern for guarding the feelings of others that might counsel an avoidance of that threat.

Aristotle teaches us that courage is a midpoint between two extremes in our possible reactions to danger: the extreme of too little, which he characterizes as cowardice, and the extreme of too much, which he considers a rash form of carelessness, or a careless form of rashness.

Cowardice   Courage   Carelessness

We typically think of courage as simply the opposite of cowardice, but it's just as different from a rash, unreasonable carelessness. A courageous action is not the deed of a person insensible to danger, unaware of its presence, or irrationally reckless in the face of it. An act of courage is a properly motivated and measured response to perceived risk by a person willing to face that potential harm for the sake of securing or promoting a greater good.

Harry often shows himself willing to confront terrible danger to save a friend. He understands what he's facing and stands up to it willingly because of something he values or someone who matters deeply to him. Real courage like that is generated by a person's most fundamental values and by the depth and intensity with which those values are held. This sort of authentic courage is then naturally displayed in a way that is both appropriate and proportionate to the needs of the situation.

This understanding of courage leads to an interesting point. A person who has no values extending beyond the end of his or her nose is not likely to display any sort of courage in the face of danger. If there is nothing ultimately more important to you than your own skin, then why indeed should you ever be willing to take a real risk? Professor Gilderoy Lockhart is a good example of this. Utterly vain and totally self-absorbed, this famous author and short-term teacher at Hogwarts constantly brags about his actually fictitious exploits of derring-do. But when confronted with real danger, he wilts and runs. He is capable of even the most despicable actions for the sole purpose of avoiding serious risk. Only values that reach beyond the narrow focus of self-protection can produce and support real courage. Love of country, love of family, a deep concern for people generally, a strong friendship, religious conviction, a love of freedom, a sense of justice, or a deep commitment to truth can generate genuinely brave action. Of course, so can a strong enough desire for fame or honor. But this sort of desire can kick into operation effectively only by an attachment to those other, broader positive values. The right values can transform a terrified man or woman into a courageous hero.

We could easily raise a question here. If the right values can generate courageous action, can wrong values do the same job? In other words, could it possibly be that it doesn't really matter what your values are—as long as you have any at all, even bad ones, can you still have the basis for brave action? The evil Lord Voldemort's followers—the men and women known as "Death Eaters"—might seem to provide us with a clear example of this. They often put themselves at risk in fighting his battles and doing his bidding, and yet they seem to lack all the traditional moral values. Instead, they appear to be selfish, greedy, ambitious, sadistic, and vindictive people who will do almost anything for their Dark Lord. It can easily look as though their bad values function in the same way that good ones ordinarily do for generating brave action in the face of danger.

Consider the soldiers of a mafia don, the direct reports of a thoroughly corrupt corporate chief, or a cell of frontline terrorists enacting the will of their evil leader. It can seem that, in their case, tragically bad values can still give rise to the good quality of courage. Or could it be that things are not as simple here as they might superficially seem?

Some traditional students of morality have believed in what has often been called "the unity of the virtues." This is the conviction that it is impossible to have one real moral virtue without all the others. A vicious person, on this account, could not display the true virtue of courage. But the behavior of Voldemort's Death Eaters can appear to refute this view. They seem to do brave things in support of evil. However, that is an illusion. It is certainly true that Voldemort's followers give him a form of allegiance and obey his wicked commands out of their own greed and ambition, as well as from other base and selfish motives, but they follow him into real danger only out of fear, not out of courage. They are more afraid of his merciless wrath than they are of the other dangers that might threaten them, and so they often place themselves into positions of serious risk, but not because of any values other than self-protection. In their own minds, they are always taking the lesser of the available risks, fearfully succumbing to the will of their wicked leader, whatever their own values might suggest. Their actions, however brave they might appear, are for this reason never examples of true courage. Authentic courage always involves overcoming some fear, not being bullied by fear.

A positive value always underlies and motivates the action of a genuinely courageous person. An individual certainly can be brainwashed or hypnotized to act as if he were brave. This is what we see in the case of typical terrorists. They are willing to go on what they know to be suicide missions of self-immolation in order to commit random murders and other acts of destruction. But no such action is an example of real and admirable courage. Without positive values, there can be no positive virtue of courage. And, interestingly, there is a flip side to this coin. Without courage, there can be no other positive values reliably manifested in a challenging world.

Courage is a fundamental virtue, or strength, without which none of the other classic moral virtues could be exhibited properly in any circumstances of perceived personal risk. An honest person, for example, a person who values truth, has to have the courage of his convictions in any circumstances where there is pressure to cover up and hide the truth. Otherwise, honesty cannot prevail. You can't reliably show the virtue of persistence or perseverance in a difficult and risky task if you let your courage falter. Likewise, no one can be a real friend without the courage it takes to stand by another person in times of need and threat. Courage is a necessary condition for consistently living any of the other virtues and for genuinely embracing any positive values that reach beyond the narrowest forms of self-interest.

It's fairly simple to come to at least a basic understanding of courage as a virtue, as well as to see that it is somehow relatively fundamental among the virtues. What's often harder is to grasp how we can cultivate and attain it in difficult situations—precisely the situations in which we need it the most. But on this question, Harry Potter can teach us a great deal. When we examine his many experiences of danger and fear, and how he gets from those visceral reactions to where he needs to be in order to act bravely, we can isolate several factors that seem to be responsible for helping him to have courage.

Anyone can cultivate courage, but like most things of value it takes work to achieve.

It isn't magic that gives Harry the courage to do what he knows he needs to do. And that's good, because most of us don't have this sort of wizardly tool available to us. We can see from all of Harry's confrontations with danger that he relies on some simple but powerful techniques available to us all. I believe that, in fact, we can find in his encounters with danger five basic strategies for summoning the courage we all need in difficult and even terribly frightening situations. I'll just list them first, and then we'll see how they work for Harry. They are completely general strategies, as appropriate for frontline workers, middle managers, top executives, kids at school, or moms and dads at home as they are for young wizards in life-or-death battles. By mastering each of these steps, we can position ourselves for courageous responses to challenging and even threatening situations. Some of the steps involve day-to-day actions in advance of any dangers we may confront, and others recommend things that we should do as the fear wells up inside us. Each step is important, but all of them used together are amazingly effective.

Harry Potter's 5 Steps to Courage
1. Prepare for the challenge.
2. Surround yourself with support.
3. Engage in positive self-talk.
4. Focus on what's at stake.
5. Take appropriate action.

THE POWER OF PREPARATION

1. *Prepare yourself for the challenge.* Nothing builds confidence and supports courage for a difficult undertaking like preparation. Listen to soldiers before a military action or athletes before a big game. You'll hear things like "We've worked hard to prepare for this, and we're just going to go in there now and do what we've been trained to do." Preparation is the first ingredient for confident and courageous action. Harry undergoes exhaustive and exhausting preparation and practice for all his Quidditch matches—the sport of wizards played on broomsticks with flying balls. And it pays off. Then, before the final of three very difficult Triwizard Tournament Challenges that Harry has to face in his fourth year at Hogwarts, he steadies his nerves and readies himself for action by remembering his preparation. He reminds himself that he has survived great difficulties in the past, that he has defeated monstrous creatures and overcome enchanted barriers, and that this time he has had the most opportunity to prepare himself for the challenges he'll confront. As a result of all the explicit preparation he's done, and everything that he's experienced to further prepare him for the upcoming tasks, he has created a new level of confidence in his own abilities and now is able to solidify that confidence by reminding himself of all this preparation.

The simple act of reminding ourselves of what we've faced and dealt with in the past can calm us and position us emotionally to face the challenge at hand. Most of us have confronted "monstrous creatures" and "enchanted barriers" in many ways throughout the course of our educations and subsequent careers. Whether we think those confrontations have gone well or badly, we at least know now that we've survived them and most likely have learned something from them. Even this simple realization can bolster some small degree of confidence in confronting a new difficulty or danger. Everything we've experienced in the past prepares us in some way for what we'll face in the future. And it can help when we remind ourselves of that simple fact. But what helps much more is any explicit preparation we make for something we know we'll be challenged to do. Preparation can inspire confidence and support courageous action like nothing else. It is foundational.

Success is the result of preparation. It is up to us to refine the skills and reinforce the attitudes we need to achieve our goals.

I should say something here about the relationship between courage and confidence, since I have just spoken about them both and Harry often displays them together. They are different but closely related qualities. Both are important for a life of excellence. And both are crucial for any leader to have. But we need to make some distinctions. Courage is a virtue. Confidence is an attitude. A virtue is a habit or tendency to act in some positive way. An attitude is a connected way of thinking and feeling, with an evaluative dimension. We speak of both good attitudes and bad attitudes, appropriate ones and inappropriate ones, while, by definition, any virtue is good and is always appropriate to have. A virtue is an aspect of character. An attitude is a cast of mind. But one further distinction will make their differences clear.

Courage is the fundamental disposition, habit, tendency, or deep inclination to act in support of great value, even in the face of great risk. Confidence is an attitude of positive expectation that a desired outcome will result from our actions. These are clearly different things. It's possible to be very confident in a situation where courage isn't even called for because there is no real danger at hand. And, on the other hand, it's possible to be courageous in a situation where you can't be very confident at all that you'll prevail but you know that, despite the uncertainty, you have to act. So courage and confidence are distinct qualities. But they are mutually supportive and very often go hand in hand.

Courageous action typically requires at least some level of confidence that the action chosen in response to a danger is the best one available, as well as that it has some chance of success. Otherwise, the action would be a desperate or empty gesture rather than a proper expression of courage. Contrast the case of a man who knowingly throws himself on a live grenade a second before detonation to save the lives of friends standing ten feet away with the very different case of a man who knowingly throws himself onto a suitcase nuke a moment before detonation to protect his friends standing nearby. The first example is clearly a case of ultimate courage, but the second we would hardly know how to categorize. So courage typically requires at least some measure of confidence. And confidence in turn sometimes depends on courage. The confidence needed for accessing your full potential for effective action is produced more easily in your life if you're a generally courageous person—one who is not daunted or cowed by obstacles and threats. I've discussed this very interesting relationship between confidence and courage at length in a book called *The Art of Achievement*, so I won't go into any more detail here. But it's important to understand at least something about this connection, because Harry often fortifies his courage in a difficult situation by building his self-confidence. We can all do the very same thing.

Sometimes, a lack of personal confidence is the only real obstacle that stands between a person and the greatness that he or she could attain. Professor McGonagall once points out this linkage to her awkward, sadly underachieving student, and Harry's fellow Gryffindor resident, Neville Longbottom, when she says to him:

"There's nothing wrong with your work except lack of confidence."
(OP 257)

A lack of self-confidence can block our path, regardless of our talents and skills, because when we don't really believe in our own best prospects, we won't venture the risks that alone could stretch those talents and skills to their heights. Conversely, when we do have a robust and healthy attitude of self-confidence, that fact in itself can help unlock our potential for many good things, including properly courageous action.

Personal preparation builds the attitude of self-confidence by giving us resources we know we can use, and in that way it enhances our ability to experience rational courage. Many things in Harry's life have prepared the way for his courageous deeds. And the same thing can be true in our lives. This first lesson in the end is simple. If you want to be brave, be prepared.

SUPPORT AND CONFIDENCE

2. *Surround yourself with support.* The best preparation can position us and ready us for almost any task at the level of personal skill, but by itself that's sometimes not enough to bring us a feeling of confidence and the reality of courage. It's always hard to go it alone, especially in circumstances of great uncertainty or threat. If we have friends and companions who believe in us, and who express that belief to us, they can encourage and support us when we need it like nothing else can. Of course, crowd psychology and interpersonal dynamics can be a two-edged sword. Other people can help us or drag us down. But the firm support of strong companions and close collaborators can strengthen us in the courage we need when things are particularly difficult.

Sometimes, just being around confident people can raise our own general level of confidence. Attitudes can be very contagious. At one point, Ron's sister Ginny reflects on what it was like to grow up around two of her other brothers:

> "The thing about growing up with Fred and George . . . is that you sort of start thinking anything's possible if you've got enough nerve." (OP 655)

We tend to become like the people we're around. If we hang around with negative doom-and-gloom types, depressed pessimists, cynical slackers, and worrywarts, it's hard to enjoy positive feelings in our own hearts. Their bad influence will have an effect. If instead we associate with positive, confident, and courageous people, we will tend to become more positive, confident, and courageous ourselves.

Our friends are a forecast of our future.

There is an old saying that we've all heard: "It's lonely at the top." Many top leaders feel isolated. And this has psychological consequences. We all need some sort of support group of friends or colleagues. That's one of the most important reasons why groups like the Young Presidents' Organization and the Young Entrepreneurs' Organization have come into existence. YPO, for example, is an international support and educational organization with chapters in major cities throughout the world that brings together individuals who have risen to the job of president of a substantially large company before the age of forty. Members can belong until the age of fifty, at which stage they may then go on to join the World Presidents' Organization or another group called, simply, CEO. Having done scores of talks, workshops, and retreats for YPO and WPO groups over the years, I have become convinced that these organizations serve many important purposes in the lives of their members and within the broader global society. Members learn from each other, from world-class resources of all sorts, and can share their loves, joys, worries, and fears, their deepest ambitions and their most daunting challenges with accomplished peers in a completely confidential setting. But another thing also happens. The members of these groups generally tend to be very positive and confident people who rub off on each other, "as iron sharpens iron." Just being around his YPO friends can lift a member's spirits during a difficult time at work or in his personal life. The collective confidence and positive spirit to be found throughout these groups can work wonders in the life of any member and bolster those same characteristics in his own heart and mind. We all need to be around people whose positive attitudes will help spark and sustain our own.

This is one sort of support that good people can provide us just by being who they are and conveying the right attitudes to us in what we see them do. But there are other, more active levels of assistance our friends and colleagues can provide us as well. They can verbally encourage us, pump us up, and cheer us on, and they can provide us with many other kinds of substantial help when we need it. Any of these forms of support will tend to boost our self-confidence in whatever challenge we face.

The best way to get the support of cheerleaders and helpers into our lives is to take the initiative and serve in that role for them. People tend to reflect back what we do for them. If we want other people to support us, we need to cultivate the right sort of relationship with them from the start and be very supportive of their needs and aims. We should encourage and help the people around us first because it's just the right thing to do. It's simply the appropriate way to behave toward our friends and associates. But a great side benefit of helping others is that, as a result, they will then be much more likely to help us when we need it as well.

Harry supports his friends when they need him. Then, when he needs help or encouragement, they are also there for him. Let me give a simple example of how he often benefits from this support. Before his first Quidditch match, our young wizard had a very bad case of nerves. We are told, simply, that he felt terrible. As he walked out of the locker room to go onto the field, he found himself "hoping his knees weren't going to give way" (SS 185). It was that bad. But then he saw something his friends had done to encourage him, and it had an immediate effect. They had made a huge banner that now flew over the crowd flashing the words "Potter for President." He instantly felt better and more courageous.

At a later Quidditch match, the Gryffindor house team captain, Oliver Wood, gives his teammates a locker room pep talk engaging their emotions and reminding them of their high level of preparation and competence (CS 167). This well-informed cheerleading then has its intended effect. They go out and win the match.

This is just basic human psychology. We all benefit from the support and encouragement of others. If we take an active role in helping and encouraging the good people around us when we see they need it, we will be preparing them to do the same for us when we are in need. Harry's friends mean a lot to him. He is touched by their problems.

He helps them. He encourages them. And they in turn encourage him. They also assist him in many other ways.

It's easier to be courageous and confident when we know we have the backup support and goodwill of others. In fact, one of the most important themes of the Harry Potter stories is the great value of friendship. Everything Harry is able to accomplish is rooted in the collaborative efforts of many people. His best friends help him. Some of the teachers help him. The groundskeeper Hagrid helps him. And the great Dumbledore often brings him crucial aid as well. Even when Harry feels most alone, he is able to accomplish whatever he needs to do because of the support of someone else.

Relationships are the foundation for all lasting success.

The motivational literature of the past half century has been geared mainly to individual goal setting and goal attainment. It is rightly described as "self-help" literature, because the focus is distinctly on the individual self and its improvement. But the greatest thinkers on human potential have always realized that there is more to true success than just the development of the individual and the solo achievement of personal goals. There is a social, interpersonal, communitarian side of success that we should never neglect. There is no self-made man or woman whose growth, development, and success didn't come as the result of the input and help of other people along the way. That's just how life works. As Aristotle realized, we are all essentially social creatures. We need other people. And they need us. We accomplish the most, and experience the deepest sense of fulfillment in what we achieve, when we have a close network of people supporting and helping us, people whom we in turn assist when they need our help.

Just having other people helping out inspires us with more confidence and courage when we need it. But it's especially nice when those other people verbally affirm their belief in us—and in doing so help us to believe even more deeply in ourselves. Before the second of three very dangerous challenges that Harry must confront in his fourth year, his huge, strong friend Hagrid goes to the trouble of pulling him aside at class time, patting him on the back, and repeatedly telling him that he's going to do fine in the contest, and actually win—he's certain of it (GF 485). Just witnessing the gentle giant work so hard to encourage his young friend can bring us all an inner smile of satisfaction at the benefits of real friendship between people, however different they may appear on the surface. But from the way the passage ends, we can tell that Harry isn't able to share his friend's confidence in his prospects.

The best intentions and wishes of others, along with their most heartfelt cheerleading, sometimes just don't fully convince us that we're up to the task of whatever challenge we are facing. When we're worried enough, we can inwardly discount the very best words of encouragement that our friends speak. We can tell ourselves they're just being nice, or that they have no idea how bad the situation really is, or how totally ill-equipped we are to deal with it. On occasion, we can work ourselves into such a lather as to be just beyond the reach of anyone's best attempts to be helpful and encouraging. This happened to Harry on the morning of his second Triwizard Tournament task. Hagrid's words of encouragement ultimately couldn't help him. And neither could the cheerful assurances of his fellow students all morning as they greeted him and expressed their belief and confidence in him. It all left him cold. He had gotten himself into such a state that nothing that anyone else said could help (GF 488).

Another interesting example of this occurs with Ron, after he has joined the Gryffindor Quidditch team and has made enough mistakes in his play to convince him in his own heart that he is really no good at all. And the more convinced of this that he becomes, the more his play deteriorates. Any error, however small, can take the wind out of his sails and get him completely off his game. We are told that:

> His greatest weakness was a tendency to lose confidence when he made a blunder . . . (OP 400)

We've all seen this happen. Perhaps we've experienced it ourselves. Each little mistake we make renders us more self-conscious, more fearful of another mistake, and somehow more expectant of exactly that result, in a downward spiral of self-doubt that can create exactly what it dreads. By dwelling mentally on his mistakes, Ron gets so down in the dumps that it's hard for anyone else to help him. Before an upcoming match, Ron and Harry walk together into the Great Hall for breakfast. Everyone there is dressed in the house colors, ready for the big game, and they all give Ron and Harry a huge, enthusiastic welcome, with cheers for their sporting heroes. But it does Ron no good. He sits down in a complete funk.

"I must have been mental to do this," he said in a croaky whisper. *"Mental."*

Harry responds to him and tells him he's going to be fine. He points out that it's absolutely normal to be nervous before a big game. Ron hardly registers what Harry has said.

"I'm rubbish," croaked Ron. "I'm lousy. I can't play to save my life. What was I thinking?" (OP 402)

Hermione walks over with Ron's younger sister, Ginny, and they sit down with the boys. Hermione asks how Ron is feeling. Before he can respond, Harry tells her that Ron's just nervous. She chirps up immediately that this is a good thing, and that she's convinced people never perform as well in school exams—her area of particular expertise—unless they feel at least a bit nervous beforehand. But nothing that Hermione or anyone says can seem to help poor Ron in the least. He is impervious to encouragement.

Hermione, however, has made an important point. Nervousness is a form of energy. It's up to us what we do with it. We can let it shut us down, or we can surf on it to success. The best people often feel quite nervous just prior to a performance or challenge. Those who rarely experience this electric emotion tend for the most part to be clueless slackers who really just don't care, and who therefore never accomplish very much. Nervousness is a sign of emotional commitment and existential, personal investment—a reflection of our values—and it can even be an indication of inner readiness.

Our fear of failure can be a secret springboard to excellence. Used properly it is a fuel for our performance.

Whenever I'm about ready to step in front of a business audience and give a talk, whether it's to a few dozen people or several thousand, I can feel my heart rate increase. I used to say to myself that I'm getting nervous and should just calm down. Now I literally smile, take a deep breath, and just say to myself, "I'm ready." What we often interpret as nervousness can serve us as a very positive thing if we govern it well and use it properly. Hermione is being a good friend to remind Ron of this, using the example closest to her own heart and experience. On this particular occasion, all of Ron's friends do their best to encourage him. But none of the well-intentioned cheerleading and expressions of support can work for poor Ron, who goes on to have a horrible game filled with mistakes, a match that was saved in the end only by his teammate Harry's brilliant individual play.

We often need something more than the encouraging support and verbal assurance of people around us. It's not enough for others to express their belief in us. We need to do something to convince ourselves that we are indeed up to the task. And we each have within our abilities the capacity to do exactly this. There is a mental power used by the most successful of people that is available to us all. It's one that Harry knows how to use when he really needs it.

THE POWER OF THE MIND

3. *Engage in positive self-talk.* Ron undermined and weakened his ability to play Quidditch at the level of the talent he did have because

of his persistently negative self-talk. He would have been much better off by trying to be a little more positive. He could have mentally identified something he was good at within the confines of the game, congratulated himself on that, and then sought to understand how he could extend that ability or skill to more aspects of the game. He could have reassured himself that his hard work would indeed eventually pay off. In even the most challenging of situations, most of us can find some leverage point for beginning to change things for the better. But that requires a positive approach. Purely negative thoughts most often result in nothing more than sadly negative results. Positive thoughts can turn us around.

Inner attitude is the doorway to outer performance. Motivational speakers have harped on this for so long largely because it's true, despite the unfortunate common tendency of too many to stretch this truth into the hyperbolic stratosphere. In reaction to the unqualified and irresponsible claims that are sometimes made for the power of positive self-talk, some intelligent people have become very skeptical of this simple strategy for building confidence. I've heard well-educated businesspeople say, "I'm a little too smart for all that baloney." But reading Aristotle and other great thinkers carefully has convinced me that the smartest people often need the benefit of a little inner cheerleading the most, since they are precisely the people most likely to understand all the ways in which things could possibly go wrong. They need to redirect their energies and mental focus into a more positive direction. We could all use this easily available form of psychological self-medication now and then. Self-talk isn't literally magical, but it can often come close.

Sometimes, Harry tries to build other people's confidence by what he says, and at other times, he talks to his friends in a way that is actually aimed at building up his own inner courage as well. Having to leave Ron in a difficult situation and walk into a worse one, with fairly compelling evidence that he might not get out alive, Harry tells Ron that he'll see him a little later, actually conveying a positive message to himself as well as to his friend (CS 304). By articulating aloud the expectation of a positive outcome, he builds his own confidence, however indirectly and slightly, in the possibility of such a result.

The human mind is very subtle and almost endlessly attentive in certain ways. When we are talking to others, our minds are listening to what we're saying and taking it all in. When we speak disparagingly of our own prospects for success, or even worry aloud, we often subtly undermine our ability to think and act with any positive degree of confidence. If we engage in too much self-deprecating humor, putting ourselves down for the amusement of others, our own minds can register the descriptive content of our witticisms and come to believe it at an unconscious level that will affect what we're able to do. Conversely, if like Harry we speak to others some words of confident expectation, those words, however forced, can register in our own minds in a positive way and make a difference for good, however small. In difficult situations, even a very small difference can occasionally make all the difference that's needed. And Harry seems to know this.

At times, we are privy to the young wizard's inner thoughts. And in them, he occasionally seems to work explicitly on beefing up his courage, as when Rowling represents him in one situation as reminding himself mentally of what he had survived in the past and how he is capable of taking care of himself. In the same scene, standing alone in his room at the Leaky Cauldron Inn where he is staying for a short time, he uses the power of positive self-talk not just inwardly but outwardly, stating aloud his confidence that he is not going to be killed. To his surprise, the mirror in the room speaks up and commends him on his verbalized attitude (PA 68).

It matters what we tell ourselves in the privacy of our own minds and in the solitude of our own rooms. Do we build ourselves up or tear ourselves down? Do we engage in persistently negative thinking, or do we employ positive self-affirmations to enable ourselves to use our talents and preparations in the best possible ways? The choice is always up to us. And the habits of choosing that we have in this regard can have long-term consequences, negatively or positively.

Positive thinking and positive self-talk certainly cannot replace talent and preparation, but they can alter our psychology in such a way as to unlock our true potential when we engage in them carefully and appropriately. When Harry talks to others or himself and represents the future in a positive way, we can understand him to be focusing his intentions and mustering everything within him to move forward in a positive direction, refusing to allow himself to be held back by doubt and debilitating fear. Positive self-talk is not infallible, but it can be extremely effective.

The first time that Harry's friend Ron does manage to overcome his otherwise persistent lack of self-confidence on the Quidditch field and actually do something great, it is because he finally learns to use the power of positive self-affirmation. As he later explains his moment of personal victory to Harry and Hermione, he recalls his stream of consciousness at the time:

"... I thought—*you can do this!*" (OP 704)

Ron had experienced a lot of negative self-assessment in his athletic endeavors, and with the accompanying negative results to be expected. He was finally just tired of it. He tried a positive alternative, and it worked.

The very next year, unfortunately, Ron is back to his old ways, feeling bad about his skills and talking himself down, and his performance is once again as poor as his attitude. Harry tries everything to pump him up and restore his positive mind-set, understanding that his problem is not really physical at all but mental. Once he realizes that nothing else will work, Harry hatches a plan. He makes Hermione suspect and Ron believe that he has furtively slipped a very rare and powerful good-luck potion into Ron's pumpkin juice, a potion they both know that he owns. As a result, Ron goes into the big game minutes later fully believing that he is invincible, and he plays brilliantly, helping the team to a huge win. When Harry is later confronted by a highly disapproving Hermione, who knows that it's illegal to use luck-enhancing potions for sporting events, he gets a real kick out of spilling the beans and confessing to them both that he hadn't actually used the potion at all. He just wanted

Ron to believe that he had, so that for once he would go into a game feeling lucky. And this had its intended result (HB 299). That is the power of the mind and the power of positive belief.

Positive self-talk represents the present and the future in a confident way. Sometimes it does this by recalling positive things about the past, whether matters of preparation and certification or any history of past success relevant in any way to the present challenge that's now being faced. When Harry explicitly remembers escaping the powerful evil wizard Voldemort on three different occasions and mentally dwells on that record of personal success, he positions his mind for more confidence and courage in facing whatever he will confront next. He is a person who succeeds and survives, and that thought fills his mind.

Displacement is a key to human psychology. We rarely ever get rid of any bad thought, emotion, attitude, or habit without displacing it, or replacing it with a more positive alternative. The positive idea or action then takes up the mental, emotional, and behavioral space that had been occupied by the negative one. People addicted to smoking, abusing alcohol, or using any harmful drug are able to stop and really shake the addiction only by using the power of displacement. They can't just toss the bad habit out the window. They have to replace it with a better one. The new habit then takes up the psychological space that had been filled by the roots of the unhealthy behavior. There is no longer any room for the old pattern easily to creep back in. The same thing is true with our thoughts. Doubt and anxiety won't just go away when we need to be confident and courageous. We can't magically banish bad thoughts by simply wishing them away. And neither can Harry and his friends. We do ourselves a favor by following his lead and displacing these negative states of mind with more positive thoughts whenever action is necessary. Positive self-talk can make a big difference.

The power of the mind for building inner confidence goes far beyond the activity of positive mental cheerleading. The ways in which we represent a situation to ourselves can have a huge impact on our experience of both confidence and courage in that situation. And this brings us to Harry's fourth strategy for bravery.

VALUES AND COURAGE

4. *Focus on what's at stake.* The more important a situation is to us, the braver we tend to be in our response to danger, in order to protect, preserve, or promote what we consider to be of great and irreplaceable value. Harry will do incredibly courageous things to save the life of a friend. In one situation, he discovers a passageway, a large pipe that opens into an underground area where a monstrously huge snake has taken one of his younger friends, the sister of his best buddy, Ron. Despite the grave danger involved and the likelihood of serious harm and even death, Harry is fully prepared to go down the pipe. In fact, he knows that if there is any chance he can save the life of Ginny, it's impossible for him not to go (CS 301). Great values defeat fear.

When Harry later is confronted by the man he believes killed his parents, and who seems poised to kill him, any fear in his heart is immediately displaced:

A boiling hate erupted in Harry's chest, leaving no place for fear. (PA 339)

Now, of course, an instance of hate replacing fear is not exactly a paradigm of something good replacing something bad. But it does illustrate the general phenomenon of displacement. With another emotion filling the space that fear would have occupied, there is no room for this more debilitating emotion to enter in and take over.

Later, again, we see in Harry's mind and heart the results of the same sort of emotional displacement:

Harry could feel himself shaking, not with fear, but with a fresh wave of fury. (PA 345)

The anger generated in Harry, the rage or fury at the man he thinks murdered his parents, is enough to push out any rational fear he might otherwise have experienced in a situation like the one he

was in, a situation of apparently imminent danger and a great perceived threat. A powerful feeling of hatred and fierce anger toward
this man is generated by the love Harry has for his dead parents and
the high value he places on them. That love and value well up into a
fury toward their apparent murderer, and the fury blocks any possible
experience of fear. When fear is eliminated, a path forward is opened.
Great values cast out fear. Great values open doors.

But we need to be careful about how this operates in our lives. When
our deepest values and commitments generate negative attitudes and
emotions like hate, anger, or fury, we are typically thrust into a distinctive form of self-produced danger. These negative states of mind and
heart are not easy to control and can often lead us to do things that we
later come to regret. They are not good for us, either psychologically or
physiologically, and they are not generally beneficial and reliable guides
to action. Harry is fortunate that his fury in this situation did not lead
him to do something terribly wrong and irreversible. He ultimately
allowed reason to prevail. But if we grant a place in our hearts for anger,
resentment, hatred, and fury to grow, we make it much more difficult to
do what is reasonable and right. Our deepest values and commitments
most properly displace fear and other inner blockages to action by
means of love, not hate, or concern, not anger. When our fundamental
commitments well up in positive emotion and powerfully positive attitudes, those altogether healthy inner states can sweep aside anything
that is holding us back from what we need to do and point the way forward in a more reliable manner.

Fortunately, the things we value most are more likely in normal situations to inspire us with love, concern, and desire rather than hate,
anger, or fury. And these emotions can link us to the people around us
while they propel us into action. It's much easier for others to get
caught up in our enthusiasms than in our anger or resentments. Before
the founding philosopher of capitalism, Adam Smith, wrote his
famous, groundbreaking treatise *The Wealth of Nations*, he expressed an
understanding of this quite well in his important and often neglected
book *The Theory of Moral Sentiments*. Negative emotions can spread

gloom and alienation. Positive emotions, by contrast, can be contagious in very productive ways. They can spread from person to person. They can bring people together. That's why the most effective leaders make it a habit to remind their associates of how the tasks ahead of them relate to the things they all value most. It's also why the most highly motivated people are to be found in organizations that celebrate and genuinely believe in the right values. People need to feel that their work serves noble ends. We all want to make a positive difference in the world. If we can help the people around us see how the deepest values we hold in common are being lived and even enhanced by our work together, we can provide in this way the basis for a confident and courageous partnership in the pursuit of excellence together.

Remembering what's at stake in our work will renew our sense of purpose and restore our energy like absolutely nothing else can.

In the second challenge of three that Harry has to face at the Triwizard Tournament in his fourth year at Hogwarts, he works hard to save his friends from a potential underwater grave without even thinking of fear. By focusing on what's at stake, he has no time to be delayed or detained by negative emotions. He just immediately takes the action he perceives as necessary. We see the same thing in his fifth year, as reported in *The Order of the Phoenix*, when Harry comes to believe that his godfather, Sirius, has been captured by the powerful Voldemort and is being tortured by him. Harry does not hesitate in deciding that he and his friends need to take immediate action, even though any form of personal involvement will be tremendously dangerous for them all. Hermione and Ron immediately express their very serious and almost frantic hesitation about taking on a rescue effort themselves, but Harry replies:

> ". . . Voldemort's got him, and no one else knows, and that means we're the only ones who can save him, and if you don't want to do it, fine, but I'm going, understand?" (OP 734)

What's at stake is so important that nothing will stop Harry. And he explains this well to Ron and Hermione. His friends then ultimately respond in the same way and follow him into what may mean death for them all, in an effort to save the life of one good man. There is no guarantee of success—in fact, quite the opposite: failure and death are frighteningly likely—but they believe they must try. None of them feels brave at all in this situation, but their action is extremely valiant.

Some of the most courageous people in all of human history have later reported that they didn't feel particularly brave at the time of their great accomplishments, but that they just knew what they had to do and then did it. They were motivated to action by knowing what was at stake. Their convictions overcame their fear and in many cases displaced it altogether. They acted despite being scared, or else explained later that they were just too busy to feel either scared or brave in responding to the urgent needs of the situation. Their values propelled them into action.

In some circumstances, personal preparation, the support and cheerleading of others, inward positive thinking, and consciously dwelling on the great values that are at stake still don't generate together any feeling or inner sense of bravery at all. But the truly brave person doesn't wait for that to change before taking action. Courage or bravery is not at all in itself a psychological feeling, but is rather an inner strength we can have whether we feel it or not. Many ordinary people who have done courageous things and reported later that they didn't feel distinctively courageous while doing them nonetheless often recall that they did feel very focused at the time. Courage is sometimes manifested only when the courageous action is already under way. The fifth strategy to produce and enhance courage that we can learn from Harry Potter is our last one, and it is sometimes the only one that works.

THE ACTION APPROACH TO ATTITUDE AND VIRTUE

5. *Take appropriate action.* Harry shows on many occasions the power of action. In one classroom situation, a large snake unexpect-

edly appears from the end of a wizard's wand and moves toward one of Harry's fellow students, prepared to strike. Fear envelops the room.

> Harry wasn't sure what made him do it. . . . All he knew was that his legs were carrying him forward as though he was on casters and that he had shouted stupidly at the snake, "Leave him alone!" And miraculously—inexplicably—the snake slumped to the floor, docile as a thick, black garden hose, its eyes now on Harry. (CS 194)

As Harry acted, fear just vanished from his heart. At the time it happened, he didn't know he had the rare gift of being a Parselmouth—that, according to Rowling, he could speak and communicate with snakes. He simply saw a situation where action was needed and he took action, not even fully realizing what he was doing or how it could possibly be effective, but nonetheless sensing the right thing to do and then just doing it.

When Harry and Ron first show up at the train station to catch the Hogwarts Express, the special train they take to school each year, they are told that the only way they can get to the proper platform is to walk straight into what appears to be a solid brick wall. But appearances can be misleading. Sometimes our misgivings over a situation can be dispelled only when we take action. Ron's mother, Mrs. Weasley, tells the obviously anxious Harry that all he has to do is to walk straight at the barrier before him, without hesitating. He shouldn't stop or even worry about it. She adds that if he feels any anxiety at all, it would probably be best for him to take it at a run rather than holding back (SS 93). In any challenge, a positive attitude is important, but it's actually getting into action that's always most important of all.

There is one sequence of events in Harry's very eventful life where we can see clearly the importance of both focusing on what's at stake in a dangerous situation and then taking action before having any firm assurance that the courageous act will work as planned, or even that it won't make things dramatically and terribly worse. I like to think of it as Harry's most vivid step of faith, an action that's symbolic of so many other similar steps in his life. He is in the third challenge of the Triwizard Tournament, making his way through a huge, intricate maze bordered by thick, high shrubs, where he has been led to expect that many fearful dangers will stand between him and the ultimate goal he's pursuing (GF 624–625).

He sees an unusual golden mist ahead of him across his path. He hesitates, not knowing what he'll find in the mist, unsure of whether it holds a powerful, dangerous enchantment, and puzzled over how to proceed. He considers doubling back and trying another path in the maze. But then he hears a girl's terrible scream from nearby, up ahead. He calls out the name of the only female contestant in the tournament and gets no response. There is an eerie and foreboding silence. Harry knows he can't hesitate further. He takes a deep breath and runs into the mist.

Whenever a great value is at stake—whenever a good person is in danger—Harry takes action. But what happens as a result of his action in this particular instance could never have been predicted.

The world turned upside down. (GF 624)

Harry suddenly finds himself actually hanging down from the ground, which is now above him, his glasses dangling at the tip of his nose, about to fall into the endless sky now stretching out ominously below him. He is utterly confused and completely filled with a mind-numbing, all-encompassing fear. His first thought is that if he does anything and even tries to move, he might make things dramatically worse in an instant. Even a single step and he might drop free-fall, plunging into the abyss of the sky, now under him, forever lost to the earth. He has to force himself to focus and think.

The situation looks bad. It's totally disorienting and very scary. Panic can easily freeze rational thought in such circumstances. Any action on Harry's part, however small, could make the situation vastly and irretrievably worse. But inaction would mean giving up on any possible chance of helping the girl who had screamed and who might be in mortal danger. The values at stake are great, and our young wizard knows it.

Harry then closes his eyes and does what he is convinced he has to do—he pulls his right foot away from the ground and steps out beyond the available evidence, in the manner of all great heroes, and acts in courageous faith. The result is nearly as startling as what had already just happened.

> Immediately, the world righted itself. Harry fell forward onto his knees onto the wonderfully solid ground. He felt temporarily limp with shock. (GF 624–625)

He breathed deeply, got up, and began again to run forward down the path, leaving behind the mysterious mist that had so shocked and challenged him.

Sometimes, when great values are at stake, you just have to take action, regardless of how things look and no matter how you feel. That is the way of courage. It's also a version of the famous "leap of faith," first vividly described by the great nineteenth-century Danish philosopher and father of existentialism, Søren Kierkegaard. It was Kierkegaard's insight that when momentous values are at stake, thinking and reasoning about what we should do can take us only so far. The evidence available will never be fully sufficient for any truly important personal decision. Confronted with uncertainty, we are tempted to engage in endless reflection for the sake of getting a bit more clarity as to what should be done, but endlessly thinking it through can actually keep us from doing anything at all. As Kierkegaard states in his famous and seminal book *Concluding Unscientific Postscript*, "Reflection can be halted only by a leap." It is this inner leap—in the present case resulting in only a small but decisive step—which Harry, in the company of every real hero, is willing to take.

Harry Potter shows over and over again how a young man fully vulnerable to all the fears that any of us ever experience can overcome those fears and nobly press on to do what needs to be done. None of us can do anything to guarantee that we will act with courage in any particular situation of danger. But we can position ourselves in such a way as to increase the likelihood of such a response. We can do five things that facilitate courage. We can prepare for the challenge, surround ourselves with the support of others, engage in positive self-talk within our own minds, focus on what's at stake, and then take appropriate action. And this just means that we can cultivate the virtue of courage in our lives—a lesson we get from the remarkable and courageous Harry Potter.

HARRY POTTER, JEFF IMMELT, AND THE REST OF US

In a graduation address to the Dartmouth College Class of 2004, General Electric CEO Jeffrey Immelt, himself a Dartmouth graduate, said to these future leaders:

> The challenge you must accept, right now, is to make yourself better every day. The era we live in belongs to people who believe in themselves, but are focused on needs of others. I call it being great and good. Great in the sense of competing to be your best, and good in the sense of building trust through compassion, humanity, and love. And if you commit to being both great and good, you will succeed in any environment.

This seems to capture the practice of Harry Potter as he grows and matures. He learns to believe in himself. He learns to believe in his own abilities to stand up to daunting challenges and prevail. He cares about others and focuses on their needs, while also competing to be the best in the areas of his greatest interest. He builds the trust of others through his basic kindness and compassion for them, and then they are there for him when he needs their support. He seems to be moving in the direction of being both good and great, the combination of qualities that has been modeled for him by Albus Dumbledore.

Immelt then offered the graduates five pieces of advice based on the wisdom that he picked up during his own college years, wisdom that he has seen born out in all of his subsequent business experience.

He refers to these pieces of advice as five values. I'll present them very briefly, using a few of his exact words, and then elaborate just a bit in the spirit of his further remarks. He said:

"First, commit to learn every day."

Greatness arises only out of knowledge. You can't be a great leader, or an exemplary contributor in any endeavor, without an ongoing thirst for knowledge. We all have to learn not to take things at face value, but to dig until we discover the real truth that alone will fuel our enterprises properly. We have to be constantly learning—from our mistakes as well as our successes. This is also an important part of the preparation for life's challenges that facilitates courage.

"Second, work hard with passion and courage."

Life isn't a short dash—it's a marathon. Any contribution to the world that is worth making will take a lot of hard work along the way. And none of us can sustain our efforts over the long haul unless we're genuinely passionate about what we do. It's one of the easily forgotten truths of life that only happy people can keep working hard at the highest levels, with the right motivations, and with the best results. But passion without courage can never prevail against great difficulty. So courage is just as important as loving what you do. And, as we have seen in Harry's experience, courage best arises out of love.

"Third, be a giver."

Until fairly recently in world history, a person could become a great leader mainly by giving orders. Things have changed. The best leaders now lead by giving in many ways. Give to others. Give your best. And give people a reason to trust you. Without a climate of trust, people cannot work together in the best possible ways. People now are very demanding. To gain trust and lead well, you must be a motivator, a communicator, and utterly authentic in your own personal life. You always have to do the right thing in order to get the best results.

"Fourth, you must have confidence."

Leaders take on tough problems. But you can't do that effectively without a hearty dose of confidence in yourself and in what you're doing. We live at a time when the world needs some real heroes in every walk of life. And to be heroic, we can't just take the safe, well-traveled path. We all need the confidence that it takes to do something new. Any other approach is just a waste of your life.

Confidence breeds success.

"Finally, be an optimist."

Expect good things. Do not fear failure. We are each responsible for what we do with every day we have. Each new day brings with it the chance of a new beginning. Use your mistakes to recalibrate your approach and you can confront the next situation with a positive attitude. Optimism is a choice. It's a way of living and dealing with any situation that arises. In work and in life, attitude is just as important as talent. Together, they create potential.

Immelt managed to say quite a lot in his short remarks. And everything he said resonates with what we learn from Harry. Notice in particular that the importance of courage, confidence, and an overall positive attitude figures prominently in his sage advice. And he recommends these qualities in the context of a strongly ethical approach to business and life. Immelt's emphases here mirror what I think the mature Harry Potter would both preach and practice as the CEO of a major company like GE, or as the head of an organization of any size. They can help point us all in the right direction.

The best leaders do the right things, and they do things right. They set proper goals based in a sound vision, and they proceed to move toward those goals in appropriate ways. In substance and form, they know how to bring others along to superior accomplishment. They realize that only a great process will produce great results over the long run, and that, in any endeavor, a great process requires good people working together with great attitudes, living with inner strength, and helping each other forward. Great leaders realize that they can't lead boldly without the virtue of courage, and that their associates also need to live courageously in their own roles, whatever those roles might be. They also understand the power of confidence when tackling new challenges.

It's ultimately character and inner attitude—the fundamental dispositions and activities of our hearts and minds—that determine what any of us can accomplish as leaders. Just like Harry and his friends, all of us face challenges, difficulties, and dangers of various sorts throughout our days. To find the real magic in business and in life, we need to find the path of courage in dealing with what each new day brings. If we are able to take the risks that we feel are right and stand up for the values that we know are best, then we can reap the great rewards that courageous living alone can bring. When we learn to relish the contests of life for the growth that they can create, we begin to live more fully, and we guard ourselves against the terrible regrets that the timid inevitably feel.

Great leadership requires great courage. A great leader lives courageously and helps those around him to do the same. The virtue of courage so strongly embodied by Harry Potter, as well as the deep values that give rise to it and support it, can be appreciated most fully in connection with the broader ethical context within which we identify more generally what the proper values and the real virtues in life are. And that's the next topic we'll address in our quest to understand the best of what Harry Potter can teach us.

3

~∞

THE ETHICS OF WIZARDS

Always with Unyielding Integrity.
—*GE Values Statement*

M ark Twain once remarked that to act morally is noble, but to talk about acting morally is also noble, and a lot less trouble. This is funny, but while it's true in one sense, it's also misleading on a much deeper level. In this chapter, we're going to talk about what we can learn from the wizards in Harry Potter's world about the moral life and the role of ethics in long-term success. But on the topic of ethics, the whole point of talk is action. When we begin to understand what acting morally, or ethically, really means, we learn very quickly that the worst trouble in life comes from ignoring the insights and requirements of ethics.

OUR CHALLENGE

Ethics is one of the most important things in business, and in life generally, and it's also one of the most misunderstood. Getting it right—properly understanding the ethical way of living, and then acting with ethical consistency every day—is the foundation of sustainable success in both our professional and personal lives. Getting it wrong is a setup for disaster, as so many business headlines over the past few years have indicated.

There is nothing more crucial for building a great career, enjoying a rich and fulfilling personal life, and leaving your proper legacy in this world than living the right ethical values in everything you do. But consistently ethical living has always been a challenge for a great many people. Before we take a direct look at some of the ethical lessons in Harry Potter's world, we're going to do a little preliminary thinking about why ethical living is such a challenge, we're going to dig up the deepest truth concerning what ethics is really all about, and then we're going to ask what it takes to live the best life we can.

Hogwarts is ethically no different from the rest of the world. There have been saints and scoundrels at every point in history. The saints have understood some important things that the scoundrels have never fully grasped. If we can share their insights, we will inevitably gain a new and distinctive motivation to resist the temptations that always threaten to lure us off the high road of ethical action.

GETTING CLEAR ABOUT WORDS

When you think about it, the word "ethics" itself can be a bit confusing. Is it singular or plural? It looks plural, but, oddly, it's both. We might say, "His ethics are deplorable," treating it as plural, but we could just as easily remark, "Ethics is crucial in business," using a singular verb as if we're dealing with a singular noun. To make things even more complicated, we sometimes use another form of the word that's obviously singular—"The Puritan ethic is fading fast." This can all be a tad worrisome for any of us who are haunted by the memory of an old English teacher, every bit as strict as Minerva McGonagall, who insisted that we get such things right. But the key to a basic mastery of the word is actually quite simple.

When we're talking about the various principles or patterns of action that a person lives by, we tend to speak of ethics in the plural—as in "Her ethics are admirable." When we want to refer to an overall concern for moral principles, or to the study of such principles and values generally, we most often use the term in a singular way—as in "Ethics always has a place in law school, medical school, and business school curricula." Could we alternatively say that ethics always *have* (plural) a place in professional school curricula? Yes, unfortunately, the sad fact is that we can, although it would be a bit less standard. There is no absolute consistency of usage for the term in ordinary language, but there are general tendencies of standard use.

One more source of potential confusion is that some people use the words "ethics" and "morality" differently, limiting the former to professional and business contexts and the latter to personal matters. It seems to me that this is ultimately a distinction without a difference, or else it's a big mistake. We shouldn't even try to compartmentalize our lives in this way, in terms of how we treat people. Other human beings deserve a certain measure of respect, honor, and care, whether the context is business or family life, the office or the neighborhood. Values like truth and virtues like courage range across the distinction between the personal and professional with no alteration whatsoever. Because of this, I like to use the words "ethics" and "morality" basically as synonyms, meaning roughly the same thing.

Respect, honor, and a concern for others are just as important at work as they are at home.

We shouldn't let language confuse us. Life is often confusing enough without allowing our words to wrap us up in needless perplexity. The predominant modern misunderstanding of ethics, however, has little to do with grammar and word usage. It's a fundamental mistake concerning what ethics is really all about. It's subtle, and it's dangerous. Seeing the real truth about ethics will help us to unmask this mistake, and once we do, we'll understand the real nature and power of ethical living. That, in turn, will help us to learn the most we can from the ethics of the wizards in Harry's world.

UNDERSTANDING THE HEART OF ETHICS

Most people nowadays seem to think that ethics is all about staying out of trouble. That's why corporate and industry discussions of ethics always center on issues of law, regulation, codes of conduct, compliance, and the Federal Sentencing Guidelines. But this is a misunderstanding of ethics that has misled people throughout much of human history, and it's a mistake that can set us up for serious problems today.

When you think that ethics is all about staying out of trouble, you can easily be tempted to accept any alternative way of avoiding trouble as a substitute for real ethics. We all saw this in the case of the Enron debacle. Some very smart executives came to believe that sophisticated deceptions involving sufficiently complex and "creative" accounting practices would keep them out of trouble, no matter what they did. But they were wrong. And disaster ensued.

The ancient philosophers saw it all much more clearly, and so have the best people in all of human history: Ethics is not about staying out of trouble. Ethics is about creating strength. And this operates at every level. Ethics is all about strong people, strong relationships, strong organizations, strong friendships, strong communities, and strong families. Ethical action produces a form of strength grounded in trust that nothing else can duplicate. And that's because ethics is rooted in a fundamental realism about human nature. There can be no substitute for it when it's properly understood.

The path to resilience and strength is through ethical behavior. Unethical conduct inevitably leads to failure.

My father had his own real estate company, focused on large residential land development. He always treated people well. He was completely honest in all his business dealings, absolutely dependable, and he went out of his way to be helpful to his clients, along with potential clients. Because of that, people instinctively trusted him. His reputation for integrity spread. And his business grew. I remember that, in the course of his career, he sold the same piece of land—two hundred and fifty acres—six times. When each buyer or group of buyers decided that they wanted to sell, they came back to my father to handle the transaction. They all did well because of their investments, and my dad did very well because of his character. Strong character is a foundation for strong business.

Harry Potter's friends look to him as a leader not just because of his many talents and accomplishments but also because of his character. They know they can trust him. They can depend on him. They are convinced that he has their best interests at heart, as well as his own. He will do anything for them, and they know it. This deep-down certainty about Harry's goodness provides a strength and resilience to his friendships. He and his friends occasionally may misunderstand each other and have fights like many young friends do, but in the end, their bond is so strong that his closest chums will follow Harry to what they know may be their deaths. Harry's fundamentally ethical orientation is the foundation of much of the good that he can do with others.

There is something else that's important for us to get straight. Morality and legality are different. Ethics and law overlap, but they are distinct things. Some people think that as long as they aren't violating any laws, they are satisfying all the requirements of ethics. One way to see the difference between ethics and the law is to consider the fact that, throughout history, ethical people have often felt they were morally obligated to disobey grossly unjust laws while working to see them changed. Harry and his fellow students, as well as some of the teachers, including Dumbledore himself, have on occasion had to resist and actually violate official Ministry of Magic decrees that were unjust and dangerous. It was precisely their strong ethical concerns that generated their stance and their resulting actions.

On the other side, sometimes the law is silent but the demands of ethics are clear. Vance Young, a good friend and star Realtor in my small town, had over eighty-three million dollars' worth of real estate closings last year. He always goes far beyond the requirements of the law in making sure that everyone in a transaction is treated fairly and well. When two friends of his were recently making competing offers on the same piece of property, among four interested buyers, he was careful to follow the ethical path of maximum disclosure to everyone involved in the whole situation, rather than be content merely with the extent of disclosure legally required. He believes that good character demands following the promptings of conscience and not just hiding behind mere compliance. And the strength of his business reflects that commitment.

In ancient Greek, the word "ethos," from which we get "ethics," actually meant "character," not "rules" or "regulations." It had to do with integrity. And that's an interesting concept. Our term "integrity" comes from the same root word as "integer," which means "whole number," and the word "integrate," which means "to bring together into a greater unity or wholeness." Integrity is all about wholeness, unity, and harmony. When you make a decision, do you bring to bear on it all of your highest values? Do you always act in harmony with all your most fundamental beliefs and commitments? Are your words united with the truth? Do you treat other people the way you would want to be treated—acting toward others in harmony with how you'd want them to act toward you? These are all questions of integrity. They indicate what makes for strong character, a strong person, and strong relationships. Understanding this helps us to avoid a second and closely related modern misunderstanding of ethics, the very common belief that ethics is really just a matter of restraint and restriction, involving lots of rules that tell us not to do what we might really enjoy and benefit from doing.

We get the English word "virtue" from an ancient Latin word, "virtu," a term that meant "strength, power, or prowess." The great moral philosophers have always understood that deeply satisfying and proper success in life comes from the exercise of certain virtues, or strengths, of character. As much as the circumstances and conditions of human life have been transformed throughout the centuries, human nature has never really changed, and this insight about success has never changed, either.

Personal power comes from being honest with yourself and candid with other people, along with being dependable, courageous, caring, persistent, and creative. These qualities are all individual human virtues, or habits of thinking, feeling, and acting that empower us. When you understand this, you no longer see ethics as mainly about restriction and restraint, although both these things are certainly part of the ethical stance. As a matter of fact, the simple restraint of self-discipline is one of the most forgotten virtues in modern life, and yet it's of crucial importance for both business success and personal happiness. The unrestrained life is, ironically, the unsatisfied life. But ethics is not just a matter of being told that "Thou shalt not" do this, or do that. It's mostly about building and being the best and strongest person that you can be.

HOW TO BE ETHICAL EVERY DAY

This last insight leads us to a third aspect of the modern misunderstanding of ethics. Many people tend to think of ethics as encompassing just big, complex, and debatable problems involving professional codes of conduct, large-scale social issues regarding such things as race, gender, and poverty, workplace problems like sexual harassment, and headline-grabbing corporate abuses of standard accounting practices. But ethics is mostly about the little things: How do you feel and act toward the people around you every day? Are you a blessing or a curse to those who cross your path? Do others see you as short-tempered, peevish, insulting, dismissive, or arrogant? Or do they rightly think of you as a kind and caring person? Are you perceived as self-absorbed and undependable, or as someone others can count on? These are the basic ingredients of ethical living. Of course, as Harry's career at Hogwarts often shows, circumstances can sometimes mislead people into misunderstanding us and ascribing to us characteristics, attitudes, and motivations that we don't have at all. But a truly ethical person will be understood as such by the people closest to him or her. And Harry's experience bears this out. When all the rest of the school seems to doubt him, he always has at least one friend who sees him for the basically good person he really is.

The little things always add up. How do we interact with those around us? What tone of voice do we use? Are we kind and under-standing? Are we honest? Do we get back to people with answers to their questions as quickly as possible, or do we ignore their needs whenever we think we can get away with it? Do we realize that great business is all about taking care of the customer, or do we think that it's really all about us—our needs and our income? Are we as good as our word, or do we expect a free pass in life? These are the most com-mon sorts of questions that constitute the small but very important concerns of everyday ethics.

In ethical behavior, everything matters.

Ethics is not mainly about mind-bending complexities and dilem-mas at all. Sometimes, of course, we do face difficult questions where ethical demands might seem to pull us in two opposite directions. This can happen when loyalties to more than one person, institution, or value are in play—as, for example, when you're both representing the interests of your company and yet also acting as an advocate for your client. We can also occasionally face other complex issues where there are no clear precedents or rules to guide us. I don't mean to say that figuring out everything we should do in specific situations is always easy. Not at all—it's sometimes quite difficult. But it always involves treating other people as well as we possibly can. It always means treating others the way we would want to be treated if we were in their place. We'll see in just a bit how this comes up in Harry's life. But for the moment, I want to provide first a little more preparation for our reading of the wizards.

I've just stated a version of the most famous ethical rule in all of world history, the Golden Rule. It's a touchstone of conduct that's been recognized by the wisest people in every developed culture, and it is every bit as relevant to modern business and life as the latest developments in science and technology. In fact, nothing may be more relevant to personal success than this one standard of action. The best classroom teachers I know govern their conduct by the Golden Rule. And then there are teachers like Severus Snape, Harry's sarcastic, vindictive, and emotionally abusive potions instructor, who seems completely unable to engage in Golden Rule behavior, at least when it comes to Harry and his friends. And this prevents him from teaching them well. The most successful retailers I know treat all their customers in accordance with the Golden Rule—even the difficult ones. Great managers and the most admirable leaders I've ever met follow its directive in everything they do. I've also seen the rich results of this wonderful rule of ethical behavior in the history of my own family's business throughout the years.

The Golden Rule gives us a test. Whenever we're thinking about doing something that will affect another person, or group of people, in any way, we should always ask the question: "Am I treating everyone involved as I would want to be treated?" Other people respond to Golden Rule treatment and will find it difficult not to return the favor and treat us well in turn. I've come to think of this one rule as the single most important tool we have for ethical living. If you haven't been acting in accordance with the Golden Rule in a certain context or relationship in the past, it's never too late to start. When you take the initiative and begin to go down this moral high road, you can change things for the better to an extent that you may never have anticipated.

Of course, consulting the Golden Rule can't guarantee that we'll make the right decision in every situation. Some circumstances are indeed complicated, confusing, and tangled up with conflicting considerations. However, using this famous rule can slow us down, refocus our minds, remind us of the likely consequences of our conduct, and nudge us in the right direction. We all need its help in living the ethical life.

Great leaders treat others the way they would want to be treated.

Sometimes you might find it difficult to do the right thing under pressure. Basically good people can be tempted to break the ethical rules now and then in the same way they might drive five or ten miles an hour over the speed limit out on the interstate. But the ethical limits described by principles like the Golden Rule aren't like highway laws. They are rooted in universals of human nature. We all know that, as important in many ways as our speed limits are, they could have been set a little higher or a little lower. It's possible to violate them on occasion without any obvious harm and for what you feel is a greater good. The problem is that this can contribute to a relaxed, loose attitude toward all limits. But as Socrates taught us long ago, when we cross the moral line and do something unethical, it always causes harm, at least to us, in our own souls. When Draco Malfoy becomes increasingly involved with evil during his sixth year at school, he gradually begins to look physically ill. And Voldemort himself suffered great harm as a result of his attempt to murder Harry. Evil wreaks havoc in the world and always rebounds on itself. There is no proper room in life for lying to clients or family members, betraying people, cheating, stealing, and putting others down. Such actions dishonor and harm the other people involved. And they degrade and weaken those who are responsible for them. It's of vital importance not to stray from the ethical path in anything we do. Unethical behavior always involves self-inflicted damage.

In our own day, more business leaders, and more people generally, are starting to realize a truth long known by the great thinkers. Unethical success is extremely fragile and is always self-destructive over the long run. As Dumbledore says at one point to Harry concerning their chief evil nemesis, recounting what happened when the Dark Lord murdered Harry's parents and chose to target Harry himself, and referring to Harry's resultant commitment to see him eliminated:

> "Voldemort himself created his own worst enemy, just as tyrants everywhere do! Have you any idea how much tyrants fear the people they oppress? All of them realize that, one day, amongst their

many victims, there is sure to be one who rises up against them and strikes back!" (HB 51)

If you habitually treat people badly, someday someone will right the imbalance of justice in the universe. And you will feel the consequences. Unethical conduct always bears within itself the seeds of its own destruction. In our daily behavior, and whenever we are called upon to make an ethical decision, we should bear this in mind.

In every situation, it's important to do the right thing. But what about the very toughest decisions, when the right choice isn't easy to see? The late British philosopher and novelist Iris Murdoch pointed out in her little book *The Sovereignty of Good* that if we think ethically and act well in the normal course of business and life, if we pay attention to the proper things and value the right things, then, when a difficult decision-making situation arises, we may find to our surprise that the choice has already been made for us by those structures of value and care that we've long been developing. Life is habit, and the right ethical habits will serve us well. If we take care in the little things, the big things won't be so hard to get right after all.

It helps to have friends and mentors with whom we can honestly discuss our trials and struggles. They can give us moral encouragement, and we can return the favor. It's much easier to live ethically when we work with other people who share our basic commitments. But ultimately it's up to each of us to remind ourselves what ethics is all about, and how the strength it creates can't be had any other way. We have to learn how to resist and ignore the occasional protests and promises of our imagination that there are shortcuts to happiness, and quick fixes of satisfaction, to be had outside the realm of ethical action. In the final analysis, as Socrates, Plato, and all the great philosophers have reminded us, we each need to ask ourselves what sort of life is best worth living and whether our actions each day conspire in favor of that sort of life or undermine it. The real truth about ethics is that, ultimately, everything we do matters, and that the ethical path is the only reliable road to a life of fulfillment and meaning.

It's that important in life, and we see its importance in the various turns and twists of Harry Potter's adventures.

Some people would object strenuously to reading J. K. Rowling's entertaining stories for their ethical lessons. We'll see what their objections are, and then we'll see what the real truth about Harry and his moral journey might be. There are deep truths that can surprise us, and they certainly can enlighten us.

MORAL RELATIVISM AND REALISM

Some adult readers have claimed that the ethics of the Harry Potter stories are simply deplorable. These books have been accused of "moral relativism" and much worse. They have even been charged with promoting the attitudes and rituals of satanic witchcraft. This latter allegation is silly. The former is just wrong. Let's look briefly at each.

Most of the witchcraft and wizardry of Harry Potter's world has more similarity with the flying brooms and pointed hats to be found in Disney cartoons than with anything in Wicca, the very small, real-world, quasireligious sect of self-proclaimed contemporary witches and warlocks, with their informal priesthood of perpetual graduate students and coffeehouse radicals. And even Wicca itself has more in common with the New Age, Southern Californian, laid-back spirituality of incense and massage oils than with anything involving evil, nefarious actions, and demonic or satanic rituals. Those critics who can't tell the difference just aren't paying attention. Harry and his friends would probably feel right at home at the Magic Kingdom in Orlando or Anaheim, but would get as far away as possible from the dirty dungeons of a modern satanic cult, as fast as their flying broomsticks could carry them. There is no ritual mutilation of animals or perversely religious sacrifice of innocent humans going on at Hogwarts. It isn't that kind of place at all. And there is nothing whatsoever in the stories to encourage anything like that in anyone's life.

As to the charge of moral relativism, critics have often complained that Rowling doesn't do enough in her books to portray a clear and absolute difference between good and evil. They claim that the good characters are not pure good and the evil villains aren't evil enough. Ask them for examples of what they mean and you'll often get answers as weak as "Well, Dumbledore is supposed to be such a good person and yet he is portrayed on occasion as getting very angry," or "After all, Dumbledore at one point knowingly encourages Harry to sneak around in an invisibility cloak and do something to undermine the adult authorities," or "Harry is supposed to be a good guy and he tells lots of lies. He even swears."

First of all, we can draw a clear and absolute distinction between good and evil without thinking that either is ever found in a pure form in normal life. Rowling's good characters have weaknesses, and her evil characters typically have at least some slim hope of potentially redeeming qualities, however deep down and presently diminished those qualities might be. No realistic depiction of good and evil in the world involves the caricature of deifying the good and absolutely vilifying and demonizing the bad. Rowling's portrayal of good and bad as intermingled in many characters' lives is not moral relativism but the most believable, straightforward moral realism.

Second, Rowling's presentation of her good characters isn't as tainted as critics complain. Consider the complaint that the good headmaster Dumbledore is occasionally described as angry. In our world, as well as in Harry's, good people can get angry, even very angry, and indeed should, when confronted with tremendous injustice or evil. There is nothing inherently bad or wrong about an experience of anger—the moral issue resides in the question of how we control and use that anger. Dumbledore experiences a righteous and robust anger when confronted with gross injustice or evil that endangers others, but he never lets that emotion take control of him and deflect him from the path that goodness demands. Anger is a natural reaction of good to evil. And in the headmaster's life, it acts as the fuel for proper action. When Dumbledore encourages Harry to put on an invisibility cloak and sneak around Hogwarts to do something that undermines an adult authority, the "authority" in question is altogether corrupt and is about to do something that is both terribly evil and irreversible and that, unfortunately, in the circumstances can be stopped in no other way.

Third, and we'll have to talk about this at length in the next chapter, it's true that the young Harry and his friends all tell lies—fairly frequently and apparently with ease. We also are informed that the adolescent Harry on occasion swears. We aren't told what he says, but only that he can speak in this way when frustrated. Rowling doesn't present lying or swearing as a good thing, or as in any way admirable or commendable behavior. She just represents it as actually going on in the lives of these young people. In particular, she doesn't portray the students' casualness about truth as right, only as rife. Again, this does not intimate any form of moral relativism; it's just a display of moral realism. By all current ethical surveys in the real world, this is, sadly, how lots of young people act. Over 90 percent of children under the age of eighteen who were questioned in a recent ethics survey admitted that they lie to their parents. They tell lies to others, too. In another survey, almost 100 percent of adults admitted that they lie, dissimulate, prevaricate, or stretch the truth beyond its proper bounds on occasion. This is how we are. It's nothing to be proud of, and it's certainly nothing to endorse, but it's part of the human condition. The only people who claim never to have engaged in such behavior tend to be either individuals with very bad memories or else people who are doing the very thing they deny in the act of denying it.

We'll return to this topic as our main focus in the next chapter, because it is so important in our personal and business lives. We live in a culture where it's become more common, more expected, and, unfortunately, more accepted to engage in unethical forms of deception. Some people in the world of business see this as a normal part of negotiating and as a standard tool in their tactical arsenal. Others, unfortunately, also view it as an inevitable element of marketing. And yet we are almost all still morally offended when we discover that we've personally been told lies and deceived. Most of us understand, deep down, that lies always detract from the best sort of life and prevent the building of the best and most healthy relationships.

Surveys have shown repeatedly that lying is remarkably pervasive in high schools and colleges throughout the nation. No wonder, then, that this can be a problem when people enter the world of work. As the poet Gerard Manley Hopkins wrote in 1918, "The child is father to the man." Princeton philosopher Harry G. Frankfurt recently wrote a surprisingly bestselling little book titled *On Bullshit*, in which he contends that, throughout the culture, we've lost our sense of the importance of truth. One man I know recently told me that he had been fired from a sales job with great responsibility. When he asked why, his boss replied, "Because of your ethics." The executive went on to explain that in this important sales position, the young man had to be willing to do whatever it took to make a sale, and that this included an openness to using even deception and outright lies whenever necessary. My friend was known to be a man committed to truth and honesty, and his moral stance was deemed to be completely unacceptable for his job. It can get that bad.

Truth is ultimately a friend, even when it looks like a threatening stranger.

From the point of view of what I know, believe, and value now, it's a source of great embarrassment for me to look back on my life so far and to have to acknowledge, even to myself, that I've actually told some lies—not as a matter of course, or at all frequently, and mostly in my youth, I'll hasten to add, but on at least some fairly rare occasions. Over a period of years in the past, to my current regret, I at times resorted to delicate and diplomatic untruth, usually to protect the feelings of another person, but on a few and especially shameful occasions, merely to safeguard myself from embarrassment or trouble. I never let this creep into my classroom work as a student, into my own professional endeavors as a teacher, or into any of my business relationships, but I allowed it just enough incursion into my life to understand from firsthand experience how the young Harry Potter could fall into this easy "out" on many occasions. Owing to the same range of experience, I also now know without any doubt that, in the final analysis, it's not a good thing to do. I didn't always skip the odd social occasion or miss the occasionally inconvenient commitment because I really wasn't feeling well, but I later actually felt pretty bad about claiming it at the time. Not even my best psychosomatic skills could cause my physiology to match my excuses every time. Now, years later, I believe that, in my maturity, I have learned my proper lessons about all this, and I wish I had understood it at a much younger age. It's been a long time since I've offered another person even the smallest little white lie to avoid offending, or used any sort of artful dodge to slip the noose of trouble I felt I didn't need. And the surprising discovery I've made is that it was never necessary at all. In addition, for all the time since then, I've enjoyed tremendously the difference of how it feels to live more thoroughly in the truth and have come to understand what good can be done and what can be built in the world, only by consistently using the reliable, unshakable foundation of fact.

Most of us normally experience good and evil in fairly subtle and less than dramatic ways throughout our day-to-day experience. All good is important, and all evil is damaging, but most of what we encounter in our normal lives in developed societies tends to be fairly far from either extreme end of the spectrum. We confront horrible evil and we see the most exalted forms of good more often in art and history than in the ordinary course of daily life. But certainly, a clear distinction between good and evil is never just something for books, movies, and crime dramas on television, perhaps in addition to what we read in the news about events in faraway places. It matters deeply in the reality of our normal daily lives. It also matters a great deal in the world of Harry Potter.

Let's think for one more moment about the charge that in the Harry Potter stories evil isn't portrayed in an absolute way. I wouldn't want to come across a figure more evil than the vile Lord Voldemort. This is a completely corrupt wizard questing for the ultimate power, an ascendancy over life and death. And he seems to enjoy killing anyone who stands in his way. He takes over lives, perverts the souls of others, and has no regard whatsoever for any positive value. The fact that he may have begun life as an apparently normal little boy, and then increasingly become so evil over the course of the years, doesn't make him any less wicked, as if he is somehow a junior upstart compared to a possible figure of eternal evil. Even the Satan of the Bible once fell from grace. A person can embody evil, and perhaps even something like absolute evil, despite the fact that it has taken him some time to get into that condition.

There are absolutes of good and evil in the Harry Potter stories just as there are in real life, but most of the characters there, just like the people here, move around day to day along the moral spectrum moderately far from either extreme. Rarely do we encounter pure good or unalloyed evil, but, more commonly, some mix of each. Most of the main characters in the magic world of Harry Potter are young people moving through a fog of insight and illusion, groping their way forward to increased moral clarity, like most of us in the real world. We shouldn't just condemn them for their foibles, but applaud the compelling depiction of their journey from a considerable degree of naïve carelessness with good and evil into a greater wisdom that clearly sees the difference. It's ultimately this that Rowling gives us. And in doing so, she helps us to appreciate the real nature of ethics in the world.

ETHICAL AND UNETHICAL PEOPLE

A genuinely ethical person believes that some personal qualities are objectively good—trustworthiness, for instance—and others are objectively bad—untrustworthiness would be an equally good example. He or she also believes that some actions are objectively right—helping a good person who is in need, for example—and others are objectively wrong—intentionally harming an innocent person for no good reason would be an uncontroversial case. The ethical person holds a conviction that the good and the right are to be embraced, and the bad and the wrong are to be avoided. From the perspective of ethics, anyone who fairly consistently embodies the good and the right, with no radical departures from that pattern, is deemed morally good. A person who embodies predominantly the bad and the wrong is for that parallel reason morally bad. In addition, any extreme and apparently irredeemable version of the morally bad or morally wrong is most often characterized by an ethical person as evil. The completely unethical or amoral person, by contrast, most often has a very different view of life. From his perspective, good and evil don't even exist as objective features of existence.

At one point, Harry discovers in a surprising way that one of his recently hired instructors at Hogwarts is secretly a servant of the evil wizard Voldemort. As their confrontation is happening and the truth is coming out, Professor Quirrell suddenly speaks of himself in the past, in his own youth, perhaps even hoping to influence Harry and win him over to the dark side, by saying:

> A foolish young man I was then, full of ridiculous ideas about good and evil. Lord Voldemort showed me how wrong I was. There is no good and evil, there is only power, and those too weak to seek it. (SS 291)

The unethical person thinks that life is one big game. Power is its goal, as well as the main implement for playing it. This philosophy of life can be found represented in human history from the earliest times, but it has perhaps its most famous embodiment in some of the work of the Renaissance philosopher Niccolò Machiavelli. It seems that Machiavelli believed the meaning of life to be just power—getting it, exercising it, and maintaining it. Everything else is secondary. You want money? Get enough power and you will be able to acquire it. Do you crave fame? Again, sufficient power can make it happen. Comfort? Security? Reputation? Powerless people can only dream. Whatever you want, the right amount of power can put it within your reach. Therefore, you should seek power, Machiavelli and all like-minded philosophers have urged. In more recent times, the nineteenth-century German thinker Friedrich Nietzsche developed a similar take on life, and his works influenced various Nazi theorists in later years.

It's ironic that the alternative to an ethical life is the unbridled pursuit of power — since the deepest source of genuine power is living the ethical life.

This is the life philosophy of the wizard referred to by people who fear him as "You-Know-Who" or "He-Who-Must-Not-Be-Named," the evil Lord Voldemort, Harry's archenemy and nemesis. Voldemort seeks power over other people, power over all of life, and ultimately power over death. He says to his followers:

"You know my goal—to conquer death." (GF 653)

Professor Quirrell's downfall was to follow in Voldemort's footsteps and serve to do his bidding in all things, hoping in that way to obtain a share in his power.

Recall the famous claim of Lord Acton in 1887: "Power tends to corrupt, and absolute power corrupts absolutely." The lust for power is an inherently corrupting quest. The more of it that an unethical person gets, the more he wants, and the further he drifts from a proper perspective on life. There is, of course, nothing inherently wrong with power. Power can be used for good or evil. Great power can put a person in a position to do great good. What is wrong, and is inevitably corrupting, is a focal quest after power for its own sake—which is to say, ultimately, for one's own sake. This is a life path that is inherently self-absorbed and that falls into the category that traditional monotheistic religions label as "idolatry." An all-consuming pursuit of power easily becomes a worship of power and plunges a person into a state of corruption that cuts him off from all the higher values in life. Like traditional forms of idolatry, this pursuit ends up being self-defeating and self-destructive.

When Harry first visits the Gringotts Bank, where the wizards of his world keep their gold, money, and other valuables, he sees engraved on some inner entrance doors a short poem about greed that is meant to serve as a warning to all prospective thieves. It actually conveys a broader cautionary word than that, and applies to any form of greed for other people's money, for power, or for any other form of desired status or personal resources. It says, in part:

Enter, stranger, but take heed
Of what awaits the sin of greed,
For those who take, but do not earn,
Must pay most dearly in their turn. (SS 72–73)

Seeking and taking anything that isn't properly ours will bring with it the unpleasant surprise of some form of proper punishment. The unethical person doesn't typically understand this, and so is often baffled at the true consequences of his greed for power or things. The danger in chasing the wrong things, or in pursuing any goals in the wrong ways, is that we'll find to our surprise that the totality of what we get will end up being very different from what we had wanted and hoped to attain.

THE DANGERS OF CORRUPTION

There is another dangerous process evident in these stories. Nearly all of the people who associate with Voldemort are thoroughly corrupted by his company as they become ensnared by his vision. This is a danger noted by all the great philosophers, and one that results from a tendency in human psychology that we've already considered in our look at Harry's courage. There is an incredible malleability to human personality. We tend to become like the people we're around. In the New Testament, the apostle Paul quotes a Greek proverb that goes back at least as far as the work of the ancient poet Menander (c. 342–292 B.C.) when he says in his first letter to the Corinthian church, "Do not be deceived: 'Bad company corrupts good morals.'" George Herbert much later said it like this: "Associate not with evil men, lest you increase their number." No greater advice has ever been given. Let's call this "The Principle of Association"—we are influenced by and in many ways eventually become like the people we're around.

I watched a small lizard outside my back door yesterday. When he was sitting on a bright green plant, he was every bit as green as the stem supporting his weight. Then he jumped off onto the brown and rusty braided wire handle of an old wicker basket. Within a surprisingly short time, he was nearly as brown as the wire. We human beings don't change our color, but our personalities and actual characters can mold themselves to our environment in unexpected ways. This is why it's so important to choose our friends and close associates wisely. Their impact on us can be dramatic, and if it's bad, insidiously so, because we're typically unaware of what's happening as we begin to be transformed by the example of their presence.

The number of widespread ethical failures to hit the business headlines in the past several years has been astounding. And in each case, corrupt individuals have had an insidious influence on their associates, corrupting them in turn, and often convincing them to do things they might not otherwise have even thought of doing. We may feel like we're strong enough to be around any kind of person without being influenced by them, but that's usually not a very realistic opinion. Bad people can have terrible effects on us in many ways, even if we're never actually tempted to follow them into their misdeeds.

We become like the people we surround ourselves with.

Rowling illustrates something closely akin to this principle in a particularly vivid way. The dementors are horrible and frightening creatures used as guards at the toughest prison for criminally convicted wizards, a place called Azkaban. Their role in the punishment of wrongdoers ends up, however, going far beyond that of providing security. Just being around them amounts to a terrible punishment itself. The good and helpful Professor Lupin explains to Harry that dementors are among the worst creatures on earth, both living in and loving decay and despair. He tells Harry that they drain or eliminate any shred of peace, hope, good feeling, or happiness from anyone and anything around them. He adds:

> "Get too near a dementor and every good feeling, every happy memory will be sucked out of you. If it can, the dementor will feed on you long enough to reduce you to something like itself . . . soulless and evil." (PA 187)

Unfortunately, this may remind you of a hated professor, or a particularly bad manager, or some other unpleasant person in authority that you've worked with over the years. It's not a pretty description. Think about the terrible effect of merely being around such a monster. Something interestingly similar to this often happens to anyone who associates closely with any sort of evil or unethical person. Their goodness, kindness, happiness, general optimism, and positive life force can all be slowly drained away, and a real transformation can occur. That is the destructive force of evil and the insidious power of association with it.

THE PHILOSOPHY OF THE UNETHICAL MIND

It has often been said that the difference between an ethical and an unethical person is very simple: An unethical person loves things and uses people; an ethical person loves people and uses things. The unethical person's philosophy of life can typically be summed up in two beliefs:

> Power is to be pursued.
> People are to be manipulated.

This second belief is just another way of expressing the old immoral philosophy of life that "the end justifies the means." An unethical person is always manipulative, never treating others the way he would himself want to be treated, but in every way using other people for his own personal ends or goals.

The Hogwarts sorting hat at one point describes the Slytherin house students in a song as "cunning" and says that they are prepared to use any means whatsoever to accomplish their aims (SS 118). Using any means can involve lying, cheating, stealing, betraying, and even killing. The great enlightenment philosopher Immanuel Kant repeatedly characterized this approach to life as absolutely wrong. He insisted that there is a universal duty never to treat another human being as a mere means to your ends and not at the same time as "an end unto himself." What this comes down to is that we should never treat other people as mere tools or instruments of our will. Human beings are not just of instrumental value. Of course, there's nothing wrong with asking someone to do something for us. We have to do that with associates and friends all the time. When you lead an organization, or if you manage other people, that's just your job. But what matters is how you use the talents and energies of others, the attitude with which this is done, and the tone with which you do it. We all have intrinsic value and we all should be treated as such—with respect and dignity. That is the ethical stance.

The great Jewish theologian and philosopher Martin Buber once made this point in a related way in his enormously influential book *I and Thou*. He explained that there are two fundamentally different orientations possible between any two human beings. One he called the "I-It" relation. This is the mind-set that treats another person as an object, a mere thing to be manipulated and used—just another piece of the furniture of the universe. The other relation he called the "I-Thou" relation, using a very formal term in his native German language for ultimate respect. This is the mind-set that treats another person as a sacred soul deserving of honor and high regard. That is the ethical stance.

The unethical person is always a user. In a moment of confrontation, one of the bad guys Harry has to face says to him:

"Decent people are so easy to manipulate, Potter." (GF 676)

And the evil antagonist, Tom Riddle—the original and secret identity of Voldemort—boasts:

"If I say it myself, Harry, I've always been able to charm the people I needed." (CS 310)

A smiling face is no guarantee of a good heart. Neither is a charming personality. Some of the worst people on earth can be amazingly engaging and pleasant to be around—as long as it suits their needs and desires for the moment. Affability is no sure sign of goodness. Unethical people can use a world-class winning smile or a pleasant-seeming personality as they use everything else—for their own selfish purposes.

Dolores Umbridge, the unqualified teacher sent to Hogwarts by the Ministry of Magic in Harry's fifth year, is a particularly loathsome creature to readers because it is so easy to see through her showy affectations of pleasantry, a forced, sickly smile and her horribly saccharine voice. Her genuinely cruel intentions are not easy for her to hide. But many of the bad characters in the Potter stories, as well as in the real world, are much better at disguising their true purposes. This is what makes them particularly dangerous. Unethical people think of every other human being as a mere object to be manipulated and used or else to be avoided, ignored, or even eliminated.

Why, indeed, is it true that decent people are often so easy to manipulate? Why are basically good people sometimes so easily charmed? It's really quite simple. Most good people are inherently trusting. They act honestly most of the time, and so they naturally expect others to do roughly the same. We all tend to view the world through the lens of what we know. Trustworthy people just instinctively expect others to be worthy of trust as well. Deceptive people, by contrast, are always on their guard. The most suspicious people in the world tend to fall into either or both of two categories: those who very often have acted dishonestly themselves, and so typically expect the same of others, and those who have been severely burned by dishonest people in the past and desperately want this never to happen again. The lesson here is not at all that good people should be less trusting of others, but that we all should be cautiously open and suitably careful in granting our trust to other people. And we should not expect the unethical individuals among us to be as easily identifiable as Professor Umbridge. Harry and his friends are sometimes fooled. And so are the rest of us.

RECIPROCITY AND RESTRAINT

So what exactly is the ethical approach to life that's exhibited by the good wizards in Harry's world? What does it require? What does it involve? How can you spot it in another person? How can you test it in yourself? Are there some general contours to the ethics of the wizards from which the rest of us can learn?

Let's answer these questions gradually. First, let me draw your attention to a common approach to life. When you carefully observe human nature as it actually is, you begin to notice something pretty soon. People tend to treat others the way they have been treated. This is not a universal law, but it is a very general tendency. To put it another way, most people tend to reflect back the conduct they themselves receive. This is what philosophers sometimes call "reciprocity." We see this habit occasionally in Harry's life—as, for example, when his uncle Vernon once growls a warning at him to behave himself when he talks to his very unpleasant aunt Marge during her upcoming visit, and Harry basically says that he'll act politely toward her if she first acts in this way toward him (PA 19). He's prepared to be a gentleman only conditionally and plans to fling back at his aunt exactly what she dishes out to him, or worse. And that, of course, isn't the ethical stance. Reciprocity is a pressure that, unfortunately, most people seem to give in to most of the time—we rise or sink to the level of the people around us. If they're nice to us, we're all smiles and sweetness, but if they're rude to us, they may be amazed at how sharp and nasty we can be in return.

In every facet of life, what you give, you tend to get.

Around Draco Malfoy, arguably the nastiest little boy at Hogwarts, an arrogant upstart from a wealthy "pure blood" wizard family, Harry often loses control of his temper and is almost irresistibly tempted to stoop to his level in retaliation. Even the sensible Hermione once completely loses her composure in response to him and slaps his face. Several times, Harry hears this malicious troublemaker speak disparagingly of Hagrid, the groundskeeper who is a good friend to Harry, and we are told that it takes all his inner willpower to resist the temptation to follow Hermione's lead and hit Malfoy squarely in the face (PA 316). The fact that Harry doesn't pummel Draco in all these situations is due more to a concern for staying out of unnecessary trouble than it is to any more principled moral stance on his part. But he is still in the early stages of his moral education.

Stooping to the level of the worst people around us isn't the moral path, and it isn't an approach to life that works very well. At one point, Harry completely loses his self-control and duels with Malfoy to defend Hermione's honor. The terrible, unintended result is that Hermione is injured (GF 298–299). The irony here is a cautionary tale in itself. Unethical means should never be employed in the effort to attain good ends.

This is not the ethical way. Reciprocity is the path of an amoral puppet, a person who lets others call the shots and pull his strings. The ethical person is an individual who always takes the initiative and tries to do what is right in any circumstances, regardless of how other people are acting. He or she doesn't just reflect back the conduct of others, but instead always seeks to do what ought to be done, even if that means swimming against a strong current or standing utterly alone. The moral person has a higher standard of conduct than just the question of which way the wind is blowing now.

There is an interesting parallel between the natural lure of reciprocity in social interactions between people and the pull of the crowd away from principled actions generally. Energy conservation is of increasing importance in our world. It matters what sort of transportation we normally rely on, how we heat and cool our homes, whether we conserve and recycle paper and packaging materials, and even how we use electric lights in our business environments as well as in our homes. Many people, when urged to exercise more caution in their daily use of electricity—for instance, turning off lights when they're not needed and taking other conservation measures, however small—can easily be tempted to reply in protest, if only in their own minds, "Why should I go to all that trouble when most people aren't? What good will it do for me to go out of my way to conserve energy when others will just continue to be wasteful?" But the ethical stance is never to measure and direct our own conduct by the actions of "most people" or the inclinations of the crowd that happens to be around us. The world needs more ethical lights in the darkness. The fact that many others aren't providing any of this light, rather than being a reason not to do so ourselves, is precisely more of a call to each of us to light our own little torches and provide whatever measure of illumination we can. An ethical person is always less concerned about what is popular, or what is customary, than with what is right. To take the ethical path, we sometimes have to resist strongly the influence of at least some of the people around us.

Although Hermione Granger does lose her composure and slap her nasty classmate Draco Malfoy in one situation, when he is making deeply insulting remarks about a good and noble friend, she is usually the voice of reason, virtue, and restraint. We often see her urging Harry not to let Malfoy and others make him mad. Once, when the opportunistically unpleasant Malfoy is mocking Harry, his wise friend steps in and tells him to completely ignore him. She repeats:

"Just ignore him, it's not worth it. . . ." (PA 96)

Harry often has trouble keeping his cool in Professor Snape's Potions class. Snape has a visceral dislike of Harry that derives from an old animosity with Harry's father in their own school days, and he allows the Slytherin House hooligans, Malfoy's friends, to torment Harry in class, often stooping so low as to join in himself. We are told at one point that Harry has about had it with this treatment and is on the verge of responding in kind when, again, Hermione intervenes with what has become almost a mantra of "Ignore them"—repeated over and over again (GF 297). Even when she is the one being insulted and Harry is about to come to her defense, Hermione offers restraint as the proper course, both telling Harry to ignore it and then showing in her own behavior how this can be done (GF 316). On these occasions, and in many other situations, Hermione characteristically displays the dignified self-control and poise of a Stoic philosopher.

The Stoics were a group of ancient thinkers who emphasized that we may not often have the measure of control we'd like over the circumstances we find ourselves in, but we can always take control of our own attitudes and reactions toward those circumstances. In particular, we can't control how other people behave, but we can govern our own emotions and actions in response to their behavior. We can choose to be wise and ignore what would otherwise make us extremely mad. We can rise above it, or—to use a philosopher's term—we can transcend it. I've often had to take myself mentally outside a difficult and emotionally charged situation while still physically immersed in it, reminding myself to "rise above it" and take up the stance of an objective anthropologist, sociologist, or psychologist observing what was going on without becoming caught up in it. And I've found that this Stoic maneuver can be very effective. When you refuse to let other people's agitation or hostility dictate your own emotions, you keep yourself in the best state for making good decisions, and you retain at least the possibility of steering the situation in a more productive direction. The Stoic sensibility does not allow external events to dictate our inner attitudes and decisions. The Stoic stands firm on her own values and rests in the dignity of her own character.

Until sometime early in the twentieth century, most educated people read and appreciated the Stoics. My father, who never went to college, had books with essays of the Stoics proudly displayed in the living room. He read Epictetus, Seneca, and Marcus Aurelius for advice about life and business. He absorbed and used their insights and passed them along to me. My dad's ongoing project of self-education immersed him in Stoic wisdom. The importance of it all came rushing back to me one day as I sat down in seat 1A on a US Airways flight about to leave Orlando and noticed the gentleman next to me reading Tom Wolfe's big novel *A Man in Full*, about a month or two after it was published. I asked him how he liked the book, and he replied, "I love it! And I really like all the Stoic philosophy in it. Everybody in the world of business needs to read the Stoics!" I heartily agreed, then asked him what had led him to this conclusion. He thought for a second and said, "I was here in Orlando for a big convention. My company manufactures golf clubs. We were going to feature in our booth the newest model that we're really excited about. But when we got here, the clubs hadn't arrived. We checked on them, and no one seemed to know where they were. People started getting really panicky. This was the night before what was supposed to be our big launch of the product. I saw some of our executives really losing it, yelling and screaming at people, being really irrational. I had just been reading in Wolfe's book about Stoic composure and Stoic cool. A big dose of that could have made a huge difference in those circumstances." He went on to explain how the situation was eventually resolved, but only when a few clear heads calmly took appropriate actions—when a modicum of Stoic objectivity and poise finally was allowed to blow like a fresh breeze through this otherwise superheated turmoil.

People in the world of business do need a dose of the Stoic perspective on life. Fortunately, it's fairly easy to find the *Meditations* of Marcus Aurelius in any bookstore. But it's much harder to locate good translations of Seneca or Epictetus that are easily available for the hurried executive. So I set it as a personal goal to discover all the best passages from these three great Stoics—one a slave, one a lawyer, and one the Emperor of Rome—translate them into the best language of our time, and help people see how to read and use their incredibly effective ideas. This ended up being a long project of study and education for me that significantly deepened my perspectives on life and how we react to it. It also culminated in a book called *The Stoic Art of Living: Inner Resilience and Outer Results* that basically provides a manual for understanding some of the most admirable traits of both Dumbledore and the young Hermione as they confront the difficulties that cross their paths. The reaction of people who have a chance to meet the Stoics in print and master their perspectives is genuinely remarkable. My seatmate was right. The world of business needs the Stoics. But, as we can see in all of Rowling's stories, so does the world of Harry Potter—and so do we all. The techniques of self-mastery that my father practiced, that Dumbledore lives, and that normally govern the emotions and actions of a young girl like Hermione are exactly what Harry Potter needs in order to best use his distinctive talents for the good of others as well as himself. It's often a challenge for Harry, as it is for most of the rest of us. But the disciplines of self-control and self-mastery described and practiced by the great Stoic philosophers can provide us with the psychological poise we need in even the most turbulent of circumstances. The Stoics give us that key to moral independence that allows us to stand firm in the right and treat people as we ought, regardless of what might be happening all around us.

We can eventually see that Hermione's repeated Stoic advice has an effect on Harry over the long term. Much later, when his friend Ron is being taunted, we witness Harry coming to his rescue with the very same advice:

"Ignore them," he said . . . (OP 290)

Sometimes a good person has to confront evil and resist it, even with force. But more often than not, the little irritations and insults of life just need to be ignored. Hermione frequently urges Harry to rise above a situation, to transcend the moment and not to let little things bother him. She is advising him to stay on an ethical path and not descend to the level of retaliating against evil with just more evil. Then Harry eventually does the same thing for Ron. Anyone who uses this advice can break the cycle of negativity that otherwise often threatens to get out of control and take over a situation, bullying even good people to do what they know isn't right. The tools of self-control that the Stoics give us with their reflections and mental techniques can make all the difference in how such situations play out and in how we later feel about what we have done. They can also make the difference between winning and losing, in business and in life.

RESPECT FOR RULES

Hermione Granger is often the coolest head among Harry's friends. Her mind works logically and rationally. An academically talented girl, she is very self-disciplined and hardworking, a real high-achiever, and she arrives at Hogwarts as someone who believes in following the rules. She respects the rules of logic, the rules of language, the rules of the school, and the rules of fair play. She watches the boys, her friends Harry and Ron, engaged in all their foolishness, and often acts as almost a mother in residence, urging them on to the path of common sense or pulling them back from the edge of trouble. The boys are a good bit more casual about rules. Professor Snape at one point expresses with tremendous irritation his belief that Harry is perversely intent on breaking rules and crossing lines whenever he can, and on another occasion confronts Harry about this, snarling:

> "To me, Potter, you're nothing but a nasty little boy who considers rules to be beneath him." (GF 516)

Snape certainly appears not to be the best judge of character, and he's especially biased when it comes to Harry. But he's right that Harry sometimes ignores, or works to get around, the rules at Hogwarts when doing so suits his purposes. And he's often joined in this by Ron, his best friend. It's not that Harry and Ron actively disparage rules. They aren't anarchistic rebels who reject all rules and break them purposely to make a point. Neither are they callous young men who just simply don't care about other people's rules and regulations. The truth is that, on one level, they are just normal kids who occasionally enjoy doing something that seems in itself harmless, fun, and exciting, even if it involves stretching or actually ignoring some school rule. And, on another level, they may even realize the limits of rules in life.

We've all had the experience of being up against rules that just seem crazy—if you're a gainfully employed adult, you may think, for example, of what you confront at tax time. Or consider how it feels when you discover that the ultimate rules in the fine print concerning what your health insurance will or will not pay for sometimes seem to have been decided by a blindfolded man throwing darts randomly at a board across the room. If you're a younger person, you may be able to bring to mind some school rule, or even a family rule, that you think isn't reasonable at all. Not all rules seem to make sense. We've all chafed under the restricting irritation of rules, regulations, and even laws that struck us as outmoded, awkwardly formulated, and counterproductive in their application. And we've usually also encountered the sort of person bound and determined to enforce the rules, whether or not they even remotely made any sense in the particular situation. I have to admit that I've been a bit amazed whenever I've seen this in my own experience.

I was the first professor at the University of Notre Dame ever to direct a Summer Seminar for School Teachers, sponsored by the National Endowment for the Humanities. Fifteen teachers of grades K–12 were going to be selected in a national competition for the best and brightest, then invited to Notre Dame to live together and discuss philosophy with me for a month. Our topic was "Pascal's *Pensées*: Faith, Reason, and the Meaning of Life." We were going to be studying one of history's great mathematical, religious, and philosophical thinkers, along with the application of his ideas to modern life. The lady who at that time ran the Housing Office at Notre Dame—like a marine drill sergeant would run a barracks—informed me that, unfortunately, there was a problem with my plan. It was impossible to do as I was suggesting. There was a rule at Notre Dame, long on the books: Men and women could not stay in the same dorm, even in the summer. This, of course, was not so different from Hogwarts, where boys and girls in the same "house" still sleep in physically different accommodations. The rule apparently was made to keep frisky young students away from the other gender in all residential aspects of campus life at this great Catholic university.

"But," I told the head of housing, "these people are mature, adult teachers, chosen in a national competition. They are allowed to live in the same dorm at every other university in the country that is honored to have an NEH seminar on campus. The residential formation of an intellectual community is part of the seminar experience, and"—to me this was the absolute clincher—"some of the selected participants are married and will be arriving with spouses. So we have to house both genders in the same dorm." This was all met with a blank look and then, after a moment, a determined one. "I'm sorry," the authoritative lady said with an obvious firmness of voice, "the rules will just not allow it." To make a very long story short, I finally got everyone in the Housing Office to see reason, or at least to just give up and let me have my dorm, but not before I had to appeal the situation to the highest levels of the administration. And still, all summer long, whenever I needed to approach the Housing Office about anything, the first response I heard would always be "Well, there's a problem with that." I learned quickly that my immediate reply should be to smile and say, "That's okay. I'm a problem solver. And I'm sure we can come up with a good solution together. What's our challenge?"

Corporate life is often no different in this respect from university life. People have turf and often control it with rules that can seem just silly, outrageous, or plain wrong. We have to expect rules to be misused in life—isn't everything else? And we should be prepared to work both creatively and persistently to overcome any rules, or applications of rules, that block sensible actions that will be for the good of all concerned. It's human nature to hide behind rules. To let this get us all worked up and angry is usually counterproductive and not at all necessary. It's a bit like getting mad at the weather. Some rage at the storm, while others simply put on galoshes, grab an umbrella, and carry on with what they need to do. I realized long ago that there is no point in getting angry when confronted by rules that make no sense. The most sensible choice in most cases is either to comply, when very little is at stake and resistance isn't worth the trouble, and perhaps create a novel route around the situation or else to take action to change those rules, or at least to alter their application in the particular situation.

The poet Ogden Nash once wrote, "In a world of mules / there are no rules." Human life depends on social coordination, and thus, on rules. Without any rules and regulations that are for the most part obeyed by people, the world would be utter chaos most of the time. No human being in a society can live in utter disregard for rules. When the rule of law breaks down in any nation, we see the sad and often terrible consequences right away. However, some of the rules of any society are quite contingent or arbitrary. They could have been different from what they are, and indeed in other parts of the world, the relevant rules *are* different—consider, for example, the rule about driving on the right side of any two-way, two-lane road in America and on the left side in Britain or, for instance, Bermuda. It's necessary only that everyone knows and obeys the rule, whatever it might be, in each individual place. Politeness still requires, in certain parts of the American South, that verbal responses to any questions and requests that have been asked by adults should be of the form "Yes, ma'am" and "No ma'am," "Yes, sir" and "No, sir," while such phrases of honor will often just elicit uncomprehending stares in other areas of the United States. And then, as a child growing up in America, I have to admit that I loved to inform my mother on a regular basis that burping was polite in China, or at least somewhere exotic far outside our house. How do you hold a fork during dinner, and where do you put it when you've finished eating? What do you wear in this situation and in that one? All these are contingent rules. They could have been otherwise. And that deeply bothers some young people before they realize the importance of social coordination in life and the value of even contingent expressions of respect and regard.

Rules are important. Rules define human enterprises and generate reasonable mutual expectations in any social activity. Likewise, rules are fundamental in early-childhood training, and for learning any new skill. Rule-governed behavior is crucial for any form of long-term business success. And so it can seem very natural for some sincere people to assume that all rules are of equally inviolable importance—as if the order of society hangs above a sea of roiling chaos by a single thread, a slender support that will be torn asunder completely by any small violation of the rules. But that clearly goes too far. Not all rules are created equal.

There are well-intentioned people who think that ethics is just all about rules. Morality, in this view, means following all the rules, in letter and in spirit. For people who think like this and believe that ethics is simply about rules, it's easy to view both Harry Potter and his creator, J. K. Rowling, as outrageously unethical individuals, because of their apparently slack view of rules. A magical map that Harry gets his hands on—a map that shows where everyone is at any given time on campus, and that also indicates secret passageways for escaping campus—is at one point described by the apparently sympathetic author Rowling as "the most useful aid to rule-breaking Harry owned" (GF 458). But she is just being facetiously playful in this passage, characterizing the map as one of Harry's school chums might, or as Harry could well be imagined thinking about it in the excitement of his own mind. She is not herself endorsing or supporting a philosophy of rule-breaking for its own sake or a worldview of contempt for rules. Any reader who accuses her of immorality or an unethical attitude from the sheer occurrence of this sort of passage is simply misreading it quite uncharitably.

A critic who concludes from such a statement that Rowling, or

Harry, isn't an ethical person is also just misunderstanding ethics. Rules play a central role in all ethical systems and in the lives of all ethical people—but not just rules, and not all rules, and not all the time. People who think that ethics simply consists of fastidiously obeying lots and lots of rules fail to see a few things that any good philosopher could point out.

Ethics can't just consist of rules. First, rules need interpreting. If the interpretation of one rule were always supplied by another rule, and the interpretation of this further rule was given by yet another rule, we'd end up having infinitely many rules to guide us in life, which is absurd and impossible. Second, rules can conflict. To settle any case of conflicting rules, we need something more than just those rules. Third, we can never have enough rules, and so we often get too many. I realize that this may sound like a typical philosopher's paradox, so let me explain it a bit more.

There can't be a rule for everything. Rules are general and always a little vague. Life is particular and always very specific. No matter how elaborate and well thought through a given set of rules is, it can never anticipate every eventuality in all its complex detail. Because of that, for every rule there is a loophole awaiting the discovery of a sharp attorney, a creative mischief-maker like Fred or George Weasley, or any other shrewd operator. We can never have enough rules to eliminate all the possible loopholes. But if we think we need to try, we end up with far too many rules. Consider the U.S. Tax Code again as a prime example. An immensely complex tangle of rules is no clear guide for anyone. In addition to having rules for life, we need a good dose of wisdom and virtue to round things out. Rules alone can never suffice. Wisdom and virtue are guides beyond the rules, and they are the interpretive powers we have for properly understanding rules. This just means that ethics is ultimately about wisdom and virtue.

Wisdom is insight for living. Virtue is the habit of acting in accordance with wisdom. Wisdom tells us what's right, and virtue helps us do it. The wise person, as Aristotle saw, understands rules and respects good ones, but is also able to see beyond the letter of the law and into the heart of justice. The virtuous person is guided by wisdom and acts in accordance with goodness, kindness, justice, fairness, patience, compassion, respect, honor, forbearance, honesty, and all the other traits we often refer to as individual virtues. As we grow in the two general qualities of wisdom and virtue, we are better able to see what we should do in any situation, and we are more reliably able to do it.

The ultimate keys to ethics are simply wisdom and virtue.

What is good? What should I do? How is this situation to be handled? There can't be enough rules, and there can't be rules good enough, to answer all our questions and eliminate for us the occasional task of hard and sustained thinking. There will never be the equivalent of a simple moral software program, an ethical calculator where you can plug in all the relevant details of your situation and you will be given automatically a specification of exactly what you should do. The world doesn't work that way, and neither does ethics. We often think of moral decision-making as being like a True-False test, where we're always hoping to get the right answer, but it's sometimes more like an act of artistic creation, where we're just trying to make something beautiful, with each stroke of the brush contributing properly to the final result.

Harry Potter occasionally breaks rules. But that doesn't prove he is an unethical, nasty little boy. He is struggling like any young person to find his way in the world, and he doesn't start off like Hermione, as an almost evangelistic follower of rules. Sometimes his rule-breaking is frivolous and irresponsible, but at other times it saves lives and defeats evil. Throughout the stories, Hermione loosens up a bit, and Harry grows in the direction of a greater maturity from his distinct direction as well. That means he grows in wisdom and in virtue. And it seems that, as he ages, he doesn't break as many rules as casually and carelessly as he once may have.

THE GOLDEN RULE

As I mentioned at the start of this chapter, there is one moral rule recognized in some form in every great human culture. It's probably the best general guide to behavior ever articulated. Like every other moral rule, it requires proper interpretation and application, and this always depends on some basic measure of wisdom and virtue. But it is one rule that is undeniably of central importance in normal human life. And we can see it being acknowledged in the conduct of every good wizard in Harry's world of magic as well. It's the famous Golden Rule, as stated earlier: "Do unto others as you would have them do unto you." Treat others the way you'd want to be treated if you were in their place.

Dumbledore lives the Golden Rule. So does his trusted associate, Professor Minerva McGonagall. Hagrid extends this rule to the most unlikely members of the animal kingdom, treating even dangerous magical beasts the way he would want to be treated if he were in their place. Examine the behavior of any of the good wizards in Harry's world and you'll see the same thing, more or less consistently. They seek to live by the Golden Rule. The bad characters are the opposite. Like his father Lucius Malfoy, young Draco is no follower of the Golden Rule. Neither are his beefy cohorts, Crabbe and Goyle. Least of all is Lord Voldemort himself. They never treat others the way they'd want to be treated. They treat others any way they please and in any manner that suits their selfish, petty personal interests.

Throughout the adventures and difficulties faced by Harry and his friends, all the good wizards tend to interact with the people around them in accordance with the Golden Rule, and the others do quite otherwise. This reflects well the fundamental truths about ethics in the world. Good people care about others. And good people treat others well. Immoral and unethical individuals stand apart by acting precisely in a contrary manner. They recognize no external constraints on their conduct, apart from any they might think could serve their own narrow and base aims.

The older and wiser Sirius Black once says something very insightful to young Harry, when talking about a man who had corrupted his own character in a fight to get to the top in a highly politicized government ministry. He advises his young friend:

> "If you want to know what a man's like, take a good look at how he treats his inferiors, not his equals." (GF 525)

A man who treats his superiors well can just be courting their favor. Someone who treats his equals well may just be hedging his bets. He might just be thinking, "Who knows? One of them may someday be in a position to be of use." We have more reliable evidence of good character on the part of another person only when we see him treat well those people around him who seem to have no apparent power to reciprocate and no immediate prospects of such power.

One of my philosophy students long ago, Kevin Fleming, is now a very insightful psychologist and much-sought-after executive coach with clients in significant positions of power and influence. Dr. Fleming has told me that he can learn a lot of important information very quickly about the character of a high-powered businessperson by noticing how he or she treats the waitstaff and other employees at a restaurant. Raytheon's highly respected CEO, Bill Swanson, also has commented on this phenomenon in his now famous booklet, privately circulated among CEOs and top corporate executives, *Swanson's Unwritten Rules of Management*, saying, "A person who is nice to you but rude to the waiter—or to others—is not a nice person." He even adds in parentheses, for heightened emphasis, "This is a rule that never fails." If we see a person living with kindness and consideration to all, regardless of position and power, treating all others around him the way he'd want to be treated if he were in their place, then we have strong positive evidence that we are dealing with a genuinely good and ethical individual. If we see the opposite, then we have right there very good evidence of a distinctly bad character.

How a person treats others is generally a good test of character.

Sirius Black voices for us here the reason that Harry, Ron, and most of us readers don't really trust Professor Severus Snape from our very earliest introduction to him. Formerly a "Death Eater," a follower of Voldemort, he has come to work at Hogwarts and generally appears to have aligned himself with Dumbledore. The headmaster trusts him to have changed his allegiance wholeheartedly. And he accordingly becomes a member of the Order of the Phoenix, the secret band of wizards who are led by Dumbledore and are working to thwart Voldemort's schemes and rescue their world from the threat of evil. Yet we see Snape often unable to live with any measure of compassion and love for his fellow man, including Sirius Black and, most notably, Harry. With some of the information about this mean-spirited professor that comes to light during Harry's fifth year, a charitable reader can easily conclude that it could just be that a background of abuse and extensive association with evil have left long-term scars on Snape's personality that will take much more time to heal. Nonetheless, if he genuinely has undergone a thorough change of heart and has come over firmly to the side of the good, there seems to be much work yet to be done before he will have become a fully good and ethical person.

At the culmination of year six, as recorded in what is perhaps the most shocking passage in all the Harry Potter books, we see something happen in *The Half-Blood Prince* that seems to untangle decisively and totally disambiguate the paradoxical character that is Snape. And still, things are not always what they seem. Many readers continue to wonder whether the full truth is yet evident about this mysterious wizard. He could be playing an important and elaborate role in the ultimate fight against evil as he engages in his most shocking actions—a role very dangerous for his own soul—or he could be showing his true colors. Regardless of the ultimate story, this much is clear: Whatever Snape is at his core, there seems to be plenty built up around that core that strikes us as morally despicable. And this is typically manifested through his many violations of the Golden Rule.

The particular Golden Rule test that Sirius Black articulates so well is one that even he occasionally fails—for example, in the way he customarily treats his family house-elf, the unpleasant and mean-spirited little creature named Kreacher. The Golden Rule is certainly a high moral standard that is difficult for most people to live up to, and consequently few of us do so with complete consistency. It is also a general litmus test for ethical living that the members of Harry's unpleasant guardian family, the Dursleys, fail all the time.

From the day he was orphaned, at about the age of one, and until he was eleven, Harry lived full time with the Dursley family at number four, Privet Drive, Little Whinging, Surrey. Since going off to Hogwarts as a residential student, he still spends most of each summer vacation in their care. For deeply magical reasons that are not revealed until the end of the fifth book, *The Order of the Phoenix*, Dumbledore entrusted the infant Harry into the safekeeping of the Dursleys right after the murder of his birth parents by Voldemort. Petunia Dursley, the Muggle sister of Harry's wizard mother, is to be his protector. Her power to keep him safe consists not in any magical skills on her part but in the nature of the blood she shares with her sister and the magical power that resides there. Harry is safe from harm by Voldemort as long as he is in her home.

But Uncle Vernon and Aunt Petunia treat Harry horribly. There is no Golden Rule in use at the Dursley house. Everything there is about middle-class appearances and the manipulation of others for the sake of social status. Vernon and Petunia view Harry as a misfit, and he is nothing more than an object of their contempt, resentment, and petty cruelty. Their son Dudley is just as bad as they are, and this of course should be no surprise. Harry is forced for many years to live in a cramped space under the stairs, he's given almost nothing to eat, and he's compelled out of absolutely no financial necessity to wear hand-me-down clothes that don't even remotely fit. His birthdays are ignored, and in every other way he is treated worse than Cinderella ever was. The Dursleys fail the Golden Rule test every day and they do so quite miserably. They model for Harry the worst sort of ordinary behavior throughout the most formative years of his childhood.

We shouldn't be at all puzzled that, as a result, he has to struggle on occasion in his own conduct to find the more ethical path. What we should be genuinely amazed by is that he does seem to have all the right core values, and that he is indeed developing along a fundamentally ethical path, despite the tremendous disadvantages of this background. There is an old saying: "A stream never rises higher than its source." Harry seems to live as an ongoing disproof of its pessimism. He has certainly risen far above his upbringing. And in our world today, that is a source of hope for many of Harry's fans.

HARRY'S MORAL JOURNEY

Harry Potter learns from every situation he encounters and from everyone he meets. His time at Hogwarts is a journey of moral awakening and moral formation. We judge him best as a person not by looking at any single moment in time, or at any one thing he does, but by tracing the whole path of his moral education and development throughout the years of his young life that we are privileged to see. He shows us flashes of courage and honor, unselfishness, and kindness in many situations. And then he tells a little white lie, or a great big whopper, or else he lashes out in anger and irritation at someone close to him, and we are set back on our heels wondering what manner of young man we actually are encountering. But if we look more deeply, and think carefully about what we are seeing, we can come to the conclusion that Harry is indeed an Aristotelian work of moral art, undergoing a deep and dynamic character formation far beyond the experience of most of his peers. He is gradually in the process of becoming what he is capable of being, with fits and starts and temporary reversals for sure, but with definite and discernible movement in the right direction. To an important extent, Harry is lured on in the right direction by his great example, Dumbledore, who acts toward him in a way that ultimately he can emulate—and in so doing he can attain for himself the high road of the proper ethical path.

All fans of Harry Potter are excited about what we think we see him becoming. It's easy to imagine him someday serving in Dumble-dore's place, running Hogwarts, serving as the most admired leader in the wizard community, and doing for some other young person exactly what Dumbledore is now doing for him. Goodness always wants to produce more of itself. That is at the core of the ethical life. But that is still a long way off, and the journey from here to there will certainly be an exciting one.

On the issue of what Harry ultimately is, and will become, we should perhaps let his older friend Hagrid have the last word:

"Well yeh might've bent a few rules, Harry, bu' yeh're all righ' really, aren' you?" (GF 391)

THE SIX TESTS OF ETHICAL ACTION

Before we leave our general topic of ethics, and go on to examine more specifically some important questions about truth and lies that are posed throughout the Harry Potter stories, we should take a moment to look at six quick thought experiments that will help all of us, workers or wizards, to make the properly ethical choice in any given situation.

Over the centuries, wise people have come up with some simple and helpful tests that we can use to evaluate the ethical appropriate-ness of anything we're considering doing. These little thought experi-ments can help us gain mental clarity in a difficult situation and get our moral bearings, especially when some measure of financial gain, power, or status is at stake, and we might be tempted to rationalize an action that we really know to be wrong. Oscar Wilde famously admitted, "I can resist everything except temptation." These tests can help us to resist even that.

Simple thought experiments can help us envision the consequences of our actions.

The Publicity Test: This test consists in asking, "Would I want to see this action that I'm about to take described on the front page of the local paper or in a national magazine?" Or "How would I feel about having done this if everyone were to find out all about it, including the people I love and care about the most?" Harry Potter has an invisibility cloak that allows him to go about and do things without being seen. Most of us, when we contemplate doing something we really know to be wrong, imagine ourselves with the existential equivalent of that invisibility cloak. We think no one will ever know. And we're very often wrong. By just supposing that people will know, we are brought to confront what we really think about a potential action, as seen by others as well as ourselves.

The Moral Mentor Test: Many ancient philosophers advised us to carry around in our minds the image of a wise and good person we admire, whether a parent or friend, a mentor in our field, or a great moral example from history, like Jesus or Gandhi, and ask: "What would my moral mentor do in this situation?" We can easily imagine Harry, Ron, and Hermione asking, "What would Dumbledore do?" By imaginatively placing an admired mentor in our position and tracing out his or her likeliest responses and initiatives, we can give ourselves the guidance that this person would most probably pass along to us if they stood by our side at the time of moral decision-making.

The Admired Observer Test: A variant on the two tests just given, this one recommends that we ask ourselves, "Would I want my moral mentor to see me doing this?" "Would I be proud of this action in the presence of a person whose life and character I really admire?" Or even: "What would make my moral mentor most proud of me in this situation?" Imagine that some person you respect and admire the most could magically witness your actions and overhear your innermost thoughts. How would that affect what you're contemplating now? Would you continue in your current train of thought, or would you shake yourself hard and quickly reverse course?

The Transparency Test: This involves asking, "Could I give a clear explanation for the action I'm contemplating, including an honest and transparent account of all my motives that would satisfy a fair and dispassionate moral judge?" Would someone like Headmaster Albus Dumbledore accept your reasoning and your conclusions? Would the stern and strict Professor Minerva McGonagall approve and endorse your action or at least understand how a morally good and well-intentioned person could have chosen it? If not, then perhaps you need to move in another direction.

The Man or Woman in the Mirror Test: Avoiding all irrelevant questions of weight, hair color, the exigencies of a very bad hair day, baldness, bloodshot eyes, bags, double chins, jowls, and wrinkles, this simple thought experiment urges us to ask, "If I do this, will I be able to look at myself in the mirror and respect the person I see there?" A mirror doesn't have to be magical like the Mirror of Erised, which we'll discuss later, in order to have an extraordinary impact on our self-awareness and self-image. That one reflection can give us the little taste of objectivity and self-reflective intimacy we sometimes need in order to get real with ourselves and face the facts of our actions.

The Golden Rule Test: "Would I like to be on the receiving end of this action and all its potential consequences?" "Am I treating all the other people involved in the way I'd want to be treated if I were in their place?" This, as we've seen, is perhaps the most powerful guide to ethical action on any given occasion for any person who has built a basically good character in the past and has any shred of the sort of empathetic imagination it takes to anticipate the likely and unlikely consequences of an action. We often forget to consider the feelings and legitimate needs of people affected by our decisions and deeds. The Golden Rule has been as important to the wise people of our world as it has been to the wizards of Harry's world. It is the best rule of thumb for ethical behavior at work and for life generally. We ignore it to our great detriment.

If a mature Harry Potter ran General Electric, I believe that a concern for ethics would be at the core of all his leadership training. He would have seen the power of Dumbledore's character and the difference it had always made to what that moral master could accomplish. And I think that Harry would not want to settle for anything less—in his own life, as well as in the lives of the people around him.

The ethics of wizards are very much like the ethics of people in our real-life world of work. There is a spectrum of admirable, acceptable, and unconscionable conduct to be seen. The very best wizards, like the most enduringly successful people in our world, follow the high path of ethical conduct, apprenticing themselves to masters who are farther along the road and leading others to join them on their moral journey. The Harry Potter stories can give us some interesting and important insights into how these issues play out in our own lives every day.

4

TRUTH AND LIES AT HOGWARTS

I think that business people leading by example can spread
better practices and can be a positive force for change. I really do.
—*Jeffrey Immelt, Chairman and CEO, GE*

We've just taken a first look at the ethics of the wizards and some of the other characters in the world of Harry Potter. In this chapter, I want to focus in on a specific ethical problem involving a particularly blatant violation of the normal rules of morality that seems wildly out of control in all the Harry Potter books. It's a feature of the novels that has offended traditionalist teachers, outraged many concerned parents, and caused a few moralists to recommend that the books be kept away from tender, impressionable young minds—like several classics before them. If the old schoolyard, rhyming taunt that begins with the words "Liar, liar" were true, nearly everybody in these stories would be running around with their pants—or robes—on fire. We will learn something of vital importance about business ethics and about the moral life in general by examining carefully the interplay of truth and lies at Hogwarts and elsewhere in Harry's world.

This topic is of foremost importance in our own time, since every ethical problem in the real world of business in the past few years has been created by lies, sustained by lies, and guarded as well as greatly exacerbated by lies. Most of these lies don't even get into the headlines. People lie to themselves about what's going on. They lie to their associates and clients by what they withhold as well as by what they say and how they say it. People spin, dodge, and try to buy time. They deflect attention from where it ought to be and hype what isn't at all what it should be. They show in many ways that they don't fully appreciate the positive power of the truth.

In all this, the people of our world are often a lot like the young wizards and witches in Harry's world. And, like them, we need to learn some lessons. We need especially to understand more deeply the importance of honesty and trust for working with other people on anything worth doing. If we can't learn this from the example of others, we'll almost inevitably and eventually learn it the hard way, and that path can be so unpleasant that it behooves us all to look for any alternative available to us. We can find such an alternative in the lessons of the wizards.

A WORLD OF LIES

The world of Harry Potter is filled with lies. At Hogwarts, students lie to their teachers, to each other, and to their parents. Some teachers lie to their colleagues and occasionally to the students. Visitors lie to those in authority. When the man introduced as Professor Moody arrives at Hogwarts with an array of special gadgets, he discovers that the overall environment of mendacity renders some of them completely useless. Harry points at one of the instruments and asks him what it is. The professor replies:

> "Secrecy Sensor. Vibrates when it detects concealment and lies . . .
> no use here, of course, too much interference—students in every
> direction lying about why they haven't done their homework. Been
> humming ever since I got here." (GF 343)

In Rowling's fictional world outside Hogwarts, it's just as bad. Journalists lie to their readers. Children at home lie to their mothers. Mothers lie to their kids. Adults in all walks of life deceive each other.

At some point, you can begin to conclude that, excluding of course the noble Dumbledore and perhaps a few others, nearly everyone in Harry's world uses lies quite casually to accomplish their ends, and on a fairly regular basis. In one of my readings through all the Potter books, when I was actually looking for lies, I began to notice so many that I was reminded of the old lawyer joke: "How can you tell when a lawyer is lying? When you see him moving his lips." Sometimes, the students of witchcraft and wizardry at Hogwarts in particular seem to put the worst legal shysters of the modern world to shame with the speed, skill, and sheer number of their deceptions.

I even found myself smiling when I came across this brief, representative, and telling piece of dialogue:

"No," Harry lied. (PA 155)

You don't even need to know the context to appreciate that one. The lies don't have to be elaborate. But they are plentiful. And many of them seem sadly, utterly pointless. Consider this:

"Harry," said Fudge jovially, moving forward. "How are you?"
    "Fine," Harry lied. (GF 581)

And this:

"What's up?" said Hagrid.
    "Nothing," Harry lied. (SS 79)

All Harry was hiding in this quick word of deception was that he had just met for the first time a fellow Hogwarts student, Draco Malfoy, who seemed a bit unpleasant, and who had said some unflattering things about Hagrid that Harry obviously didn't want to repeat. But why lie? There was really no reason. It had just become a habit. There are many such examples throughout the books.

We don't have to wait long to find our first lie in the sweep of these expansive and intricate tales. On page one of book one, *Harry Potter and the Sorcerer's Stone*, we come across the first reported deception: Rowling tells us that the Dursleys, the family raising Harry, are concealing the real truth from everyone else, the secret that this young man in their care is a wizard. They are embarrassed by his wizardly parentage and his magical powers, and desperately want what they consider a "normal" family life. They are Muggles of the worst sort, and they try hard to hide the truth about Harry from everyone around them. For years, they even hid it all from Harry himself.

The Dursleys lie to Harry about all sorts of things. They withhold truth from each other. Their son, Dudley, lies to his parents. And Harry acts in kind. He regularly deceives them all. We first see Harry when he is a tiny baby and has just been rescued from the scene of his parents' murder at the hands of the Dark Lord Voldemort. Hagrid arrives at number four, Privet Drive with him, and Dumbledore takes him to the doorstep of the Dursley home so that Mrs. Dursley, the sister of Harry's mother, can raise him. We next see the young wizard-to-be more than ten years later, right before his eleventh birthday. And he is by then a master of deception, a skill that seems necessary for any form of survival at the Dursley household.

When Harry finally is contacted on his birthday by Hagrid, keeper of the grounds at Hogwarts, and learns the truth about his parents and his powers as a wizard, he is completely amazed. In the course of what he's told, he is also informed that there is a governing body for wizards and other magical beings, a Ministry of Magic, whose primary purpose is to keep the truth about the existence and powers of wizards away from all the nonmagical people in their world. Here we have even what seems to be an official institutionalization of deception. Harry is a bit puzzled and asks why there would be an office of people whose job is to hide such a big truth from the general population. He's told that it's necessary because, otherwise, all the ordinary, nonmagical folks would be bothering the wizards all the time, wanting all their problems solved by magic (SS 65). Perhaps this is a good reason for the existence of the wizards to be kept secret. But it does serve to reinforce our sense that truth is a rare commodity in Harry's world. There is a cynical and witty old saying—"Truth is precious. Let us use it sparingly." This could be a general operational philosophy for most of the characters we come across in these stories.

THE QUESTION OF MORAL JUSTIFICATION

People lie and deceive for all sorts of reasons. They tell fibs and whoppers, little white lies, and sometimes terribly damaging falsehoods. In almost every case, it absolutely shouldn't be done—there's no excuse for it at all. It's just wrong. And it reflects either a weak and careless, or else just a downright dishonorable, spirit. But sometimes things are a little more complicated. And we need to understand these rare complications in order to grasp more deeply the overall importance of honesty in normal circumstances. Consider, for example, any situation where an act of deception is engaged in or a lie is told to prevent something really terrible from happening—say, the murder of an innocent person—something that, in the situation, can be prevented in no other available way. Whether we think the act of lying or deceiving is morally right under such circumstances, or that it's still wrong, however understandable and perhaps even unavoidable, most people would acknowledge that, in these particular circumstances, it may be uniquely justifiable, or at least excusable, and so at some level, in some sense, at least minimally morally permissible, however regrettable in itself it still might be.

Let me give you a fairly uncontroversial example of what I mean. And to make the point as clearly as possible, I'll simplify and idealize just a bit. When a soldier fighting for a noble cause, defending innocent people from the attacks of a terrible aggressor, tricks an enemy combatant so well that he is able to surprise and capture him without bloodshed, and in this way save the people who had been targeted for murder, this is normally thought to be morally preferable to simply attacking that enemy and severely injuring or killing him. Was the good soldier's act of deception that avoided bloodshed morally right? Some ethicists say yes. Others say that, whether or not it was right in the sense of "morally good" or "commendable," it was at least justifiable, as long as it, or something very much like it, was literally necessary for the prevention of a much worse wrong. In the story just told, the act of deception prevented our soldier from having to wound or kill his enemy, and, at another level, we can suppose that it prevented the enemy combatant from murdering a number of innocent individuals.

Some people believe that the biblical commandment about truth and lies is simply "Thou shalt not lie," and will draw our attention to the evident fact that this proclamation as stated is absolute and does not allow for exceptions. It doesn't say, "Thou shalt not lie *except* to prevent a worse evil." And no theologian has ever suggested that whenever God condemns lying in the Bible, he must have really meant something like this, something a bit more complicated and nuanced, like morally unjustified lying, or lying that isn't necessary for some greater good, but that the Creator was presumably willing to sacrifice precise accuracy for the sake of catchy, rhetorical punch. However, the Bible does not state quite so simply, "Thou shalt not lie." It seems to be news to most people that the relevant commandment in the Bible, in the famous Ten Commandments passage found in the Book of Deuteronomy, actually says: "Thou shalt not bear false witness against thy neighbor." The commandment is about a specific form of deception—false accusation. It's not quite as universal and blunt as normally represented. When the phrase "Thall shalt not lie" occurs in the King James Bible, it has nothing intrinsically to do with fibbing, as we can see from the fact that on one occasion it ends with the clarifying phrase "carnally with thy neighbor's wife " and on the other it's immediately followed by the phrase "with mankind, as with womankind," which, as is clear from the context, has nothing to do with widespread gender-specific collaborative deception (Leviticus 18:20, 22). But of course, the Bible in many other passages clearly shows very little tolerance for lies and liars generally, despite the apparent ease with which some of the patriarchs and other biblical characters engaged in this activity. The moral imperative that can be derived from its many relevant passages is just commonly stated by use of the simple phrase "Thou shalt not lie," and is most often captured in the equally simple ethical judgment "Lying is wrong." Many good people seem to infer that lying is always wrong, regardless of the circumstances. It couldn't be any simpler than that.

But even simple truths can sometimes have complex applications. It could be that the lie told by the soldier in my example, or the act of deception he engaged in, is still—considered in itself—morally bad, but that it is nonetheless at another level morally excusable in these precise circumstances and even strongly advisable, to the point of being morally preferable to any alternative available to him. Some philosophers draw a careful and very useful distinction between bad and wrong as applied to actions. And this isn't just academic nit-picking. They say that an action is bad when it is in itself the sort of thing we should avoid whenever possible, and that an action is wrong when it is in fact blameworthy in the situation within which it occurred, all things considered. Using this distinction, we can say that not all bad things are wrong in all circumstances. I know, this can sound like the sort of verbal shell game that philosophy professors seem to play with their students for their own perverse pleasure, but it's really not. Sometimes, as in the case of our hypothetical soldier, something that may be intrinsically bad (lying, tricking, or deceiving) has to be done to prevent something much worse, and so—all things considered— we don't in the end judge what's done to have been wrong. Since it is an altogether understandable and excusable action, the soldier who engages in the deception is not at all to be morally censured, held blameworthy, criticized, or punished for what he has done. Many people would actually find him praiseworthy—even if not so much for what exactly he did as for the fact that by doing it he was able to avoid doing something much worse, while nonetheless succeeding in his effort to prevent what would have been a terrible evil.

Legitimate moral categories aren't ever meant to keep us from doing what morally needs to be done. They are intended to guide us in taking seriously the difference between good and evil. They are meant to keep us from engaging in patterns of conduct that will damage our own souls and harm the people around us. A world in which no one ever had to deceive anyone else about anything would seem to be a better world than the one we're in. I have no doubt about that. But we live in a world where some individuals and groups motivated by greed, hatred, or just evil will sometimes attempt to do great harm to other people, and a soldier, or policeman, or anyone else, can occasionally find himself in a position where some small ruse may stop such a rogue and lead to his capture and restraint. As bad as the most morally sensitive among us may feel about any act of deception, it would be hard to argue that trickery is never under any circumstances preferable to the alternatives of allowing a brutal murder or else just seriously harming or killing someone yourself to prevent the terrible realization of his murderous intent. The philosopher Immanuel Kant seems to have thought otherwise, but that just shows once more that no great thinker is right about everything. This, again, isn't a conclusion of moral relativism; it's just an implication of moral realism.

I addressed the charge of moral relativism in Chapter 3. But let's return to it for a moment. It has often been claimed that the pervasiveness of lying in the Harry Potter stories, along with the lack of any explicit condemnation of this activity by the author, shows that she is a moral relativist. She allows her characters to get away with things that are just wrong. But she never labels these things as wrong. Let's assess this criticism by first defining carefully what moral relativism is.

Moral relativism is, simply put, the view that there are no moral absolutes, and that judgments of right and wrong or good and evil always depend on context—that they're always "context relative." To point out that a good person can sometimes be justified in deceiving an evil individual bent on inflicting terrible harm is not to reject absolutes and embrace relativism. It is, on the contrary, an endorsement of the view that it is always absolutely wrong to allow evil to prevail when we are in a position to prevent it, and that we absolutely must take action whenever we can to block serious evil from happening, even when that means doing something we might still consider bad, if we're rationally justified in believing that it's strictly necessary for preventing the occurrence of a major and horrific wrong and that nothing else will work. The act of deception may still be a sin, or morally bad, on its own—perhaps of spiritual danger to the liar, and so something to be regretted, confessed, and repented—but it can also be an act that is morally justified, in at least the sense of "morally excusable," under such extreme circumstances. This is never a determination or judgment to make lightly, but it is one that sometimes must be made. This is the moral philosophy, and judgment, that lies behind the Potter stories. And it's not at all a philosophy of moral relativism. Nor can it by any stretch of the imagination be used to justify lying as an acceptable tool of business or ordinary social interaction, as we'll see below.

In real life, good people accept serious deception only when it is absolutely necessary to prevent a much worse harm from happening.

If Harry Potter puts on an invisibility cloak to sneak out of Hogwarts and break school rules for the purpose of getting some ice cream with his friends, we are confronting one sort of deception. When he puts on that cloak to hide his actions in the effort to help an innocent person escape imminent and wrongful execution, a murder planned by powerful people, and one that can't be prevented in any other way under the circumstances, we are faced with a very different sort of deception. Drawing a distinction like this isn't even a small warning sign of relativism. It's merely common sense. And it doesn't mean that there are no absolutes in the world of wizard ethics; it just means that simple slogans can't always replace the difficulties of real moral reasoning, judgment, and wisdom. Rowling's stories display the level of moral complexity that we often face in the real world. But by embedding them in a vivid overall battle of good against evil, she gives them a power to capture our imaginations and illuminate our real moral understanding of life.

So there is in these stories an absolute difference between good and evil. But this doesn't mean that every action and every person falls completely and clearly into one or the other of these categories in an unambiguous way. Life is sometimes messy. Using a common name for the category of those wicked people who have chosen to follow the evil Voldemort, Harry's godfather tells him that the world isn't divided simply into two groups, good people and Death Eaters (OP 302). The fact that our experience in the world is often an encounter with moral ambiguity and moral complexity doesn't at all imply that there is no real difference between good and evil. It just means that it's sometimes hard for us to discern what should be done, and it's occasionally difficult to evaluate properly what the people around us are doing.

Since I have pointed out that it can sometimes be morally acceptable to engage in deception in the most extreme of circumstances, where human lives, or other great values, are at stake, I should hasten to add that such circumstances rarely if ever come up in the world of business. For all the top executives and well-intentioned motivational speakers and writers who often compare business to war, there are crucial differences that make all the difference in the world for the ethics of the actions we might consider in the two contexts.

People who really believe that "business is war" tend to go looking for their models of business virtue, or strength, primarily from among history's great warriors. The original Western paradigm for these warrior virtues is to be found in *The Iliad* and *The Odyssey* of Homer, but the same qualities can be seen portrayed and praised in many ancient military epics and manuals of strategy. A couple of classic examples of the warrior virtues would be the two very different qualities of courage and craftiness. The importance of courage in times of war cannot be overstated. And, as we have seen in Chapter 2, this quality has great value in many other human endeavors as well. Certainly, it plays an important role in the world of business. Where courage is lacking, innovation stalls. It can often take courage to do the right thing, however unpopular it might be. It takes courage to face up to difficult realities and risk failure in order to accomplish something important. Courage can make the difference between just average results and the attainment of excellence in the life of a company or an individual. As a warrior virtue, it's clearly also a transferable, or universal, virtue. But, by contrast, the warrior virtue of craftiness—understood as the ability to deceive both subtly and skillfully—is a very different matter.

Craftiness is certainly a virtue in war, one that the hero Odysseus was much praised for having. It's clear that the ability to deceive an adversary is a vital skill for avoiding an unnecessary loss of life, sometimes on both sides of a conflict. In most circumstances, it's been the judgment of many great military strategists that it's better to trick an enemy than to kill him. And certainly, it's better to trick him than to let him kill us. Deceiving an adversary in war is often the first step toward defeating him. The most perceptive philosophers who have ruminated on this fact have concluded, as I have explained above, that the same moral judgment can be made about any circumstance where a person's life is threatened by a wicked or deranged individual bound on inflicting severe bodily harm. You can justifiably hide a gun from an enraged killer and deceive him about its location. Such actions will bring you no moral critique, and, especially if you're successful, you may very likely be thanked and praised for helping to prevent an instance of great harm.

Here's a problem that confuses many people and gives them the wrong idea. The most morally scrupulous individuals allow as acceptable some forms of deception even outside the most dramatic life-and-death situations. Certain kinds of deception seem to be completely fine, and morally permissible, in sports as well as, of course, in Las Vegas magic acts and in preparation for surprise birthday parties—but even there, within limits. Consider for a moment the context of sports. We are properly outraged when a championship Little League player lies about his age or an Olympic athlete tries to get away with taking banned performance-enhancing drugs. But we think it's altogether allowable for a quarterback to fake a run when he knows quite well that he really plans to pass the ball. In many sports, an art of craftiness is carefully cultivated, within prescribed limits, without any ethical concern arising at all. The trickier a player is on the field or on the court, the more formidable he may be—and all the more admired.

If you truly thought that business is war, or even that business is really just a very intellectually challenging form of sport, then you might be inclined to embrace all the warrior virtues that seem to facilitate winning. Just as it's not only permissible but necessary to be courageous on occasion at work, you might naturally conclude that it's perfectly okay, and even necessary, to be cunningly duplicitous every now and then as well—when it helps you win, or at least helps you to prevent an opponent, or competitor, from winning. "All's fair in love and war, and I sure love to win" could be the sincere expression of a mentality focused on winning, as uttered by a basically well-meaning, highly competitive person.

But business isn't literally war, and it's not just sport either. When Odysseus fools the Cyclops, we approve. He saves his own life and the lives of others with a clever trick. But the stock market is no Cyclops, despite its nearly singular gaze at the bottom line, and no one's physical safety directly depends on how an analyst rates a stock. What's arguably allowable in war is just simply not permissible in commerce. Apart from the occasional applicability of shared metaphors, these two activities are almost as different as life and death. In much the same way, we can admire the head fake that a great basketball player uses to throw off an opponent in a fast move to the basket, without thinking for a second that business is no different from roundball, and that faking it with investors can appropriately get you to your proper goal. The context of sport is distinctively different from the real life of business in crucial respects.

However, here's the rub. There is a measure of gamesmanship in any competitive endeavor. As the patron saint of corporate accomplishment, former General Electric CEO Jack Welch, says in his book *Winning*:

> Business is like any game. It has players, a language, a complex history, rules, controversies, and a rhythm. (293)

Any business has tactics and strategies for winning. We rightly admire the person who surprises the competition through clever strategy and by keeping his own counsel well. There is an element of the game in many business contexts. Perhaps there is even a whiff of battle. People aren't supposed to die, but product lines and even companies might. So several of the classic warrior virtues do apply, like courage, patience, fortitude, energetic industriousness, commitment, adaptability, prudence, constancy, and persistence. But not all the warrior virtues are properly operative in the business domain. Confidentiality isn't the same thing as deceit, and creatively surprising moves in taking a product to market don't require morally offensive lies on the part of any of the players. It's a failure to see the difference that has contributed to unethical behavior and self-destructive patterns of activity in many highly competitive companies in the recent past. Throughout his book on winning, Jack Welch commends candor, or forthcoming honesty, in business contexts and actually uses a sports metaphor to condemn what he calls the frequent "head fakes" of businesspeople who are not courageous enough to be candid in all they say and do.

The metaphors of war and sport can help us understand some aspects of business. But business isn't literally war. And a body block near the fax machine isn't normally good business behavior.

Harry Potter may learn a lot on the Quidditch field that will help him in later life and give him extra insight for running a large organization. He will certainly learn a great many things from his ongoing moral combat with evil. But neither sport nor battle will teach him that duplicity pays off in the normal course of working with other people. Wisdom will tell him a very different story.

Again, the simplest moral rule for everyday life should be Harry's guide, as well as yours and mine: Do unto others as you would have them do unto you. Treat others the way you would want to be treated. No one wants to be duped about the conditions of his employment.

No one wants to be deceived about her investments. No one wants to be tricked into conduct that may one day result in a legal mess. And it's also fairly uncontroversial to suppose that no normal person wants to be humiliated, vilified, and financially ruined. If the chief malefactors in modern business over the past several years had just taken this one rule, and these few facts, to heart, things might have gone very differently for them, their associates, and their investors.

Real, sustainable, and deeply satisfying success never requires immoral or unethical behavior. In fact, as the great American philosopher Ralph Waldo Emerson saw over a hundred and fifty years ago, following such profound thinkers as Plato and Aristotle before him, a lack of proper ethics will unravel any appearance of success over the long run. Dumbledore sees this clearly. And I fully believe that the mature Harry Potter will, too.

LIES OF ALL KINDS

We can learn something important by examining the variety of lies we encounter in the Harry Potter stories. There are many different sorts of deceptions that we come across in the books and in the actions of the characters. Reflecting for a moment on some of the differences can be very instructive. Let's categorize at least roughly the various kinds of lies that a person can tell, basing our categories on what the liar is hoping to accomplish. These categories will be nonexclusive, which just means that a particular lie can potentially fall into more than one of the types. I'll start with the most heinous of lies, the ones we view most seriously and condemn most vigorously, and then move in the direction of less harmful deceptions. We tend to judge the first categories more harshly and the last categories less severely. If you're inclined to object that, in the end, "A lie is a lie," I'd reply that while this is obviously true on one level, on another and more careful analysis there are some interesting and important distinctions to be made—and we make them all the time.

Within the realm of intentional falsehood, there are:

1. Lies of malicious intent
2. Lies to protect the guilty
3. Lies of self-aggrandizement
4. Lies of convenience
5. Lies to help a friend
6. Lies of legitimate self-defense
7. Lies to preserve or promote a noble cause in the fight against evil
8. Lies to protect the innocent

Let's examine each of these categories briefly. They are all to be found in the Harry Potter books, and we come across each one of them in real life as well. Knowing the differences will help us to assess what we face in both the stories and our lives.

1. Lies of malicious intent. These are lies told for the sole and conscious purpose of harming another person. They can be told to damage the reputation of the other person, to get that person into trouble, or actually to lead to the individual's being physically hurt or wrongfully killed. Ethical people abhor lies of this sort as the worst kind imaginable. They are always wrong.

In book one, *The Sorcerer's Stone,* the Slytherin student Draco Malfoy once deceives Harry by challenging him to a duel later that night in a place on the school grounds they are forbidden to visit at such an hour. The young Malfoy, whose name derives from the French words for "bad faith," has no intention of showing up and informs a school staff member that a student will be there in violation of Hogwarts rules, setting Harry up to be punished or expelled from school. Draco has deceived Harry just to get him into trouble. In book five, *The Order of the Phoenix,* Voldemort misleads Harry into believing a close friend is in mortal danger specifically for the purpose of luring him into a trap where he can be killed. Many other examples of this category could be given from the stories. We always properly judge such lies to be morally wrong. They are wicked, despicable, and utterly inexcusable. And this is the judgment the author clearly intends for us to make.

2. Lies to protect the guilty. These are lies told to cover the tracks of the liar himself or of another wrongdoer. In his own case, the liar acts mendaciously to cover up some other act of wrongdoing he has committed. In the case of another person, he lies to protect someone else he knows to be guilty of a wrong act. These lies amount to complicity in the crime or evil of the person being protected and are usually thought to be every bit as blameworthy as the original offense itself. The more serious the wrong being covered up, the more seriously wrong the cover-up lie is. The less serious the wrong, the less serious the cover-up lie typically is, but there is one exception to this rule.

Imagine that a person commits a fairly trivial misdeed, perhaps under pressure and without really thinking about what he's doing. Let's suppose no one is seriously hurt in any way as a result. The wrongdoer is suspected of having committed the act and is accused of it publicly, but he vigorously and repeatedly denies it. The elaboration and repetition of lies meant to cover up the original misdeed can grow to the point of being more blameworthy than the incident itself. By lying, the wrongdoer digs himself a deeper and deeper hole. The reason we sometimes judge the dodge worse than the deed in such cases is that more reflection and intent has likely gone into the cover-up than went into the disavowed act, and, most often, trust has been violated with more people. The net result is a real mess, and can be far out of proportion to the instigating event. We often see this happen in the worlds of politics and business, where it is unfortunately a rare leader who will own up to even a small moral failing in public and voluntarily accept responsibility for it.

Cover-ups always make a bad situation worse. Admitting our mistakes, while taking courage, is always the best course of action.

One further complication in our judgments concerning deceptions meant to protect the guilty is that if a person lies to protect a family member or a close friend he knows to be guilty of a wrong act, this is often judged a bit less harshly because of traditional considerations of loyalty. Friends support friends. Family members stand by close relatives. Lying to protect the guilty is always wrong. But we can still make some important distinctions. Consider the salient differences between these two cases:

a. A basically good person lies on one occasion to protect another basically good person—a close friend or relative—who has slipped up once and broken a fairly low-level law or rule in a situation where detection by a corrupt and unduly harsh authority would most likely lead to a disproportionate and unjustly harsh punishment.

b. A fundamentally wicked person lies on a particular occasion to protect a fellow terrorist or gang member—a very bad man who characteristically engages in violent, criminal behavior—from being caught for committing a serious crime.

Even if we judge both cases of lying to be morally bad, the second case seems to most people much worse than the first. We are more likely to understand and even forgive the first kind of lie than the second, or we are more likely to assign a less harsh penalty to it. The first liar is, at least in his own intentions, trying to prevent an act of injustice, while the second liar is trying to prevent an act of justice. That doesn't necessarily make one of them right and the other wrong, but it does mean making some moral distinctions in light of the differences. An inability to make any such nuanced distinctions shows a lack of wisdom about life in the world. Right is right and wrong is wrong, but like the popular jelly beans in Harry's world and those in our world as well, they do come in many flavors.

At Hogwarts, students lie to those in authority all the time to protect their energetic and sometimes impish friends from punishment for minor rule violations. Pranks are frequently enjoyed throughout the environment of Hogwarts, then quickly disavowed and denied. George and Fred Weasley are almost constantly protecting each other and defending themselves to avoid any penalty for the pranks they pull. In most cases, fibbers covering for their friends are just trying to do a buddy a favor. However inappropriate and inadvisable their behavior might be, and however bad we think it is at some level, we typically don't judge it to be deeply immoral or outright criminal. Contrast this with any case where one follower of Voldemort might lie to protect another Death Eater so that they can continue in their path of terribly destructive evil. This sort of lie is at a completely different level of wrongdoing. The moral status of the lie is typically proportionate to the status of the crime committed by the person being protected. All such lies may be morally bad, but some are clearly worse than others.

3. Lies of self-aggrandizement. These are lies told in order to gain for the liar himself money, power, status, fame, possessions, pleasure, satisfaction, or security. They can also be told for the sake of holding on to whatever quantity of those things the liar already has. They are unfair and contemptible efforts to circumvent the truth and obtain or hold on to an unfair advantage over other people. They are behind only malicious lies and illicit cover-ups in their moral culpability. They are perhaps even more common in the world of business than type 1 and type 2 lies, but all three types unintentionally create havoc in the lives and careers of the liars and are ultimately self-defeating in their consequences.

The Dursleys often tell lies in their quest for a more secure and more exalted social status. These are simple lies of self-aggrandizement. But there are much worse lies of this sort. Many of Lord Voldemort's supporters were arrested and put into Azkaban after the Dark Lord unsuccessfully tried to murder Harry as a baby and lost most of his power, but many others have reentered normal wizard circles by simply lying that they have seen the error of their ways and have reformed. Sirius Black at one point confronts his old acquaintance Peter Pettigrew and accuses him of exactly this. The evil man is lying about his ultimate allegiance, like many of his former associates, in order to secure his own safety and future prospects as well as he can, in circumstances where the tide has turned against his true affiliation (PA 368). This could be seen as just a case of lying to protect the guilty, but the pretense of reformation could also and perhaps more insightfully be viewed as an exercise in self-aggrandizement, as the followers of Voldemort are seeking to protect themselves while waiting and hoping for their own power and status to be increased if their Dark Lord is able to reappear from hiding and gain the ascendancy he seeks.

Gilderoy Lockhart, of course, offers perhaps the most extreme and egregious example of self-promoting prevarication in all the Potter stories. He has traveled the world for the purpose of interviewing other wizards with great accomplishments and then wiping their memories clean, putting a forgetting spell on them and subsequently claiming their achievements as his own. He has built a career out of lies and has become the most widely read and commonly quoted authority on many wizardly subjects, completely unjustifiably. He comes to Hogwarts as the Defense Against the Dark Arts teacher in book two, *The Chamber of Secrets*, and is found out as a fraud by Harry and Ron. His lies end up being viewed as disgusting and pathetic, characterizations that then attach themselves to him as well. He winds up as a pitiful, pathetic, addled character in a home for the incurably insane.

The juxtaposition of these three examples within a category—the Dursleys, Lockhart, and the Death Eaters—can be taken, once again, as in the last category of lies, to show that, in addition to there being an overall scale of moral seriousness and moral disapprobation that runs between different categories of deception, we can also draw interesting and important distinctions within a category. The followers of Voldemort can clearly be seen to be the most despicable and evil in their lies of self-aggrandizement, Professor Lockhart can seem somehow slightly less evil, however wicked, in his use of such lies, and the irritating Dursleys can appear merely bumbling and relatively harmless by contrast, however wrong and objectionable their deceptions of this sort nonetheless are. Again, if distinctions like these can be drawn even within a category of deceptions, this shows once again the subtle nuances of the ethical. Ethics is a matter of right and wrong and good and evil, but it is also a matter of many specifically weighted judgments as well.

4. Lies of convenience. These are small fibs told typically for the sake of personal convenience rather than to harm anyone, to protect the guilty, or to acquire and maintain any unfair advantage. The basic aim of these lies is not intrinsically unethical. There is nothing inherently bad or wrong about the goal of personal convenience. We aim at that frequently and are for the most part morally innocent in doing so. But even though the end is acceptable, many of the means to it may not be, including even the smallest of lies.

These intentional falsehoods encompass what we often call "fibs" and "little white lies" and are thought by some people to be the unavoidable grease of social harmony. Such a lie is told for the sake of saving time, minimizing effort, simplifying a situation, or extracting someone—the liar or another person—from a potentially embarrassing, awkward, or difficult set of circumstances. Most people disapprove of little white lies, at least in principle, but many who might disavow them in theory will nonetheless tend to use this dodge to some extent when caught off guard in an awkward situation. How many husbands and boyfriends have learned that the universally advisable answer to "Do I look fat in this?" is "No, not at all," despite what the real truth might be? And convenient falsehoods often rule in even less emotionally charged situations.

Imagine you're walking down the hall toward your office and a coworker you barely know zips around the corner, smiles, and greets you with a friendly, casual "How you doing?" Despite a bad back, car trouble, marital tension, and a recent career disappointment that has been on your mind, not to mention a moderate dollop of midlife existential angst, you smile and say, "Fine, thanks, and you?" It isn't the time or place to articulate the truth and recite your woes. But your reaction is literally the saying of something you believe to be false, as if it were true, intending to get your listener to believe it. Strictly speaking, it's a lie of convenience. Maybe you rationalize saying what you do by telling yourself that in most ways you're fine, or that in enough important, relevant ways you are, or even that, within the confines of that specific hallway, on that specific spot, and at that particular moment in time, nothing particularly bad is happening. But it could be that you just say the socially accepted thing, even though it's literally false and you know it is. Lies of convenience are traditionally characterized as wrong, but they are not as seriously censured as the lies that fall into the previous categories.

This is the typical category for many instances of:

"Fine," Harry lied.

Sometimes, Harry just doesn't want to put other people or himself to the trouble that truthful reporting may involve. Occasionally, he's dodging a difficulty that he knows is really not necessary to grapple with head-on in the circumstances. At other times, he's avoiding an awkward moment and trying to make someone else feel better.

Parents reading the Harry Potter books aloud to their children can become quite dismayed over all the lies explicitly attributed to the story's hero and presumed role model, Harry. It's perfectly appropriate to take any particular instance of this as a teachable moment and point out that Harry didn't have to lie in these situations but rather could have answered the other person's greeting, deflected the other person's curiosity, or avoided the other person's discomfort and possibly hurt feelings in another way. Children can learn from Harry's mistakes, as well as from his successes, if we will just take the time to engage them over these issues, ask for their thoughts, and candidly share our own.

As common as lies of social convenience might be in both Harry's world and our own, they are rarely unavoidable and typically can be replaced with equally effective or even more effective means, except perhaps in the case of at least some questions about some articles of clothing on some close lady friends—but probably even then. I'm just kidding with this last remark, of course. But "You look amazing!" followed by a big hug is usually a safe and reassuring statement that can be true under numerous different and even widely divergent interpretations.

It's important that adults and kids have the right perspective on this category of deception. Telling lies of convenience will not by itself make you a terrible, wicked person, but it will keep you from being the very best person you can be—a truly good person. Good moral character requires the courage to avoid lying whenever you possibly can, not just when it's easy and convenient. There is no general moral obligation to tell everyone all the truths you know all the time, regardless of feelings and circumstances. But there is a general obligation to respect truth and other people as much as you can and in as many ways as you can, compatible with all your other duties. Anyone who engages in lies of convenience inevitably becomes more comfortable with small deceptions generally, and this can lead to problematic and morally dangerous compromises when the stakes are much higher.

The "little white lies" of social convenience can subtly erode our moral sense and weaken us to the lure of easy deception in other more serious forms.

---

5. Lies to help a friend. These are fabrications or deceptions engaged in only for the purpose of making a friend feel better or giving him a psychological boost when that may help his prospects in a difficult task or situation.

In our chapter on Harry's courage, I outlined how Harry once deceived Ron into thinking he had slipped a powerful good-luck potion into his drink. Harry had tried to help Ron with his self-confidence in every other way, in preparation for an important upcoming sporting event, and nothing else had worked. We get the impression from the context that Harry wasn't doing this out of his own need to win the game as Gryffindor Quidditch captain, or for the good of the team, so much as he was just trying to help his good mate. Harry couldn't stand to see Ron feeling so miserable and with that bundle of negative emotions setting himself up for a defeat that would make him feel even worse. So Harry deceived him into believing something that would boost his self-image, make him feel very lucky, and in this way open him up for a full access to all his real skills. As we've seen, it worked, and Ron helped win the game.

This sort of lie is an altruistic effort on behalf of another person and so is more easily excused, or less heavily condemned, than lies that are told or deceptions that are engaged in for evil ends or even just purely selfish purposes. Friends want to help friends, and so we easily forgive this sort of act, even if we still judge it, as long as it is a deception outside the context of an extraordinary threat to body or life, as in fact wrong. It is understandable, and can be even a bit endearing, even if we believe that it was in fact morally mistaken.

It's easy to notice that most cases of friends lying to help friends throughout the Harry Potter stories fall under our earlier category of lies to protect the guilty and should be judged mainly as such. But as the case of the good-luck potion shows, not all instances of deceptive friendly help are of this type. And those that are engaged in purely for the perceived good of the friend are clearly of a different moral weight and seriousness than efforts to help a buddy avoid the trouble that naturally arises as a consequence of his misdeeds.

6. *Lies of legitimate self-defense.* These are intentional falsehoods propounded for the sole purpose of defending oneself from unmerited harmful consequences that are otherwise judged to be not easily avoidable. They fall into two simple subcategories:

a. *Lies of self-protection*—These are lies that are intended to protect the individual from some form of harm, unjust censure, disapproval, or injury.

b. *Lies of self-preservation*—These are lies meant to protect oneself from severe bodily harm or death.

The interesting feature of self-defense is that it is usually morally justifiable, under basic conditions of reasonable belief and reasonable response. If you reasonably believe that you are being threatened with imminent harm, and you reasonably respond to that threat with the purpose of protecting yourself or preserving your life, you are generally held to be morally justified in doing whatever you felt you had to do in self-defense. The conditions of reasonableness are necessary, though, to prevent people from being irresponsibly excused from otherwise blameworthy conduct because of irrational beliefs they wrongly held and to prevent them from getting away with extreme actions, potentially involving serious harm to others, that were not at all necessary, or reasonably called for, in the actual situations that gave rise to them. In most circumstances, it's not reasonable to respond to a bully's actions with a shotgun blast to the gut if he has merely pushed and punched you black and blue. In most such cases, that would not count as reasonable self-defense. But if an effective deception is the only reasonable ploy that can stop his attacks, then that will likely be judged very differently.

The typical moral judgment made in a case like this is that it's really too bad that any sort of deception had to take place at all, and of course nonmendacious means are usually to be preferred, but if it took a deception or an intentional falsehood to defend yourself against a significantly serious, undeserved attack, and possibly dreadful harm, and under the circumstances nothing else could reasonably have been thought to have any good chance of achieving the same aim, then the deceptive action can be considered morally justified, or at least morally excusable, however regrettable in some sense it might remain. Many women confronted late at night by would-be attackers have reported later that they escaped the situation by falsely claiming that their husbands or boyfriends were coming along any second, and consequently by this sort of deception discouraged and thwarted what could otherwise have been a terrible sequence of events. They are to be congratulated for having had their wits about them and for having acted effectively in self-defense, and they are properly consoled, but they are not at all to be castigated and morally condemned for their act of deception.

A conservative Christian or Jew, or any religiously sensitive person, may judge any lie of self-defense to be a sin but, in the appropriate circumstances, perhaps a sin that was both understandable and unfortunately necessary for the avoidance of a greater evil. You can see how this is a much milder moral judgment than is typically rendered in the case of any lie falling into one of the previous categories. Even people who fervently believe that no lie is "right" or "morally praiseworthy" will somewhat reluctantly excuse lies falling into this category of legitimate self-defense, especially if it seems that the threat of harm was both serious and imminent and that no successful protection of the self could reasonably have been expected to be accomplished in any other way.

One more thing to notice: This category of lies should most properly be understood to have nothing to do with the protection of one's own reputation, social standing, income level, or personal power in a corporate context or within the broader community. It is concerned only with the most serious forms of bodily harm. No one can get a moral pass for lying to preserve their status in an organization or their financial take from a pending deal. The Dursleys may think they're justified in lying about Harry to protect their standing in the community, but they're just wrong. Only very extreme circumstances can justify or excuse what we ought to think of as the extreme measure of deception in any situation of self-protection or self-preservation.

7. Lies to preserve or promote a noble cause in the fight against evil. This category would encompass the sort of deceptions necessary on the part of the French Underground in World War II as they fought the Nazis. Another example might be the careful fabrications and dissimulations necessary for the safety and efficacy of CIA operatives as they seek to penetrate and disable terrorist cells around the world. This is not just a subcategory of our next and last general category—lies to protect the innocent—because one freedom fighter can lie to protect a comrade who is actually guilty of some crime under the laws of the repressive state they are battling and perhaps even guilty of some crime deserving in itself of punishment. But a lie may be told to protect this one individual on a particular occasion in order to protect, preserve, or promote the overall movement itself or one of its important operations. So this is a distinct category of deception. If the cause is sufficiently just, and the enemy is sufficiently evil and threatening, this sort of deception may be even more excusable than simple self-defense, because it is perhaps in principle nobler and more altruistic. But this is a judgment that can be dangerous to make. There have been plenty of people in human history who have done terrible evil in the mistaken belief that they actually were accomplishing something genuinely good for a noble cause. Nonetheless, this is still a category of great importance for the potentially legitimate justification of acts of deception.

In the Harry Potter stories, we come across at least one very striking example of this sort of lie. The morally good and paradigmatically virtuous Albus Dumbledore surprises us all and tells government officials an outright lie—boldly, quickly, and with no apparent sense of regret. In order to explain why, let me first establish some background.

A classic and commonly witnessed form of moral corruption in our world involves people in leadership positions becoming so concerned about the preservation of their own reputation, position, and power that they perversely come to ignore, and actually act contrary to, the needs of the people they lead and the ultimate good of their organizations. Seeking to appear firmly in control, they ultimately lose control of both their organizations and their careers because of their misdirected actions and the inevitably destructive consequences that flow from such a dereliction of responsibility.

It's always dangerous to place appearance over reality, or career over service.

In Harry's world, the top administrators within the Ministry of Magic want more than anything else to cultivate and perpetuate the impression that they are firmly in control of things. They deeply fear any development that could threaten their assiduously contrived image of themselves as thoroughly competent and absolutely dependable leaders. Because of this, they are doubly terrified by the rumors, hints, and bits of evidence they are hearing that the terrifyingly dangerous, evil wizard Voldemort is somehow still alive and planning to overturn the entire order of things on which they depend for their sense of self-importance. On one level, they viscerally fear Voldemort himself and any prospect of his return. But they fear almost as strongly any widespread perception that such a thing could even possibly happen, because they worry that this will erode any public sense of them as great and prudent leaders who always have things well managed and completely under control.

Cornelius Fudge, the Minister of Magic, is especially agitated over Dumbledore's claims that Voldemort is alive, growing stronger, and planning a war against the general wizard society. He knows that Dumbledore is widely viewed as an impressive and very credible individual. But rather than taking the time to look into his alarming allegations, Fudge will do almost anything to dismiss the headmaster's warnings about their evil enemy—and that includes launching a concerted effort to discredit him thoroughly as an addled old man who lives in a realm of fantasy. It's amazing how far Fudge will go to banish any thought of danger looming on the horizon.

The students at Hogwarts have always been trained in Defense Against the Dark Arts as a normal part of their education. But the corrupt and paranoid authorities now seem to think that any ongoing practical instruction in defensive skills of combat may be misinterpreted by people in the current climate as an indirect acknowledgment that there is or could be some sort of danger that the students need to be prepared to face, and the Ministry doesn't want to allow even the least suspicion of such a thing to arise. So they send to Hogwarts a new Defense Against the Dark Arts teacher to represent Ministry interests and provide the students with only theoretical, textbook-oriented lessons to prepare them for written exams. She is completely unwilling to offer them any real-world training in useful techniques of self-defense.

The students realize that this change in their curriculum and method of instruction is wrong and that it puts them in dire jeopardy. They need realistic preparation in how to protect themselves against dark magic now more than ever. And so they rebel, taking matters into their own hands and going off on their own to learn magical self-defense, in direct violation of a Ministry decree. But they are found out, and Ministry authorities, including the top man himself, immediately descend on Hogwarts to take the ringleaders into custody and punish them severely. When Headmaster Dumbledore learns what's going on, he intervenes to protect his students and calmly tells Fudge an outright lie to deflect any blame from them and take it all himself (OP 618).

This leads to Dumbledore's sudden dismissal as headmaster and to his pursuit by authorities as a law-breaker. He had lied, pleasantly and cheerfully, and had sacrificed his own position to protect the children who, in his eyes, were engaged in a noble and vital endeavor, an activity that might one day soon save their lives as well as the lives of many others. As it turns out, he was absolutely right in this belief. He certainly could have protected his students in many other dramatic ways—by instantly killing the Ministry officials who had come to the school, by paralyzing and imprisoning them, or by obliterating their memories with a powerfully dangerous spell—but he took the least damaging path available to him, the alternative of simple deception, and it was also arguably the least blameworthy of his otherwise unpleasant alternatives for preventing what would have been a great and damaging wrong.

Dumbledore could have been reasoning inwardly that Fudge and the others, through a pattern of abominable and destructive conduct, had given up any right to the truth that they otherwise properly would have expected. As a consequence, he is absolved of any duty to give them the truth. The basic philosophy here would then be that duties correspond, in at least such instances, with rights. They go hand in hand. If the relevant right is given up, the corresponding duty releases its hold. But again, a man like Dumbledore would use this perspective very cautiously. And so should we. It wouldn't necessarily mean that the lie was morally praiseworthy or even completely justified—only that it was, under the circumstances, excusable and compatible with Dumbledore's being a morally strong person committed to living a life of truth. Even if we judge that all lies are wrong, and so that this act of Dumbledore's was wrong, we are still able to admire him for being willing to incur the inner sacrifice of his own commitment to truth on this occasion for the sake of what he properly believed to be the weightier good of protecting his students. He gave up his own position in order to protect and promote a noble cause in the fight against evil.

An exemplary leader is able to put the needs of others first.

Good leaders are guided by a sense of what is in the best interests of their communities, their organizations, and their associates, as well as what is best for maximizing their positive impact in the world. Corrupt leaders are motivated and guided by a false and distorted sense of self-interest alone. The worst of leaders can convince themselves, and some-times at least many of the people around them, that they are acting ultimately for the sake of a noble cause. And they can use this as an excuse for what is really inexcusable behavior, including deceptive and mendacious conduct. But the fact that such clear, self-deluded abuse is possible doesn't in the least eliminate the generally accepted moral possi-bility that good people can sometimes be justified in resorting to decep-tion in order to protect and promote a noble cause, on rare occasions and in extreme circumstances where no better alternative is available.

Clearly, there have been businesspeople throughout history who were so self-deluded that they actually believed their ambitious deceptions and cynically calculated, tactical lies were necessary "to preserve or promote a noble cause in the fight against evil"—whether they had in mind the perceived evil of their competitors' existence and success or the supposed evil of their own potential failure and subsequent fall from wealth and position. To put it in as morally blunt a way as possible, you can't just pretty-up the worst sort of Machiavellian maneuvering as a moral necessity and thereby receive a cosmic "Get Out of Jail Free" card. The vast majority of business and life never puts us into a situation where the preservation or promotion of some noble cause in the fight against evil falls squarely and dramatically on our shoulders in such a way that we are justified in deceiving another person. We may entertain fantasy rationalizations to the contrary, but this is not how life most commonly works. The moral acceptability of this category corresponds to the extreme rarity of its legitimate application in the course of most normal lives. We should beware of ever entertaining it as an excuse for possibly duplicitous conduct in dealing with others when we really know that conduct would be wrong.

8. Lies to protect the innocent. This seems to be the least condemned category of lying, because it is in principle the most altruistic or concerned entirely for the good of another person. A falsehood intentionally uttered only to defend an innocent person against some form of serious harm has as its goal something that can in itself be a morally praiseworthy result—the protection of the innocent. Such a lie is still never typically considered a good thing in itself, but is usually thought to be justifiable, or at least morally excusable, if and only if it is reasonably believed to be the only way available for preventing great harm to an undeserving victim.

This category admittedly has to be employed creatively in looking at the Harry Potter stories, because there is almost no one in them who isn't guilty of something, so we have to be especially generous in our application of the label "innocent." But of course, when you really think about it, that's pretty much true of the real world as well. The concept of innocence would be rarely employed, except perhaps in the case of a newborn baby, unless we were accustomed to using it contextually, generally, and relatively speaking. So understood, it does have proper application in both our world and Harry's.

The only times Headmaster Dumbledore ever gets angry is when an innocent person has been endangered by neglect or attacked with malice. The only reason he ever engages in deceptive action—and this is very rare indeed—is when an innocent person or a just cause needs to be protected from a very serious threat, and there is no other way available to accomplish that end. Does this mean that the great Dumbledore has a personal philosophy that "the end justifies the means"? Whenever a good end is in view, is he prepared to use simply any means to accomplish it? No, nothing like this is implied at all. Any reasonable philosophy can acknowledge that a sufficiently noble end can on rare occasion justify, or at least excuse, extraordinary means applied in its support that would otherwise never be undertaken or employed. That understanding does not turn a person's philosophy into a relativist or a situational worldview in any worrisome or inappropriate way. A morally committed person will always be extremely cautious about applying this rare option, but can acknowledge that it does exist within a reasonable moral framework, precisely for use in dealing with extreme and extraordinary situations where great evil can be resisted, and great good secured, in no other way.

The honorable Dumbledore early on promised Harry that he'd never lie to him. And he never does. But he keeps certain truths from Harry until he thinks the young man is prepared to hear them. And he withholds truth from others who might misuse that information for evil purposes. In various places we come to see that even this great lover of truth is prepared to deceive other people who are bent on evil when that is the only way to prevent a terrible tragedy. So Dumbledore's own commitment to the truth, absolute though it may be, is at the same time nuanced. He understands that the truth can be used as a weapon, and so it must occasionally be kept from those who would employ it to accomplish great harm.

The careful reader gets a clear impression that Dumbledore would always prefer to get things done with truth alone, realizing that if he could persuade even extremely corrupt people to acknowledge all the right truths, they might abandon their paths of wickedness and not seek to abuse any given piece of information that they might come to possess. He says at one point to Harry and Hermione:

But I have no power to make other men see the truth . . ." (PA 393)

Since he can't make people see the whole truth, he must sometimes keep a particular piece of the truth away from anyone who would most likely use it to harm others.

The truth, like almost anything else, can be used to help or harm. How we use it is up to us.

In a series of events recounted in book three, *The Prisoner of Azkaban,* that I have alluded to before, Dumbledore helps Harry and Hermione slip out of the school infirmary, travel through time, and elude their enemies in order to rescue an innocent man as well as a good animal from horrible fates (PA 393–420). The headmaster misleads two other adult wizards—the Minister of Magic, Cornelius Fudge, and the Hogwarts teacher Severus Snape—to help his students pull off this rescue without dreadful consequences. He never actually lies, in the strict sense of intentionally uttering a falsehood as if it were true, but he carefully positions individual truths in such a way as to keep Fudge and Snape from discovering the one truth they are seeking. Dumbledore's act of deception is for an extraordinarily worthy purpose. It alone allows Hermione and Harry to accomplish a great good and stop a tragic evil from being inflicted on an innocent man. It is understandable, excusable, and even justifiable, because it was necessary for the prevention of an irreversible wrong of the greatest magnitude.

My aim in laying out this slightly complicated eightfold moral taxonomy of lies is not at all to intimate or argue that we should be more open-minded about lying. I don't think that this is Rowling's aim in representing all these forms of deception in her books, either. I wouldn't want for a second to appear to be defending in any way the one activity that perhaps has caused the most trouble for modern business and for our current society generally. Lying is intrinsically bad, is corrupting to the soul, and always introduces a tear into the social fabric. And it always compromises the liar. No good society or organization can exist or flourish without truth, honesty, and the trust that these things alone make possible. No good relationship can exist except on a healthy foundation of truth. Deception should never be seen as just one more perfectly acceptable tool in the overall toolkit we have for making things happen.

I have gone into all this detail because understanding it will help us to understand some common rationalizations of lying, identify them for what they really are, and resist them. It will also help us to understand how the strong moral principles on which good lives and good businesses are based are compatible with the judgments we also make about those rare and exceptional cases where deception seems to have a very different ethical status. To know and understand the exceptions well can be enough to see how infrequently they apply to our normal lives. And that realization in itself is important. But to be able to take in and comprehend the whole moral topography of truth and lies will always put us in a better position to understand ourselves and those around us more deeply, in our highest strivings and in our worst failings. It also helps us to read Harry Potter more deeply and use what we learn there in the best possible ways.

A LIE AND A FRIENDSHIP

Quite a few of the lies that we come across in the Potter stories seem completely unnecessary in the judgment of any of us who are ethically concerned adults. But I suspect that many children find some of them more natural and understandable. Let me give an example. In *The Sorcerer's Stone*, Hermione surprises Harry and Ron when she tells a lie to get them out of serious trouble. Because of some harsh words she has overheard them say about her before they actually knew her well, she has secluded herself, crying, up in an old girls' bathroom, just before a giant troll is discovered in the school. All the students are told to go to their residential houses immediately, but Harry and Ron realize that Hermione is not present in the Great Hall when the announcement is made, and so she doesn't know of the danger. In violation of the teachers' orders, they go looking for her, find her in the bathroom just as the troll discovers her, and fight the great beast, saving her life. The moment this chaotic battle ends, the teachers come in and begin berating Ron and Harry for disobeying their explicit instructions, being away from the other students, and endangering themselves. Hermione speaks in their defense, at first truthfully, but then she spins out a lie to extricate them from trouble, by taking most of the blame herself. She truthfully says that the boys were looking for her. But then she lies that she had gone searching for the troll herself, thinking she had read enough about these creatures to be able to deal with him. Ron is utterly shocked to hear Hermione, of all people, actually lie to a teacher (SS 177).

She succeeds with the lie in her goal of getting them all off and avoiding any sort of punishment. In context, she could likely have been just as successful by telling the whole truth. She was in the bathroom and didn't know about the troll, and Harry and Ron indeed broke away from the student body and went wandering down the halls when it was forbidden to do so, solely for the purpose of finding and saving her in case she was in danger. So the actual truth most likely was noble enough to get both her and the boys out of trouble. The lie on her part was therefore completely unnecessary for its intended result of saving her fellow students from punishment.

But it could be that Hermione didn't want to tell the truth in that situation for another reason. She didn't want the teachers to know that she had been upset over what she had overheard the boys saying, perhaps finding it in retrospect just too embarrassing to repeat. So it could well be that the lie was spun not just to save Ron and Harry from getting into trouble for being where they weren't supposed to be on school property. It was also intended to bring this about in such a way that Hermione could save herself some embarrassment as well. And the unintended side effect that this lie seems to contribute to regarding Ron and Harry is every bit as unexpected as the act itself: Rowling tells us that from this moment on, Hermione became their friend (SS 179).

If you're surprised or even shocked that Rowling would depict a lie as giving rise to a foundationally important and subsequently wonderful friendship, don't worry. She makes it clear that she doesn't trace the origin of this central friendship to the lie itself, but rather to the overall situation that had transpired. She writes:

> There are some things you can't share without ending up liking each other, and knocking out a twelve-foot mountain troll is one of them. (SS 179)

At the heart of any great friendship is the desire to help and protect your friends. By going to search for Hermione, Ron and Harry were already treating her in the way they would a friend, despite any mean or insulting things they may have said to each other about her earlier. She recognized this and reciprocated. She also unnecessarily engaged in what may have been nothing more than a face-saving lie of convenience. But the lie itself impressed Ron and Harry that Hermione was perhaps a little more like them than they had thought. And even this contributed to breaking down walls between them, although it really shouldn't have. But it was fundamentally the spectacular dangers both shared and survived that day that really created and cemented their relationship. And that is something in itself worth comment.

There is an insight about human nature that's behind the occasional popularity of ropes courses, Outward Bound, and other weekend-warrior corporate challenges that are engaged in for the sake of leadership building and team building. Successful struggles can create

healthy friendships. Confronting and overcoming an initially daunting challenge is a bonding experience. This is deeply rooted in human
prehistory with the fellowship of the hunt, and it can be reproduced
in rustic, mountainous, woodland, riparian, or nautical settings today.
But the cementing-of-friendship effect is strongest yet when people
join together to accomplish a real task of significant difficulty that
results in a substantive and recognized good. Corporate groups on
retreat who have renovated a dilapidated community center in the
hottest of summer weather, or who have cleaned up some vacant lots
in an inner city environment, and who can then see the beneficial
results of all their efforts, often find it a seminal experience for creating new relationships and a deeper form of trust between people.
Fighting a troll had exactly the same result for Harry, Ron, and
Hermione. If you can find a real yet metaphorical troll to fight with
your associates in any business or organizational context, you can
position yourself to create or firm up a new level of trust, respect, productive friendship, and teamwork among the people around you. This
is often all that's needed for the building of great relationships—and
that's no lie.

LIES AND MORAL REFLECTION

J. K. Rowling often uses situations of moral choice to get her readers
thinking. The case of Hermione and the house-elves is particularly
interesting in this regard. Themes concerning the ugliness of racism
and the unjustified nature of prejudice run throughout all the Harry
Potter stories. The Malfoys are a family of "pure-blood" wizards, who
detest "mudbloods"—those wizards who have at least one parent or
ancestor who isn't a pure-blood witch or wizard. The children at the
center of the story, and their moral guide Dumbledore, clearly see this
as the immoral prejudice it is. We also learn that most wizards hate
and fear giants, holding many negative views about their character. As
a half-giant, the good and kind Rubeus Hagrid has to deal with suspicion and distrust from many of the adult wizards around him. Most

wizards, it seems, also distrust and fear werewolves such as Professor Remus Lupin and clearly discriminate against them. Rowling presents us with enough details about the real violence of some giants and the actual dangers involving werewolves so that we can understand how these prejudices and their associated forms of discrimination got started and took root among large numbers of wizards, but we are also given enough specific information about actual individuals in these categories that we can see how unfair the generalizations and attitudes are that these people have to live with and strive to overcome.

Perhaps the most overtly downtrodden of all the groups in the Potter stories are the house-elves. These little creatures work as servants in wealthy wizard homes, as well as in wizard institutions like Hogwarts. They do the cooking, cleaning, mending, and many other errands for their masters and live more like slaves than hired help. In fact, they are even said to belong to their masters as property. When Hermione Granger, a young lady who grew up in a nonwizard family, suddenly learns about the plight of house-elves, she is shocked. She sees it as a completely unacceptable arrangement and calls it what it is—slavery (GF 125). When she further discovers there are house-elves in service even at Hogwarts, she is beside herself with shock and anger. She is utterly astonished that these individuals are expected to work for the staff and students entirely without pay. But she is informed that they don't want any sort of monetary compensation. She is even told that the little elves enjoy their servitude. Ron confidently insists that they like their situation (GF 224). His brother George Weasley chimes in as well and assures Hermione that the Hogwarts house-elves are quite happy as things are. But she refuses to believe that they could possibly be content in their enslavement, or, if they are, that they should be.

Hermione becomes totally passionate about elf rights. She starts her own organization, S.P.E.W.—"The Society for the Promotion of Elfish Welfare." She makes signs and badges, writes petitions, and generally annoys her friends with her crusading attitude toward righting the terrible wrong to which they've all grown accustomed. And then she comes up with her own immensely clever plan to free the elves working at Hogwarts—starting with the ones who clean Gryffindor. Her plan can accomplish its aim directly and quickly without the need of persuading anyone else to help eliminate this injustice, but the problem is that it requires deceiving precisely the individuals whose good she hopes to be securing. If she can trick them all, she can free them all.

Hermione begins to put her plan into action and believes she is doing the right thing. Harry and Ron don't think so at all. Ron points out to her that by going through with her plan she is deceiving the elves into a sudden change of their overall life condition—an instant freedom—they may or may not be prepared for and actually might not want. And he tells her quite bluntly that the tactic of deception she's using is just wrong. She refuses to see it this way and emotionally expresses her underlying conviction that, certainly, all of the elves really want to be free (OP 255). Hermione undeniably means well in all her actions, but whether it can be ethical for any of us to trick other people into doing something we think is good for them, regardless of what they may want, is the issue. It's not a question that Rowling ever answers, but it is something that she invites all her readers to contemplate. It may be one thing for a mother to sneak some chopped spinach into her homemade coleslaw, whether the kids want it or not, because they need the nutrition, but it seems to be quite another matter for a social crusader to work by thoroughgoing deception and actually force someone both abruptly and without preparation into a new and possibly frightening life situation.

Hermione tries to deceive the house-elves into a change that she feels is best for them. From our perspective, it certainly seems like something that is indeed best for them in the long run, but perhaps this will be true only if there are larger-scale changes in the surrounding wizard culture that will make free life possible for them in a fulfilling way. Hermione's first mistake is that she's taking shortcuts and is trying to liberate the elves from their servitude without doing enough of the hard work that will be involved in creating a better social environment for their lives. Trying to help, she is just as likely to hurt and make miserable any of them she successfully deceives, as Rowling shows us in one particular case.

This is an important cautionary tale about deception. The best of people can go wrong in using it. As we try to make our proper mark on the world in our work and in our broader public lives, it is rarely a proper, safe, and desirable strategy to tell a lie or trick another person, even with the best of intentions in mind. Deception is a dangerous thing. As we've seen, it may unfortunately sometimes be necessary, under the most extreme and threatening circumstances, but it's never to be entered into lightly. Every other option should be considered before any deceptive act is ever employed in service to a good end. And we should allow ourselves such a course of action on any occasion only if all the other alternatives available to us would be much worse.

I think that Rowling shows us Hermione acting in this way as an ethical warning. Good people can do bad things with the most noble of intentions. Normally fine and upstanding individuals can deceive themselves and rationalize behavior they should never even countenance. This is a problem we all need to recognize and strive to avoid. We are shown the quintessential good girl, Hermione, doing something morally dubious in the course of her ethically well-intentioned crusade against discrimination and slavery to remind us that it isn't just scoundrels who can go wrong when departing from the truth.

Rowling never expects her readers to think that lying is in general a good or useful thing, but she wants us to understand that it is a pervasive thing in the world. She gives us plenty of reasons to examine it critically and ask ourselves how we stand on this crucial ethical issue. The answers are not always easy. And that's one part of the truth she wants all her readers to see.

A FINAL WORD ON DECEPTION

Looking back as far as we can into human prehistory, I believe we can see that we originally developed language for a number of purposes:

1. To warn
2. To call
3. To express or exclaim
4. To create
5. To inquire
6. To inform
7. To deceive

When we consider each of these uses of language, we can come to see something very important.

Early humans used sounds to warn each other of danger. The more articulated and differentiated the sounds could be, the more detailed the warnings could be. Our ancestors also used vocalizations to call each other in ways that didn't involve warning and danger. One person could call others to come hunt or to come eat. The more detailed language became, the more differentiated calling could be. We have also always used sound to express hurt, excitement, anger, joy, and many other emotions. Vocal exclamations from the basic beginnings of simple grunts and screams became more expressive as they became more differentiated. A vocabulary of expression evolved to capture what needed to be expressed or exclaimed.

Language allowed creative thought to crawl, walk, and then run. With the use of language, people could create plans, schemes, tactics, strategies, poems, philosophies, laws, stories about wizards, and songs, as well as many other interesting and important structures. Under the right circumstances, an ordained minister utters the words "I thee wed" or "I pronounce you husband and wife" and thereby creates a legal and religiously sanctioned marriage. Language is used in many ways to create—an atmosphere, a firm resolve, a community, and even a nation. Think for a moment about how the language of the Declaration of Independence and the Constitution of the United States has functioned to create and structure a sovereign national government.

Language developed also for the purpose of inquiry. We learn about the world by asking questions. Early human beings needed to learn a great deal about their surrounding environment and about each other. Language became a tool for learning—for investigation, for analysis, and for the purposes of memory and the subsequent use of what had been learned.

When most people are asked the question "What is language for?" they tend to answer, "It's for the communication of information." But that is just one of the many functions language has, as we can see. It is a vitally important use of language to inform others of information we have. But it's not the only use, and it's not the only purpose of vocalization or verbalization. Nonetheless, informing is a paradigmatic use of language and is central to civilized life.

Language has also been used, from the earliest times, to deceive. One man says, in however primitive or sophisticated a manner, "Look! Over there!" and steals his companion's food, tool, weapon, or otherwise valuable item while the other's attention is diverted. This is a use of language, interestingly, that does not and cannot stand on its own. If it weren't for the prior warning, calling, expressing, creating, inquiring, and informing uses that language has, it could never be used to deceive. If there were no such thing as truth, there could be no such thing as trickery. This seventh, and last, use of language is dependent on all the others. And it is also, interestingly, the only use that when implemented well enough and frequently enough, would undermine all the others completely. The ability to deceive, through language and other means, can be, as we have seen, an important weapon in the arsenal of any good person defending great value against the onslaught of unyielding evil, as unfortunate as its use might always nonetheless be. But it is always a dangerous weapon to employ, as its successful use can contribute, in however small a way, toward undermining and ultimately defeating all the other uses of language and thereby its own extreme option. Trickery always destroys trust. Lying erodes the foundations of collaboration and community. Deception is insidiously damaging to the overall enterprise of effective human communication. So we have had to establish strict rules governing its use.

Lying undermines the foundations of community necessary for true success in the world.

But we also have had to create rules governing the use of any of these linguistic functions. Warning is, for example, a fine activity to engage in, unless certain limits are violated. We should not warn needlessly, frivolously, with unwarranted exaggeration, with undue harshness, or too late. Warnings should neither be needlessly shrill nor pointless. There are also rules for expression or exclamation. We should never express ourselves too loudly, too often, too crudely, or at times when it is just inappropriate. These are typically thought of as rules of etiquette, as distinct from ethics, but as rules nonetheless. Deep down, of course, ethics and etiquette are intimately related, despite their obvious differences—manners and morals are both about proper deportment and other-regarding behavior. The rules of both ethics and etiquette are necessary for any civilized society. The biggest difference between the two is that large stretches of etiquette are contingent and regional, however universal and absolute its fundamental intent, whereas the entirety of ethics is in principle absolutely universal in scope.

It's interesting to note that the rules we have for most uses of language take a certain form. Warning is fine *unless* certain conditions hold. Expressing is fine *unless* certain limits are violated. The rules governing deception are quite different. It is not fine unless certain conditions hold or unless certain limits are violated. The opposite approach applies here. This use of language is wrong unless certain extreme circumstances threaten. As I have indicated in this chapter, the general, traditional, enlightened moral consensus is that we should never deceive another person unless deception is absolutely necessary to prevent extreme and wrongful harm to someone else or irreversible, very serious physical or mortal harm to ourselves. It's very important to put such severe constraints on deception, or lying, because of its potential for undermining all our relations, defeating all the other uses of language, and rendering civilized society impossible.

Rowling writes nothing to contradict any of this. She says nothing to make us think that she takes a casual view of lying or that she thinks deception is ever right or even excusable, outside the most extreme circumstances. Critics of her books have not made careful enough distinctions in reading and interpreting the actions of the characters in these novels. And we need not follow them in rendering any sort of negative judgment concerning the moral underpinnings of the stories or the ultimate take on ethics they display. We can also stand just as strongly in judgment of any character within the stories who plays fast and loose with the truth, knowing the genuine ethical status of honesty and its importance in all of human life. In the end, I believe, this is something that Harry will join his moral mentor Dumbledore in understanding and living.

5

_~σδ_

LEADERSHIP ALCHEMY

You are an alchemist. Make gold of that.
—*Shakespeare*

One powerful ancient and medieval predecessor of modern science was the discipline and dream of alchemy. In its simplest form, alchemy was the quest to create a substance, known as "the Philosopher's Stone," that could be used to turn base metals into gold, and to help brew a potion that would confer everlasting life. The original title of the first Harry Potter book, and the title under which it is published in England, is *Harry Potter and the Philosopher's Stone*. Rowling makes the magical art of alchemy, and its ultimate product, the centerpiece of the book. Alchemists thought of themselves as engaged in a spiritual enterprise. They defined their activities as comprising an art and science of transformation and transmutation. Interestingly, many modern-day leaders think of themselves in much the same way. They take basic ideas, raw materials, ordinary human beings, and classic organizational structures and seek at least metaphorically to turn them into gold, while attaining a form of immortality along the way. At a time when the traditional quest of alchemy is no longer taken seriously by scientists, and its centuries of striving are thought of at most as a historical curiosity, it can itself be transformed into a powerful metaphor for all great leadership.

As historians of politics and analysts of business have increasingly come to understand, leadership is at its core a transformational endeavor. Leaders don't just manage what is, they seek to produce what should be. They aren't just guardians and stewards of what they are given. They are alchemists of achievement, magicians of metamorphosis, artists of accomplishment. The best leaders create genuinely amazing results in their organizations and have a lasting positive impact on the lives of the people they lead. And many consider what they are engaged in to be a spiritual task. Nothing less is now acceptable as leadership excellence.

THE ROLE OF A LEADER

One of the most important personal discoveries about leadership that any of us can ever make is that it's really a dynamic, informal, and changing role more than anything like an official institutional status. In its essence, it's a role that any properly prepared individual can play, and should play, whenever the time is right. Sometimes the role and the status coincide. But we should never confuse the two. Leadership is always fundamentally a relational, interpersonal role. It's a function any of us can perform.

The real leaders in Harry's world aren't necessarily the people with the organizational or institutional status and title. Cornelius Fudge, until right before the start of Harry's sixth year at Hogwarts, is the Minister of Magic, holding the highest public office in the world of wizards. But he isn't much of a leader at all, being more concerned with protecting the status quo, guarding his own reputation, and maintaining a public perception of proper order than with actually doing what needs to be done at any given time. He is unable to accept the truth that Voldemort has returned as a terrifying threat to the whole way of life in the world of the wizards, and he would prefer to live in denial, dismissing and vilifying anyone who seeks to speak the truth rather than facing it himself. He is not really concerned with the good of those he is supposed to be leading, but is personally greedy for all the perks of position and power that he enjoys in his official capacity. Rufus Scrimgeour then follows Fudge as the new Minster of Magic at the beginning of *The Half-Blood Prince*, and he soon shows his true colors as cut from the same basic cloth as Fudge. He may be tougher and shrewder than Minister Fudge ever was, but he is still more concerned with appearances than realities and tries repeatedly to recruit Harry into masquerading as a strong supporter of the Ministry, despite a long history of unhelpfulness and outright animosity toward both Harry and Dumbledore on the part of many Ministry officials. Scrimgeour reveals his basic approach to leadership when he says to Harry:

"It's what people believe that's important." (HB 344)

He then asks Harry to come around the Ministry offices now and then just to be seen there, with the idea in mind that this will lead people to think that Harry is supporting and working with the Ministry. And that will improve the public mood. The Minister makes it clear that he's not seeking any reality of partnership or mutual collaboration, but merely the public appearance of it. It's all a shallow and manipulative public relations ploy.

Just like the Dursleys, Scrimgeour is more concerned with creating the right impression than with producing the right reality. The Ministry has never really supported Harry or his friends. And Scrimgeour knows that because of this, Harry will have little motivation to go along with his suggestion. As a result, he dangles in front of Harry a not-so-subtle bribe, hinting that while he was visiting the Ministry for purely PR purposes, he could get to know the head of the office in charge of the occupation that he had told his teachers he might eventually like to pursue, that of Auror—a sort of FBI agent for wizards. The Minister also implies that Harry's future in such a job could be secured if he were just to play along with the plan.

Harry knows exactly what's going on and what the Minister is trying to accomplish. He makes it clear that he will not engage in any such charade and create the false impression that he approves of the Ministry's ongoing actions. He won't allow himself to be used as a pawn to foster the illusions the Minister seems to value so much more than realities. Once again, an official in a leadership position shows himself to be much less than real leadership material. Having known Dumbledore for quite some time by this point, Harry is in a position to recognize the difference.

Dumbledore might on the surface seem to be an example of those instances where status and role come together. He is officially the Headmaster of Hogwarts, appointed to that post of leadership by the Ministry of Magic and supported by the governors of the school. And this is undeniably so. But what is more interesting for our purposes is to note that the full scope of his real leadership reaches far beyond the walls of Hogwarts and throughout the realm of the wizardly populace. Dumbledore not only leads the Order of the Phoenix—the group of dedicated wizards throughout their world who are acting as the front line in the war against Voldemort and his Death Eaters—but he is the rallying point and guide for all good wizards who wish to resist evil in their day. He has not been appointed by anyone as the "Official Leader" for the forces of good. He has risen naturally into that role and has chosen to serve in it by his own initiative and then the acceptance and acclamation of others. He has shown himself to be a natural leader, stepping up to do what needs to be done, and he is recognized as such by those who realize they need a leader to direct their efforts.

Leadership doesn't require a title. It's taking the initiative to accomplish whatever needs to be done.

Harry Potter is much the same. No one has appointed him to an official post as a student leader. He isn't a Prefect at Hogwarts, and he hasn't been put in charge of his residential house or anything else. But when his fellow students realize that they need some serious practical training in the Defense Against the Dark Arts, so that they will be able to protect themselves and those around them if attacked by

Voldemort or his evil minions, they ask Harry to teach and lead them. They naturally look to him for signs of what needs to be done, and many of them instinctively follow him when he launches into important action to remedy some serious wrong. His skill and character also result in his becoming captain of the Gryffindor House Quidditch team during his sixth year. But even before he became captain, he was looked to as an unofficial leader in the arena of play. People with the right skills often find themselves in a position to assume a leadership role, regardless of whether any official power has appointed them to the task or not. And then, with the right character, they are accepted as such by those they lead.

I was in a major airline's hub recently, waiting in the gate area for a flight across the country, when I noticed a large group of young soldiers wearing their desert uniforms, heading out for what would surely be hazardous duty in the Middle East. They were all joking and laughing together. After just a few minutes of observing their interactions, it became clear to me who the de facto leader of the group was. He had no extra stripes, bars, or stars on his uniform. But the others clearly looked to him. Their postures and actions showed me that they followed his verbal and nonverbal signals, and perhaps unconsciously sought his approval. He came across to me as a young man of great self-confidence and bearing, completely comfortable in his own skin. Leadership is often like that. You don't have to be hired as a leader or in any way officially appointed as one in order to function in this capacity. People naturally gravitate toward certain individuals and look to them for guidance, accepting their suggestions about how to move forward, and wanting to please them with a job well done. Other folks who might not strike us initially as natural leaders can choose to step up and offer direction at a crucial time when it's needed, and often the people around them who are looking for some sense of structure, direction, and initiative will respond positively to their recommendations and follow their forward motion.

Albus Dumbledore is a quintessentially natural leader. So is Harry Potter. They both display the two most important qualities of a leader—high competence and deep character. They are both guided by the right fundamental values, and both have a quick intellect to go along with the energy level and skill that they bring to bear on anything of importance to them. We can see Dumbledore grooming Harry throughout their years together for a greater responsibility of leadership, beyond his immediate circle of friends and even the broader ranks of young people his age. The headmaster has been protective of Harry from the very start, but he has also given his prize student unusual scope for creative initiative and action from the earliest times. He praises Harry when he does well, and when he critiques Harry's lack of suitable performance, he does so calmly, gently, and yet seriously, so as not to discourage him, but rather to encourage increased effort on his part. And it has its intended effect.

During his sixth year at Hogwarts, Harry is given an important task by the professor and it's clear that he doesn't fully understand its significance. He is to approach another teacher and ask him to recount some events from the past that are very important for Harry and Dumbledore to know. The man's memory of an event long ago will be a crucial piece of a puzzle that can help Harry eventually defeat the very powerful and evil Voldemort. But Harry has other things on his mind. He allows them to get in the way of what he is supposed to achieve, and he really doesn't put the effort into this endeavor that it requires. When he is asked later whether he has succeeded in the task, he truthfully tells Dumbledore that he tried but couldn't manage to obtain what he was seeking. Dumbledore takes this as a teachable moment for Harry. He knows he has to dig a bit more deeply into the situation.

> There was a little silence.
> "I see," said Dumbledore eventually, peering at Harry over the top of his half-moon spectacles and giving Harry the usual sensation that he was being X-rayed. "And you feel that you have exerted your very best efforts in this matter, do you? That you have exercised all of your considerable ingenuity? That you have left no depth of cunning unplumbed in your quest to retrieve the memory?" (HB 428)

When Harry admits that he was sidetracked by an unrelated problem and didn't manage to use all his most creative efforts to get the job done, Dumbledore very calmly reminds him of the crucial importance of what he had been asked to do and makes it clear that everything they have planned requires the assignment to be successfully accomplished. We are told that:

> A hot, prickly feeling of shame spread from the top of Harry's head all the way down his body. (HB 428)

Dumbledore didn't get angry, shout at Harry, or berate him in any way. But his clear disappointment in Harry's lack of continued effort was enough to shame him deeply. Harry tries to explain to his older friend the reason for his lack of real persistence in the job on this particular occasion, and a silence falls between them. Rowling writes:

> Harry felt strangely diminished, as though he had shrunk a little since he entered the room. When he could stand it no longer he said, "Professor Dumbledore, I'm really sorry. I should have done more ... I should have realized you wouldn't have asked me to do it if it wasn't really important." (HB 429)

The headmaster responds immediately with as much concern for Harry as for the vital task in question, thanking him for saying what he did and expressing a hope that Harry would take a stronger interest in the job and see it to completion. Harry responds very positively with a renewed conviction and determination to get the job done. He has been corrected, but he has not been insulted or humiliated. He leaves with a new sense of mission, and as a result experiences success after all.

Dumbledore did what anyone in a leadership position should do in such circumstances. He was candid but calm, he questioned Harry, and he reminded him of the importance of the assigned task. He didn't react to failure with emotional agitation, anger, or recriminations.

He dealt with Harry straightforwardly, with kindness, and yet also, at the same time, with the highest standards for what he expected Harry to achieve. When a leader can control his own emotions and focus on his associate properly, using the powerful technique of appropriately probing questions, he can usually attain success in turning a situation around.

Asking the right questions, upholding high standards, and showing how much you care are the keys to movitating others to be and do their best.

Dumbledore cares about his colleagues, his associates, and his students. And they see this in his actions toward them. They respond by caring about him and about what he's trying to do for the benefit of them all. They resonate to the best in him and most often bring him their best in turn. This is one more application of the Golden Rule in practice. A leader treats his colleagues with dignity, regardless of their level of performance, seeking at the same time to elicit the highest degree of excellence from them in future performance.

A great leader is always teaching. A wise leader often uses difficult experiences and the most challenging of times to convey crucial life lessons to those around him. In one author interview, Rowling has emphasized the importance of what Dumbledore said to the assembled students at the end of Harry's eventful fourth year at Hogwarts, when he reveals to them the full truth about the death of one of their fellow students, Cedric Diggory, who had been murdered by Lord Voldemort—an evil wizard not widely believed at that time to still be living and menacing their world. The headmaster remembers Cedric as "a good and loyal friend, a hard worker," and as a person who "valued fair play." He then reminds the students of what they will need as they move forward, especially now that Voldemort has reappeared on the scene:

"I say to you all once again . . . we are only as strong as we are united, as weak as we are divided. Lord Voldemort's gift for spread-

ing discord and enmity is very great. We can fight it only by showing an equally strong bond of friendship and trust. Differences of
habit and language are nothing at all if our aims are identical and
our hearts are open." (GF 723)

Dumbledore embraces diversity in the service of unity. He uses
this traumatic event and very tough time to impart an important lesson about what will be needed for success in the future, against difficult odds. He then offers the ultimate eulogy for Cedric, conveying a
lesson needed by any group of people who hope to do anything of
importance. In powerful words, he asks them all to keep in their
hearts a vivid memory of their fallen classmate—a genuinely good,
kind, and courageous young man. He urges them, whenever they
might face a choice between doing what is right and doing what is
easy, to remember their friend Cedric and act appropriately.

The distinction between what is right and what is easy is one of
the most important contrasts that can guide us in our lives and in our
careers. And it's a distinction that captures what Harry is able to do at
all the most crucial junctures in his life. He is a heroic character precisely because he is able to choose what is right over what is easy
whenever he understands that great values are at stake.

I've mentioned the ancient philosopher Aristotle's student Alexander the Great a couple of times in passing. The history of his military
leadership is fascinating. At his best, he displayed in many ways what
Dumbledore is talking about here. Of all the many attributes that
contributed to his quick and stunning world-historical success, a few
stand out. Alexander knew how to gather information quickly. He
was able to act decisively on whatever he learned. He always led from
the front. He was willing to take a risk when it mattered. He never
asked others to do something he wasn't willing to do himself. He
rewarded his soldiers, showing a generosity of spirit toward them that
inspired them. He displayed an unusual degree of respect for the people he conquered. And he tried never to do things the easy way, but
always the right way, however difficult that might be. Because of this,

his adversaries were often surprised by his tactics and thwarted in their efforts to defeat him.

Every leader confronts a classic conflict between integrity and inertia in his own heart and in the hearts of the people he leads. Integrity is all about doing what's right. Inertia is about doing what's easy. Integrity is a condition of success. Inertia is more like an effective inoculation against it. A good leader has to be able to choose the right over the convenient in his own actions, however difficult that might sometimes be, and he equally has to be able to motivate others to make this occasionally very tough choice. Most people naturally seek safety and comfort and try to avoid risk and challenge as much as they can. But challenge is often the doorway to real accomplishment and a deep sense of personal fulfillment. The easy way is very seldom the path of real achievement.

The way of integrity is also the way of truth. It's certainly right and highly advantageous to seek and accept the truth about a situation, however hard and frightening that truth might be. Dumbledore often has to contend with the common fact that people prefer to believe what's easy to live with and assiduously avoid confronting difficult truths. At the end of Harry's fourth year at Hogwarts, and well into his fifth year, both he and the headmaster have to work in the challenging circumstances of seeing almost everyone else in their world refusing to believe the harsh realities of what they've discovered. And of course people won't rise to struggle with a demanding situation they don't even acknowledge. So our heroes have to fight the good fight against evil with very little support until they can bring others around to the point of seeing the truth. The best leaders don't give up when things get tough or when people seem recalcitrant, but they continue to educate, prepare, and then motivate the people around them to see what needs to be done and then to do whatever that requires, however hard it might seem.

Dumbledore is educational in his approach to leadership, whenever it's possible, and he is also motivational. He is not hesitant to remind his associates and students of what really matters and of all the most important values that are at stake in what they're doing. He seeks to rouse his charges to unity and then to appropriate action, whenever it's needed. When Harry finds himself in a leadership role, he doesn't hesitate in doing the same thing, as we've seen in our chapter on his courage. He will always vividly remind Ron and Hermione of what's at stake in a dangerous situation, and by doing so, he is able to move them to the point that they are willing to risk their lives to help accomplish what needs to be done. Dumbledore and Harry can motivate people by appealing to their basic values because these friends and companions know that the headmaster and his prize student authentically share those same values to their core. They are absolutely genuine in their own motivations and are seen by their compatriots to be utterly trustworthy in times of challenge and difficulty.

A good leader guides, teaches, and inspires.

No leader can succeed over the long run unless he or she is trusted. And the most effective leaders motivate their associates most powerfully only because they are thoroughly authentic in who they are and in what they say. Neither Harry nor Dumbledore ever asks another person to do something he wouldn't himself be fully willing to do. In fact, both wizards noticeably lead from the front and never from the rear. They are already in motion, planning and moving, as they elicit and direct the movements and actions of the other people around them.

Both Dumbledore and Harry are looked to as leaders by others because of who they are, what they've done, and what they are believed to be capable of doing. Their reliable strength draws other people to them. They are both immensely respected by their most enlightened peers—other like-minded wizards—and, because of that, they can accomplish forms of great good with the assistance of those other people that they never could have achieved by just operating alone. But to gain the most assistance from others, and to see others give their best efforts, these paradigmatic leaders are always alert to the need to motivate their friends by connecting their efforts to their values in a way that gains emotional leverage.

This topic of motivation and its importance has become an issue of controversy in the very recent past because of some statements in an enormously influential book that has been widely read in the business world. It will benefit us at this point to take a moment to examine its comments about the role of motivation in success.

MOTIVATING OTHERS

The best leaders know how to motivate the people around them and keep them motivated. But that doesn't mean they necessarily have a propensity to give fiery speeches and engage in loud, raucous cheerleading. Dumbledore motivates primarily by example and by the subtleties of teaching and reinforcement that he uses to keep people on task. Harry also motivates his peers mostly by example. But he is not at all averse to pointing out what's at stake in a particularly challenging situation. Every effective leader understands the importance of motivation and realizes that people are ultimately best motivated when a clear and imaginative connection can be made between what they're being asked to do and the deepest values they already hold. Most business analysts and peak-performance psychologists acknowledge and emphasize the importance of motivation in any life of accomplishment, and especially in any case of people working on difficult projects together. But not all experts on organizational excellence and sustainable group activities recognize this need of human nature.

In one of my favorite business books over the past few years, a runaway bestseller that has become enormously influential, *Good to Great*, the generally very insightful business analyst Jim Collins investigated a number of companies that were able to move from competence to excellence, and he drew some very interesting conclusions from this research. Most of his conclusions are well grounded, insightful, and true. But I believe that he got at least two important things wrong. And I don't say this to be in the least disparaging. Even the best thinkers sometimes make mistakes. Plato and Aristotle didn't get everything right. Not even the great Dumbledore is infallible, however wise that he is.

Perhaps the most refreshing aspect of Jim Collins's book is his emphasis on the importance of people. In my own work, I've been seeking to help top executives understand more deeply that we can preach product quality and process efficiency nonstop, but if we don't take care of the spirit of the people who do the work, nothing will have the results, long term, that we hope to achieve. Collins underlines repeatedly the importance of getting the right people into the right positions in any organization. And his advice is absolutely on the mark. We see in all the Harry Potter stories what happens when the headmaster hires a new teacher who isn't what he or she should be. Having the right people in any institution or task is crucial for its greatest potential success. But Collins infers two conclusions from this focus on finding the right people that I think are just wrong. First, he concludes that the issue of organizational vision isn't really much related to results. And then he states that providing any resources for the purpose of motivating people is a total waste of time. It will be worth a few moments to investigate these claims, because of how they seem to conflict with what we're learning from the experiences of Harry Potter and Albus Dumbledore.

An organizational vision is rooted in its values, and it is also one of the chief expressions of those values, as it guides people into the future. The best forms of motivation appeal to the deepest values that people have. And it's hard to connect our values to our work when we have no clear and compelling vision for where we're going. As we saw in Chapter 2, Harry Potter's repeated examples of success in courageously doing what needs to be done, despite the extraordinarily difficult, dangerous, and even immensely frightening situations that confront him, remind us of the importance of getting in touch with the values at stake in any situation of challenge. It's precisely through providing a clear vision and motivating people properly that this is most often effectively done. So it may be illuminating for us to understand what Collins says to the contrary and perhaps why he says it.

You can't overemphasize the importance of people to any business or to the accomplishment of any daunting and complex goal. But you can overstate it. Collins says at one point, "Great vision without great people is irrelevant" (GG 42). I appreciate the sentiment, but let's think for a moment about the exact claim. Benjamin Netanyahu, the former prime minister of Israel, was once a member of the most elite group within the Israeli armed forces, perhaps the most effective and feared antiterrorist fighters in history. In a November 29, 2001, appearance on the MSNBC show *Hardball*, while discussing the success of this unit, he said to the host, Chris Matthews, "Excellent soldiers with a mediocre strategy can't go very far. An excellent strategy with even mediocre soldiers can go quite far." Maybe he was just being humble. But I think he was being both honest and incisive. What he said seems diametrically opposed to the claim made by Collins that great vision without great people is just irrelevant. Netanyahu asserts that an excellent strategy with even mediocre soldiers can go quite far. No one, of course, would conclude from this that we should all go out and recruit mediocre soldiers. Great is of course better than mediocre. But this applies to visions and strategies as well as to people. We can appreciate the absolutely crucial importance of having the best people we can possibly recruit in our enterprises without concluding from this that vision and strategy are, by contrast, not really that important in the end. It's not a zero-sum game. Both elements are vital. A great strategy gives great people a chance for tremendous success. Dumbledore doesn't just act and goad others into acting. He first conceives a plan and by doing so makes the probability of successful action much higher. And, of course, great strategies should always serve great visions. A strong vision for any enterprise connects the people in it to their deepest values and points them toward a future they can glimpse. It steers them forward in a way they can believe in. It provides both overall direction and daily inspiration. It serves intellectual and emotional purposes for the people who do the work.

But now let's dig a little deeper into what Collins claims about vision and what he says about motivating people. In the Bible, the Book of Proverbs states, "Without a vision, people perish." Collins seems to disagree. Let me quote a few passages from his influential book, beginning with a rhetorical question that he imagines someone posing, and that he then answers:

> "Doesn't motivation flow chiefly from a compelling vision?" The answer, surprisingly, is "No." Not because vision is unimportant, but because expending energy trying to motivate people is largely a waste of time. One of the dominant themes that runs through this book is that if you successfully implement its findings, you will not need to spend time and energy "motivating" people. If you have the right people on the bus, they will be self-motivated. The real question then becomes: How do you manage in such a way as not to de-motivate people? (GG 74)

He clearly considers this point to be important, because he repeats it a few pages later:

> Spending time and energy trying to "motivate " people is a waste of effort. The real question is not, "How do we motivate our people?" If you have the right people, they will be self-motivated. The key is not to de-motivate them. (GG 89)

And then, speaking of the lesser-performing comparison companies in his study, he says:

> We found a very different pattern at the comparison companies. Instead of a quiet, deliberate process of figuring out what needed to be done and then simply doing it, the comparison companies frequently launched new programs—often with great fanfare and hoopla aimed at "motivating the troops"—only to see the programs fail to produce sustained results. (GG 178)

Here's what Collins seems not to see. We need to try so hard to get the right people involved in our enterprises, not so that motivating them will not be necessary, but so that our best efforts at motivation can work. Great people are the most fertile soil imaginable for proper motivation. They are indeed much more self-motivated than mediocre or lazy people, almost by definition, but they are still human and have normal ups and downs like all other mere mortals. They need periodic renewal. They can use a little extra inspiration now and then. Everyone needs a lift on occasion.

In the earliest documents of the Bible, the God of Abraham, Isaac, and Jacob, the all-powerful and all-knowing Creator of the universe, is represented as having selected some very special individuals for leadership positions, and then he sometimes still has to do quite a lot to motivate them. Jesus of Nazareth later carefully chose twelve disciples, and that's where his real work began. Getting the right people into an enterprise is never the end of the job—it's just the best possible beginning. Our need for guidance and motivation, for inspiration, and for a new puff of wind in our sails now and then is perennial—even for the very best of us.

Who is more self-motivated than a marathoner? It's one of the ultimate volunteer activities for overachievers. It takes a masterful self-starter with the highest level of resolve to go out running five, six, or ten miles a day for weeks or months to prepare for a marathon. And yet we hear stories from every marathon race in the country about how these runners were motivated when they really needed it by the big, cheering crowds, by individuals handing out water and shouting encouragement, or by something else they saw or heard along the way. Motivation is never a wholly do-it-yourself task.

I can't think of anyone more self-motivated than I am. I'm a philosopher, doing what I love, learning every day, working at my own schedule, and bringing people ideas that can change their lives. I even get to read books like the Harry Potter stories as part of my job! And I think I'm perfectly suited for the enterprise that is my business. I'd hire me any day. And I often commend myself on a job well done. Of course, I'm joking a little bit here, but it's still true. Yet there are nonetheless many times when I can use a little extra motivation, even when I'm not aware of the need until after that extra boost is provided.

Today, I got a letter from an inmate in a maximum-security prison unit in Texas. He's incarcerated in a town I once passed through as a young man, long ago. When I stepped off the bus and walked into a gas station, I happened to notice the thermometer on the door—112 degrees. Not a particularly pleasant location. This man just wrote to tell me what a difference my book *True Success* has made for him. I have no idea how he got it, but he says that it has helped change his perspective on life. He will be released in a little over a year, he goes on to say, and with this new start wants to have the sort of success that will bring good into the lives of other people.

I thought I was maximally motivated before reading this letter, but it put even more wind in my sails for what I'm doing. Plato said we're all imprisoned in illusions. It's great to hear of one man beginning to find his way out. I immediately sent him another of my books as a result of his letter. But I'm the one who has really benefited. Good people and even great performers aren't above the need for motivation. We just use it well.

"Motivating the troops." That's the phrase used in an almost dismissive way in Collins's book. But he acknowledges in other passages that, ultimately, there is really nothing more important than the troops. So what's the problem? Is "motivating" somehow itself a suspect activity? Only if we view it as nothing more than empty cheer-leading, with hollow assurances of the most exaggerated sort, delivered at a maximal decibel level, that we can do literally "anything we want," regardless of what it is, that the universe is poised to make our every wish a reality, and that the impossible is only something that takes a little longer to accomplish. The short-term manipulation of emotion that too often passes for motivational speaking almost never gives rise to positive results that last. Motivating people long term can't depend on smoke and mirrors, mere rhetoric and illusion, or hype and cleverness. It has to be grounded in hard-earned truth, connected to the deepest possible values, and conveyed with heartfelt encouragement. At its best, it involves reminding people of their potential, grounded in real power, skill, and opportunity, and bringing to their attention the deepest wisdom we have for utilizing our talents and resources, while inspiring them with a vision for their work that provides for the noblest possible construal of their actions, however small, day to day. True motivation involves reconnecting people with the vision and values necessary for lasting success in the world. Are great people somehow above the need for this? Absolutely not—great people need it and will benefit the most from it, when it is done in the best possible way.

Despite the intellectual allure of all analyses to the contrary, real-world business is never best understood as an ultimately impersonal structure supporting rational processes that allow each individual participating in it to calculate and accomplish whatever is necessary for narrowly self-interested financial ends. Every business is a community, and every business endeavor is an opportunity to live and use our values in the company of like-minded people, or else it's just a waste of time. In one of the most remarkable organizations I have served as a philosopher, the founder and top executives frequently talk about the deepest values of the company and of the people who work there. They often speak of family and faith and their shared sense of mission in their work, not in cynically manipulative ways, merely for the sake of "motivating the troops," but just to express what they really feel from the heart, and in a manner that rings true to all their associates. The result is a deeply committed and highly motivated workforce of courageous professionals who are able to find creative paths forward in even the most challenging of times. Most people will fight for what they believe in and will do almost anything that is needed for people they care about, regardless of the difficulties and dangers involved. This is shown in many ways in the life of Harry Potter and his friends.

Astute businesspeople understand that one of the central activities of business, and, for that matter, of any ongoing interpersonal enterprise, is negotiation, and that this is an activity that turns on the ability to motivate people to engage in appropriate action toward desired

consequences. A good leader is a good negotiator, and a good negotiator is a motivator. Harry shows his grasp of this fact in a crucial
negotiation during his sixth year at Hogwarts.

**Leaders are negotiators. You can lead people well only when you
inspire them to give their best.**

Professor Dumbledore asks Harry to get some crucial information—a set of repressed memories—from his new colleague, Professor Horace Slughorn. He also impresses on Harry the importance of
accomplishing this soon. But the information in that particular set of
memories is something Slughorn very much wants to keep private.
Harry and Slughorn are thus at an impasse. But then, with the assistance of a bit of good luck, Harry hatches a plan to motivate the man
to give him what he needs.

Professor Slughorn is a person who loves money, comfort, and status, and gathers around him students who either come from wealthy
or famous families or else at least show significant promise of becoming powerful people themselves. The professor relishes a sense of social
connection with such people. He views Harry as the ultimate catch for
"The Slug Club" of high achievers and social connectors. He has often
approached Harry about coming to parties and dinners, and our reti-
cent young wizard has carefully avoided these events as much as he
could. But with a new need, Harry approaches the professor and offers
to confide in him a secret. Slughorn's interest is piqued. Harry tells
him that Hagrid had been keeping a giant spider in the forest and that
this beloved pet has just died. He invites Slughorn to go with him to
the private burial. The professor knows that he can surreptitiously take
some extraordinarily valuable venom from the giant spider's body that
he can easily sell at a later date, and so eagerly agrees to go along.
Hagrid is very sad and is comforted to have some company. Slughorn
gets exactly what he wants and, after he says a beautiful eulogy over
the body, begins to drink wine with Hagrid. Harry pretends to sip
along with them but stays alert, watching it all. He observes the pro-

fessor become very sentimental as he gets more and more tipsy from glass after glass, and then Harry begins to speak to Slughorn about his mother, Lily, whom Slughorn had taught and had particularly liked. Harry recounts her terrible death at the hands of Voldemort, and just when Slughorn can't bear to hear any more about the tragic end of his beloved student, our negotiator makes his move:

> "But you won't help her son," said Harry. "She gave me her life, but you won't give me a memory." (HB 489)

Slughorn knows that the memory in question is of an event crucial to understanding the power and hidden weakness of Voldemort. But he immediately objects to Harry that no purpose would be served by giving him the memory. Harry explains that it would help him greatly. He then confides to the professor that he is "The Chosen One" meant alone to kill Voldemort, and that he needs what Slughorn has to destroy the evil man who had killed his mother and who is now killing so many more in their world. Harry knows that Slughorn is terribly afraid of revealing any information that Voldemort would not want to be known. So our young wizard says:

> "Be brave like my mother, Professor. . . ." (HB 490)

The professor confesses that the memory Harry wants is of something he did that may have resulted in "great damage." Harry speaks again quickly:

> "You'd cancel out anything you did by giving me the memory," said Harry. "It would be a very brave and noble thing to do." (HB 490)

And that's all it took. People have a need for nobility. And people want to feel brave. Slughorn immediately accedes to Harry's request and gives him exactly what he needs.

What finally motivated the professor to do as Harry had wanted?

A complex appeal to his values—first to his baser, more immediate interests, then to his finer sentiments, and ultimately to his deeper sense of what is of importance in life—got the job done. And, interestingly, Harry had learned this skill at negotiation by watching his mentor Dumbledore do something very similar in his efforts to get Slughorn to take a position at Hogwarts in the first place. If you understand what motivates people and ultimately appeal to their sense of self as well as to their higher nature, it's amazing what you can make happen, despite any obstacles that may seem to stand in the way. This is true whether you're working in difficult negotiations or you're just involved in the ordinary course of aligning people behind important tasks. A good leader understands the need to motivate people by appealing to their values.

STRENGTHS AND WEAKNESSES

Dumbledore is a great leader. I hope I made that abundantly clear in Chapter 1. But he's not a perfect leader. And that's largely because, like all other leaders, even he has limits and weaknesses. But unlike many leaders in his world and ours, he is willing to acknowledge his limitations. He is able to admit it when he makes a mistake, even one that results in disastrous consequences. I once heard an insightful journalist make a telling comment on a famous institution he had been visiting for a year. He said, "This place would be great if they didn't pretend they were perfect." The ability to admit imperfection is a part of true greatness. There is no such thing in the real world as a perfect sphere, a perfectly straight line, a perfect place to live, a perfect relationship, a perfect organization, or a perfect leader. Dumbledore's life shows that you don't have to be perfect to be great. But you do have to be self-aware and utterly honest.

At the end of Harry's fifth year at Hogwarts, as recounted in the book *The Order of the Phoenix*, a complex situation arises that leads him to go to the rescue of a good friend he believes to be under the imminent threat of a violent death. Some of Harry's classmates accompany him on this dangerous mission. It turns out that he has been misled and lured into a trap by Voldemort and his henchmen. Harry's friends are injured to various degrees, and one good person is killed in the terrible fight that ensues. Those who are saved have Dumbledore to thank for their rescue. When Harry is later back in Dumbledore's office, in total shock and dismay, waiting for the headmaster, an elderly wizard in a painting on the wall speaks to him:

> "Dumbledore thinks very highly of you, as I am sure you know," he said comfortably. (OP 822)

Harry is filled with guilt, remorse, hurt, anger, and even rage at what has happened. Since the beginning of the school year, he has felt at times a new and growing resentment toward Dumbledore because of a belief that the headmaster is keeping him in the dark about many developments in the war with their evil adversaries. He is confused, frustrated, and now stunned. All his adolescent emotions are ready to erupt. When Dumbledore arrives and tries to reassure Harry that his schoolmates will recover fully from their injuries, the conflicted young wizard explodes in pain and shouts back at the man who had just saved his life. The headmaster remains calm. This enrages Harry more, and he begins to pick up several fragile scientific instruments that belong to Dumbledore, throwing them around the room and smashing them to bits.

In any major corporation, security would have been called long before this point, and Harry would be roughly escorted from the building, straight into the waiting arms of the police. But Dumbledore quietly responds by saying that it's natural for Harry to feel such pain, and that, in fact, his ability to do so is his greatest strength. When Harry starts to lash out in uncontrolled fury again, the older and wiser wizard reacts in a surprising way that is bound to make all philosophical souls smile. With utter equanimity of spirit, he speaks quite simply:

> "By all means continue destroying my possessions," said Dumbledore. "I daresay I have too many." (OP 825)

And then the great headmaster does something else that is nearly as surprising, something that few people in leadership positions nowadays seem capable of doing. He takes responsibility for what has happened. He candidly admits his mistakes.

The ability to admit a mistake is a sign of strength, not a signal of weakness.

Dumbledore confesses to Harry that in many ways it is ultimately his fault that a good man has just been killed. He goes on to explain that some of his decisions and tactics in the current fight against evil have been faulty because they have not taken full account of the personalities and characters of the people involved. He realizes now that he never should have assigned a brave and energetic man in the prime of his life to a task that involved mainly staying in one place on guard duty away from all the action while his friends were out hunting and fighting evil wherever it could be found. When this underutilized wizard suddenly learned that Harry was in danger, his pent-up frustration led him to leave his post and go to the boy's aid, an act that resulted in his untimely and terrible death.

Dumbledore also admits that he has made a mistake with Harry as well. He should have explained more of the overall situation to him from the beginning. He should not have withheld potentially important information from Harry. Because he had left Harry in the dark in certain ways in an effort to protect him, Harry ironically ended up being vulnerable to the trickery that lured him into danger and eventuated in the injuries to his friends, as well as in the unexpected death that was now so painful to him. Dumbledore admits that if he had been more open with Harry, it's likely that none of this would have happened. He then continues:

> "Harry, I owe you an explanation. . . . I see now that what I have done, and not done, with regard to you, bears all the hallmarks of the failings of age." (OP 826)

Dumbledore had forgotten what it was like to be Harry's age, or even the age of his younger adult colleagues. He failed to remember and understand the motivations and emotions, energies and desires that these younger men would have. And this set him up to make some dangerous miscalculations.

The headmaster then goes on, in one of the most remarkable passages in all the books, to explain to Harry the specific mistakes that he has made in his efforts to guide him well, all of which center on a natural instinct to protect Harry from truths that might have been too difficult for him to hear. A man so committed to the truth had withheld important information from his young charge because he had been too concerned about whether Harry was old enough, and ready enough, to deal with its implications. He now understands that a full and proper access to the truth could have prevented a calamity.

There is an interesting parallel here with the way many parents have worried about whether their children should be exposed to some of the more sophisticated and "dark" themes in the Harry Potter books, with their vivid portrayals of evil and the reality of death in the world. It's often a surprise that the children themselves seem a great deal more prepared to hear and process the ideas in these stories than their parents would have guessed. Keeping our children away from important and difficult truths about the world can be a strategy that backfires, as Dumbledore learns to his great sadness and regret.

At another level, this is a mistake that many corporate and organizational leaders often make, seeking to put on a happy face, or their best "game face," and wanting not to "de-motivate" people by telling them the whole truth about their situation, when the facts might be a bit harsh and hard to take. But of course, people can't effectively fight an enemy they don't yet see, and they can't deal well with realities of which they're uninformed. In my experience, corporate leaders who have taken the risk to be more open and candid with their associates about difficult truths have generally been both pleasantly surprised and even greatly impressed at how well people have dealt with the information and have used it to find a path to success. We all want to see more of the puzzle so that we'll know how to use the pieces that are already in our possession. Any leader who forgets this sets his people up to be blindsided by things they didn't see coming. Generally, the more people know, the better they can perform. That's true of Harry and his friends, and it's just as true for any of us.

The more information we have, the better equipped we are to deal with any challenge we face.

As Dumbledore continues his remarkably confessional conversation with Harry, he recounts the times that Voldemort had confronted and attacked the young boy in his first and second years at Hogwarts and reminds Harry that when he had asked him at the time why this was all happening, he had declined to answer. The great man is filled with regret and says:

"Why did I not tell you everything?" (OP 838)

He then answers his own question:

"I cared more for your happiness than your knowing the truth, more for your peace of mind than my plan, more for your life than the lives that would be lost if the plan failed." (OP 838)

Even the most well-intentioned people can make serious mistakes in how they handle the truth—especially when they allow their concerns for the short-term comfort, convenience, and feelings of others to prevent them from conveying a difficult though important piece of information. But the normally insightful Dumbledore here overstates the problem. He didn't care too much. It's impossible to care too much for other people. And he really knows that. But what he did do is to express that care in a mistaken way. He allowed his emotions to misdirect his reason and his actions toward Harry. He should have told Harry more of the truth than he did. Then Harry would have been empowered to act appropriately when he was, inevitably, outside the close direction of his mentor.

Some real-world leaders keep the full truth from people because they believe that truth is power and they don't want to share any of the power they think they already have. This is usually a big mistake, and it's based on a false mental model for what the sharing of truth involves. Truth is not a limited-quantity item whose sharing reduces our portion of it. Sharing the truth always multiplies the truth, and it can increase power all around. But a desire to hoard truth and power is certainly not the only reason people might withhold truth from their associates. Many are a bit more like Dumbledore, even when their context is very different from that of protecting the feelings and sensibilities of a young boy. Leaders, like all human beings, too often shy away from difficult conversations and naturally put off talking about unpleasant facts that loom over the horizon. They don't give their associates all the information they need to make sound decisions and engage in appropriate actions, because, deep down, they believe that they themselves will be able to deal with the problems and ultimately make them go away. But this is a formula for disaster.

In my earlier book, *If Aristotle Ran General Motors*, I explain at length how truth is one of the four fundamental foundations for working well with other people. All our dealings with others need to respect the universal human needs for truth, beauty, goodness, and unity—these four things make all relationships and all enterprises go better. They are the foundations for sustainable excellence and for a sense of individual fulfillment in anything we do. As the insightful author Susan Scott has shown in her masterful book *Fierce Conversations*, we all need to learn how to have the sometimes difficult, utterly open and honest conversations with other people that alone will keep these four foundations alive in our relationships and operative in our enterprises.

In any positive relationship or group endeavor, the more truth that's provided, the better things can go. Dumbledore made a classic mistake that many well-intentioned and otherwise perceptive leaders are prone to make when he thought that he could always be Harry's protector and that, because of this, it wasn't yet really necessary to share with the young man the full truth about his circumstances and challenges. People need the right equipment to be able to protect themselves in difficult situations and to provide for overall effective action. A true understanding of the full reality within which they live and work is always an important part of that equipment. Great leaders tend to be people who understand the alchemistic, transformative power of the truth. And when, like Dumbledore in this one instance, they temporarily trip up and lose sight of that important piece of wisdom, they need to call themselves back to the proper path of communication and disclosure.

The headmaster goes on now to tell Harry the full truth about his situation and the difficult future he has to face. This provides our young wizard with the basic understanding that he will need in order to survive and conquer through all that is to come. As is the case with almost all of us, Dumbledore's greatest weakness is closely tied to his greatest strength. He is a man whose life is centered on love. That makes him a caring, trusting individual. Even if it's not possible to love or care too much, it is possible to express love and care in mistaken and self-defeating ways. And it certainly is possible to trust too much or to grant trust too easily to someone who doesn't really merit it, on merely the most hopeful of signs that he or she might. We can easily want to trust another person because we want to believe the best about him, whether his heart and mind really justify that trust or not. This charitable and perhaps even noble proclivity on Dumbledore's part apparently sets him up eventually for what seems to be his greatest defeat, at the end of Harry's sixth year. Even if things are not what they seem in this dramatic event, Dumbledore clearly has trusted and hired more than one person over the years who didn't deserve that trust. It's possible to express our care and concern for other people generally in improper and self-defeating ways. Whenever loving concern shades into paternalism, as it did with Dumbledore's treatment of Harry, or blinds us to aspects of reality that we'd prefer not to see, as it perhaps has in a few of the great man's relationships with others, trouble is never very far away.

Professor Dumbledore also has the significant weakness that often accompanies unusual strength. Many great warriors and extremely skilled high achievers become accustomed to solving problems and defeating foes by the sole force of their own power. Individual excellence can sometimes keep a person from learning the full importance and power of collaboration. When you don't fully appreciate the need for partnerships in challenging tasks, you don't naturally cultivate the right relationships with the people around you. And, in addition, you don't recognize the vital importance of sharing information at every step along the way. Dumbledore is a highly accomplished wizard, probably the greatest of his day, and perhaps one of the greatest of all time. That makes it very difficult sometimes for him to really understand his own limitations, and so he doesn't always do what needs to be done to create the network of collaborative partners he actually needs for accomplishing the most difficult of tasks. That's another reason he doesn't grasp from the start the need to keep Harry in the loop of what's going on. He understands that Harry will one day have a crucial, individual role to play in the defeat of Voldemort and his evil Death Eaters, but he wrongly assumes that he can achieve what needs to be done in the meantime without bringing Harry into the innermost circle of information.

One other strength that is also closely tied to a weakness in this great leader involves Dumbledore's age. Because of his advanced age, he has seen a lot, done a lot, and as a result he knows a lot. His experience is immense and his wisdom is extensive. But, as he admits to Harry, age has its limitations as well. An older leader can forget what the daily struggle is like for his younger associates. He can lose sight of what their day-to-day concerns and emotions are—what frustrates them, what interests them, and what goads them into action. But any lack of empathic imagination between people can create problems, and the problems can become especially big when the disconnection in question is between a leader and his or her associates. J. K. Rowling's ability to put herself into the place and mind-set of an eleven-year-old or a fifteen-year-old is part of the magic of her storytelling and is in part responsible for the enormous appeal of her books. Her noblest character, Albus Dumbledore, finds this at times to be a most challenging thing to do. And that sets him up for some of his biggest mistakes.

A second problem attending age is also beginning to show in Dumbledore's life during Harry's fifth and sixth years at school. He is becoming tired. His immense energy is waning. He no longer has the full reflexes and stamina of a young man. It is increasingly dangerous for him to lead always from the front, like the great warrior leaders of history. It is a noteworthy and important strength of his that he continues to have, despite his advanced age, quite unusual energy and prowess, beyond that of most wizards in the prime of their lives. But the weakness associated with this is that he may easily overestimate what he is now capable of doing and thereby unintentionally endanger both himself and others around him. Age surprises us all. It sneaks up on us and insidiously robs us of powers and potencies that we've long relied on for the successes we've had in the past. But all this is very gradual, and it's a largely invisible process. Because it can all be so subtle, we're often unprepared to adapt to it, and we neglect to begin to delegate to others some of the more strenuous tasks that we've long been accustomed to carrying out ourselves. The greatest apparent disaster of book six, a turn of affairs that has left most avid Potter readers in a state of shock and tremendous sorrow, seems to be a direct result of this problem. Our weaknesses are indeed often related to our strengths, and sometimes in surprising ways.

Our greatest strengths are often the source of our greatest weaknesses. To understand your vulnerabilities, look to your strengths.

Harry, like Dumbledore, experiences this strange and powerful connection between his own greatest strength and his most endangering weakness. He cares about people deeply. And he has a sense of justice that will not allow evil to prevail. In one particularly tense scene in *The Order of the Phoenix*, Harry has just frantically told Ron and Hermione that he has had a vivid mental vision of Sirius being tortured and that they should go immediately to his rescue (OP 733). Hermione is instantly worried and tentatively suggests that Harry just might have an overdeveloped psychological need to save people, a compulsion that can cause him to anticipate bad things that might not actually be happening and to leap into action before he knows for sure that he's really needed. Harry asks what she means, and Hermione very hesitantly begins to recall his recent history of making numerous heroic efforts to save people he thought were in distress, whether they really were or not. He can't believe what he's hearing and recalls aloud a remark that Ron once made about his having wasted time acting like a hero in the second of the three Triwizard Tournament challenges. Harry then defensively demands to know if that's what Hermione thinks he's doing now. She explains quickly that their adversary Voldemort knows Harry's character and his immediate, overwhelming desire to save any close friend he believes to be in trouble, and that this cunningly wicked man might well be using such knowledge to lure Harry and the rest of them into a trap.

Hermione, as usual, is right. But Harry can't accept even the possibility that she might be onto something important here, as emotionally committed as he is to intervening when friends are in danger. He does have, in her words, "a saving-people-thing," and it's one of his strengths as well as one of his weaknesses. It can result in great good—and it often has—or, as in the current situation, it can set him up for terrible disaster.

Harry later realizes all this and learns from it. In fact, I believe that he learns not only from his most serious mistakes but also from seeing the mistakes that his great mentor makes. Perhaps Dumbledore realizes this, and that's in part why he goes to so much trouble to admit his mistakes to Harry and to offer his best explanations as to how they happened. The professor takes many difficult moments to be teachable moments in the lives of his students, and especially in

Harry's life. The older man genuinely loves and admires Harry and sees in him a level of promise and potential greatness that Harry cannot yet see in himself. Dumbledore is grooming Harry for a life of challenge, leadership, and victory. And he is wise enough to know that this requires an absolute candor in helping Harry to learn from the mistakes that even he can make at his advanced stage of wisdom and life.

One of the most important lessons in these stories for leaders in our day is that you don't have to be a perfect leader in order to be a great one. And you don't have to be seen as perfect in order to be followed as a strong leader. The best leaders are the most candid with their associates and use every opportunity in the present to prepare those around them for better and greater things in the future. We can teach other people out of the richness of our accomplishments, but we can also teach them, sometimes the most powerful lessons of all, from the wisdom that has come as a result of our failures. Great leaders understand this alchemy and live it every day.

PASSING THE TORCH

In Harry's sixth year at Hogwarts, as recounted in *The Half-Blood Prince*, Dumbledore gives him some very important private lessons on certain evenings. He keeps in his office a magical bowl, called a Pensieve, that can literally contain objective memories of past events. By putting a wand to his temple, an advanced wizard can literally remove a memory, captured in a slight physical form that looks as if it has some of the features of a solid, a liquid, and perhaps even a gas. This wispy substance can then be put into the Pensieve, where it swirls around in something like a liquid form. Any wizard can then lower his head to the liquid, make physical contact with it, and as a result find himself magically transported into a full, three-dimensional re-creation of the original events remembered. He can move among others there as if he were a ghost and can witness what transpired from his own new point of view, as if he had been an independent observer present in the midst of the original events. Dumbledore has found and brought into his office Pensieve some important memories concerning Voldemort's birth parents and then some episodes from the wizard's youth. He wants to use this information to help Harry come to understand his adversary more deeply. By literally entering into some of the formative events before the birth of Tom Riddle (Voldemort), as well as later events in his life, Harry will perhaps gain knowledge that will help him ultimately defeat the Dark Lord.

When he receives and uses the additional memories that Harry has obtained from Professor Slughorn, Dumbledore is also able to confirm his suspicions as to how Voldemort has planned his own immortality by taking a series of measures that, as long as they remain in place, render him ultimately invulnerable in battle. Dumbledore and Harry enter the Pensieve together on several occasions and, on one of these trips into the past, discover that Voldemort has used some very rare dark magic to protect his life. There has always been a bit of a mystery about how, as a result of his attack on Harry as a baby, he had lost nearly all his powers but escaped death. Now Dumbledore knows what happened and why.

The headmaster explains to his young friend that Voldemort has used the ancient vehicle of an object called a "horcrux" to protect himself from death. The story is briefly this: When Voldemort first murdered someone, that act of evil in itself rebounded on him naturally and split his soul in half. But he was then able, by a very difficult and dark form of magic, to put one now independent half of his soul into an object other than his ordinary physical body, where he believed it could be safe even if his normal body were completely destroyed. Dumbledore deduces further that Voldemort has done this numerous times, committing many murders and further splitting his soul, placing its distinct fragments into a total of seven different horcruxes, protective objects that will keep the fragments safe, regardless of what happens to his primary physical body. In this terrible and unnatural way, he has schemed to be able to survive any attack on him, relying on the fragments of his soul that remain in the safekeeping of the horcruxes that he has enchanted, protected, and hidden in various places where he believes they can't easily be found. Dumbledore explains that the only way Harry will be able to fight Voldemort effectively and finally defeat him will require that he already have found and destroyed each of the horcruxes on which his current invulnerability relies. He then tells Harry that one of the horcruxes was the magical diary that had enchanted Ginny Weasley and led to her capture in the Chamber of Secrets during Harry's second year at Hogwarts. Harry already destroyed that object in the process of rescuing Ginny. Dumbledore has recently found and eliminated a second horcrux. So there are five objects remaining that Harry and Dumbledore have to identify, track down, and destroy. The headmaster tells Harry that he thinks he's close to locating and going after one of them. Harry asks if he can go with him and help get rid of it. Dumbledore pauses for just a moment, looking carefully at his student, and agrees. He then says, simply:

"I think you have earned that right." (HB 507)

This signals a significant change in how the professor relates to his student. And Harry understands that right away. Dumbledore had once sent Harry, Ron, and Hermione out on a short crucial mission, when there was nothing about the task that would likely endanger their lives. But this is different. Dumbledore had already incurred a serious and apparently irreversible injury to his hand, leaving it withered and blackened, when he destroyed the one horcrux that he had discovered before explaining the whole story to Harry. And now he is willing to take Harry along on a very dangerous adventure. The master understands that his apprentice will never fully be prepared for what is coming soon unless he is allowed to risk participation in truly difficult and even dangerous tasks in the presence of his teacher and protector. This will be an important stage of his preparation for what he may one day have to face alone.

They go together into dramatically perilous circumstances, and to retrieve the object they seek, Dumbledore has to drink large quantities of an unknown liquid that may be a powerful, slow-acting poison. It weakens him tremendously, almost beyond his ability to withstand it. As they attempt to escape with the object in their possession, things are extremely difficult, and Dumbledore is dangerously compromised, to the point of barely hanging on to consciousness. Harry realizes that he will have to do something to save them both and, with a new level of focus, says to his teacher, "Don't worry." The response that he hears shows us clearly that an important corner has been turned in their relationship:

> "I am not worried, Harry," said Dumbledore, his voice a little stronger despite the freezing water. "I am with you." (HB 578)

This is a passage of great poignancy and significance. In one statement, a new dynamic has been acknowledged. What Dumbledore says here is the ultimate display of approbation, respect, and trust on the part of the great wizard. For the first time, Harry has become his mentor's protector, and he recognizes Harry as such. This prepares Harry, like nothing else possibly could, to begin to think of himself as a leader of substance. The man he has so completely relied upon is now clearly relying on him. The torch has been passed. Harry is suddenly in the position that only Dumbledore has previously occupied. And he is ready for it. He steps up and does what is necessary. He gets them both safely out of their very hazardous situation.

Only a short time later, the unexpected and unthinkable happens. When they arrive back at Hogwarts, a battle is raging between some invading Death Eaters and many of Harry's friends. Dumbledore seems to know what's coming. He immobilizes Harry, who is hidden under his invisibility cloak, so that he can't intervene, be spotted, and be killed. Dumbledore knows that Harry will have a more important battle to fight at another time. And because of this, Harry has to watch, in total paralysis, while his beloved teacher, mentor, and friend is murdered on the spot, too weakened to resist. The great Dumbledore sacrifices his life to protect one more time the one person he knows can alone eliminate Voldemort, and in this way he seeks to protect all those on the side of good from the worst threat they face.

Harry is horrified, numb, and disbelieving. But as Dumbledore expires, the enchantment keeping Harry immobile is lifted, and he springs into action immediately, chasing the culprits through the castle and out onto the grounds, where they escape before he can prevent it. But he is ready for the next battle. And he is poised to take the lead in doing what needs to be done. He has been fully prepared for all of this by his forward-thinking mentor. And he now has the sense of self, and the basic awareness of his capability, that only the words and actions of his admired teacher could have given him.

One of the chief challenges of a leader is to put the tools for success into everyone's hands.

The alchemy of great leadership transforms ordinary people into extraordinary performers. It prepares people to be their best and do their best. It unleashes talent and guides it to appropriate accomplishment. It lays the foundations for enduring success and inspires others to follow the best paths forward. Leadership alchemy never leaves things unchanged, but improves things qualitatively, radically, and sometimes as if by magic. It always leaves a legacy.

6

THE WISDOM OF THE WIZARDS

Nothing is mightier than wisdom.
—*Socrates*

The Harry Potter books are full of wisdom about life. Some of this insight for living is explicitly articulated by one character or another. Some is just shown in the exciting action and developing story line. The most important pieces of advice explicitly stated in the books often come from the mouth of Headmaster Dumbledore. For example, we see him saying, in various places, such things about life as:

"It does not do to dwell on dreams and forget to live . . ." (SS 214)

This great leader is both a thinker and a man of action. He lives life to the fullest, and in the best possible way, and wants his students to enjoy the same approach to their time on earth. Dreaming is great, but doing is greater.

Dumbledore also articulates what may be one of the most important pieces of wisdom in the whole series of stories when he says:

"It is our choices, Harry, that show what we truly are, far more than our abilities." (CS 333)

Dumbledore is an existentialist of the most important sort. No preexisting categories need determine our identity or decide our fate. We have the chance, through choice, to carve out our own identities and create our own futures. The ancient philosopher Heraclitus once said, "Character is destiny." Since anyone's character is ultimately a result of the choices that he or she makes, it's an even deeper realization to see that "choice is destiny." In the recent movie *Batman Begins*, one of Bruce Wayne's oldest friends says to him, "It's not who you are underneath, it's what you do that defines you." Dumbledore takes this insight back to the source, to that factor over which we always have some control, the element of choice.

It is our choices that create our future and determine our legacy.

Dumbledore also says wise things about death as well as about life. At one point he makes an enigmatic and fascinating observation reflecting the wisdom of Socrates when he remarks that, to the well-organized mind, death is just "the next great adventure" (SS 297). It's an insight of the most profound thinkers that life is a series of adventures. Dumbledore joins some of the very greatest philosophers by extending that exciting concept beyond the grave and seeing death itself as in this way an extension of life. And with that in mind, he explains at a much later time that when people fear death and darkness, what they really are afraid of is nothing more than just the unknown (HB 566). The headmaster understands that wisdom about life must encompass wisdom about death, and he does not hesitate to pass on what he has learned to his students, who will inevitably face this one adventure at the end of all the others they will ever confront.

Many other wise perspectives of equal importance are never explicitly stated but can be gleaned from the behaviors of various characters and the consequences of their conduct. Rowling doesn't try at all to be professorial, pedantic, or preachy in her approach to sharing wisdom. But she clearly considers the wisdom to be learned from the world of the wizards to be an important element in the overall sweep of the events that she portrays. In this chapter, I want to survey briefly some of this wisdom about living that we can derive from the stories. There is no particular order to the insights and perspectives I'll offer here for comment and consideration. But they all add up and fit together to begin to outline a powerful, and powerfully good, worldview. Rowling's intellect and perceptiveness—her philosophical sensibilities and visions—shine through all her stories in both simple and subtle ways. I believe that she understands quite well that we can lead our lives, and lead other people, in the best possible ways only when we root everything we do in the deepest life wisdom we can find.

First, I should make it perfectly clear what wisdom is and what it isn't. It isn't esoteric knowledge or deeply hidden truth about life that is extremely difficult to discover, grasp, and master. That's a false model of wisdom propounded by the gnostics and sophisticated hucksters in almost every world culture. It's also a model that has gained unfortunate ascendancy in our own time. Real wisdom isn't some sort of highly secret key to life that is well hidden from ordinary people. The truth is simple and powerful. Wisdom is just great insight for living. And it's often conveyed by simple statements that serve to remind us of what we've already learned as we've walked this path of life from our earliest years to the present day.

Oddly enough, we often forget the insights we've already had about living as we continue in our adventures, and we typically do so precisely at the times that we need those insights the most. Of course, our forgetting is never complete. When reminded of something that we long ago realized, we usually recognize the truth of the insight immediately. It was still buried in memory, locked safely away deep in our neurons, ready for retrieval. But somehow we had forgotten that we knew it. It was no longer "top of mind." It had lost its proper grip on us. We had neglected to use it to filter our further experiences or to help us govern our emotions and chart out our actions in the subsequent relevant situations we've faced. And so we need to be reminded of what we really know.

The great wisdom literature of the world often serves to help us recapture insights that we've already had. And it helps us to clarify those thoughts. But it sometimes gives a great many of us new insights as well, things that we had never thought of, and novel perspectives that we can test in our further experience. Even these new insights often ring true instantly as we understand them in the light of our previous experience. They capture patterns that we might at some level have noticed but never thought much about. We may not have made the connections they explicitly give us, but we can see them when they're shown to us. These nuggets of new wisdom often open for us some new doors into the future based on what's been learned in the past. And in many ways they can guide our path as we move forward into each new day.

Human beings have always enjoyed capturing their most common insights about living in pithy statements that allow for ease of memory and readiness of use. But wisdom is not always to be found in the form of well-known truths. It's occasionally captured in a statement that may be surprising to many people, such as Dumbledore's comment about death's being the next great adventure. But even surprising wisdom shouldn't be thought of as involving technical or difficult lessons available only to the greatest gurus and their most devoted long-term students. Wisdom about life can be distilled from the process of living by anyone who pays enough attention.

In our previous chapters, we've looked at how Dumbledore embodies wisdom and virtue, how Harry experiences one of the classic virtues, what the wizards in general show us about the distinction between ethical and unethical living, how important issues of truth and deception can come to a new measure of clarification through these stories, and what Dumbledore and Harry can teach us about transformative leadership. In this chapter, we'll survey some of the main nuggets of wisdom to be found throughout the Harry Potter books, bits of insight and perspective that can help us all to live better and more meaningful lives. And then, in the next chapter, we'll confront the most fundamental issue of meaning more directly.

Meaning and wisdom are both crucial to the living of a good life.

We all seem to know this at some level. But what is not as widely understood is that meaning and wisdom are as important in organizational contexts, and in all sorts of business endeavors, as they are in our personal lives. When we look closely at the lives of very successful and admirable people, we often see that the greatest achievers have plugged into some fairly deep wisdom about life and human nature. They know themselves and the people around them in a penetrating way. They have a sense of what really matters and what isn't so important. And that's what allows them to concentrate their time and energy in the best possible ways. Wisdom empowers. Meaning directs. As we move deeper into a new era, it will be increasingly important in corporate and executive life to understand and embody the insights of our greatest philosophers and the wisdom of the greatest wizards of excellence who live among us. The life wisdom that runs through the Harry Potter stories, and the deeper understandings that crop up at various places in these remarkable narratives, can be expressed in terms of some very simple, clear insights. Let's look at a few.

LOGIC AND LUCK

The Wisdom Insight: *Logic and luck are both important for solving life's problems.*

Some people think that life is all just a matter of luck—good, bad, and indifferent. Certain individuals seem to have more good luck, and others appear to have more of the bad sort. At some times in our lives, the good luck is rolling, and at other times the bad luck just won't stop. But most believers in the concept of luck think there is nothing we can do about it and we just have to accept this sad fact. We live our lives, come what may. The universe, in this view, is like a big casino of random rewards and punishments that happen to cluster at some times in little bursts—momentary or extended—of good or bad fortune. Nobody really gets what they deserve, but rather whatever the roll of the cosmic dice happens to bring them at any given time.

More insightful philosophers have surmised that only about fifty percent of life is luck. The rest is to some extent within our control. Other profound thinkers suspect that everything we tend to categorize as luck is really the nonrandom result of complex causes outside our purview, and some suggest that this may include the outworking of an inscrutable divine providence. If we broaden the concept of luck to include everything that happens to us that's outside our control, whatever its true cause might be, and we entertain some notion of human freedom existing alongside that realm, we can easily find ourselves persuaded that life is, at most, only partially dependent on luck. We clearly have no control over many of the things that happen to us. And much that comes our way doesn't seem particularly deserved. But we can carve out some limited territory in the world where we appear to be at least mostly responsible for what happens, however ridiculously small that territory may sometimes seem. And this means simply that when we're thinking more deeply about life, we tend to realize at some level that it can't just be all luck. As Hermione says to Harry during their sixth year at school:

"Luck can only get you so far, Harry." (HB 517)

There is an old saying that luck is where preparation meets opportunity, so even if we believe that a lot of things in life just come down to luck, we should work hard to prepare ourselves in every way we can to take advantage of the opportunities that inevitably at some point will come our way. That's how we can maximize the benefits of good luck and minimize the damage of bad luck. When we take care at least to try to prepare for whatever we might face in life, we put ourselves into the best position to be able to deal with whatever crosses our paths, whether it gladdens our hearts or whacks us in the head.

When things go terribly wrong, lots of people talk about their bad luck and in that way seek to avoid any sense of responsibility for whatever has happened. When things go extremely well, however, fewer seem inclined to talk about their good luck, unless they have publicists or coaches instructing them to do so. Many people seem to prefer to ascribe extraordinarily good fortune to their own talents and hard work. But Harry Potter is not one of these people. He is prepared to admit it when he sees luck as playing a big part in his accomplishments. One of the great passages on this is in book five, *The Order of the Phoenix*. Ron and Hermione are trying to convince Harry to give his fellow students some practical lessons in Defense Against the Dark Arts. Harry is protesting that he shouldn't be anyone's teacher. Ron then begins to recall all the great things that Harry has done, year after year, to defeat evil whenever he has been attacked. Harry tries to deflect the praise, saying he was lucky on one occasion, helped on another, and on a third, it was really a magical device that gave him the time he needed to achieve what he was able to do. Ron and Hermione are enjoying his protests immensely and find it quite funny that he has no real sense of how good he is in combat with evil. Finally, Harry has just had it with Ron's confident-sounding recitation of his accomplishments and reacts like this:

> "Just listen to me . . . all that stuff was luck—I didn't know what I was doing half the time . . . I just did whatever I could think of, and I nearly always had help . . ." (OP 327)

Harry has a moment of real humility here, saying that he's just a lucky boy who's benefited from the assistance of others whenever he's needed it. But then, that's true for all of us who have ever lived through any real difficulties and come out the other side. We've had some help. And we feel lucky to have made it through safe and sound.

But Harry really knows deep down that it's not just luck. There is something more. He goes on in his response to Ron and Hermione and remembers aloud what it actually felt like, in the intensity of the moment, to face the evil Voldemort. He says:

> "The whole time you're sure you know there's nothing between you and dying except your own—your own brain or guts or whatever . . ." (OP 328)

I love the word choice that Harry uses here to depict what he felt he had to rely on in the situations of tremendous danger he's faced. Brain and guts—intellect and courage—are the two ingredients he identifies for dealing with the most challenging situations it's possible to encounter. We've already discussed Harry's courage in Chapter 2. His intellect is just as important.

Standardized intelligence tests and formal school exams check for our abilities to memorize and analyze when confronted with ink on paper or words and drawings on a computer screen, but they can never register our overall ability to think on our feet in a tense or stressful situation outside the artificial setting of an exam room. But there are many forms of intelligence that can be tested only in real-life situations, and then only over a longer stretch of time. The ability to think through a situation from where we are to where we want to be and then take the right actions to get there, adjusting and adapting as we go, is known by philosophers as "practical reason." It's a form of intelligence and a life skill important to have. And it's one that Harry enjoys in generous measure.

Harry's friend Hermione Granger is, of course, the poster girl for intelligence and logical reason in all its manifestations. When any problem arises, she wants to get busy with research right away, to position herself to know whatever is already understood about the many elements of the challenge she faces. If Hermione is ever in doubt about anything, she hits the library. You can easily imagine her on a computer and Googling in all her free time. But in the world of Hogwarts, she is immersed in books. And the information she picks up is almost always helpful. Rowling shows us through the character of Hermione the practical impact of knowledge—the vital importance of research and study outside the classroom as well as within its walls.

At the end of her first year at Hogwarts, headmaster Dumbledore gives Hermione a special student award for her ability to use logic to find a path forward and then reason her way along it in even the most difficult and dangerous of situations (SS 305). She is no useless book-worm with a brain full of theoretical facts that are of no practical value. She is a young woman who can think clearly under great duress, when many people would panic and mentally shut down. I love it that Dumbledore characterizes Hermione as being able to engage in what he calls "the use of cool logic in the face of fire." That's a great expression. Logic can cool down many superheated situations and create some degree of inner calm amid even apparent catastrophe and terrible panic. It can carve out room for courage to operate. It can serve us like a searchlight in a dark cavern and show us the way out. The ability to think through a situation from all relevant angles and take the right path forward can make all the difference between victory and disaster.

Not long before the awards banquet of the first year, Harry and Hermione are in pursuit of a very powerful object and are trying to get through a series of dangerous obstacles in order to locate it. They suddenly find themselves in an underground chamber surrounded by flames, and their only option for escape is provided by a complex-looking riddle written on a piece of paper. They both read it. Hermione looks relieved. She says:

> "This isn't magic—it's logic—a puzzle. A lot of the greatest wizards haven't got an ounce of logic, they'd be stuck in here forever."
> (SS 285)

With that one statement, the most intellectually engaged young wizard around signals the importance of logic and reasoning. The mind can do things that no magic can match. And this is a point that Rowling wants us to appreciate. Because of Hermione's ability to think and reason, literally as well as metaphorically, "in the face of fire," she is able to solve difficult riddles throughout her life and, as a result, deal successfully with the many challenges she encounters.

An effective leader encourages critical thought.

In the famous Triwizard Tournament during his fourth year at Hogwarts, the last of the obstacles Harry has to face involves a riddle

(GF 628-629). Again, the ability to reason well is crucial for success in the situation. And this time the logical Hermione is not around to save the day. But Harry is able to focus, think clearly, and move forward. He uses logic to do something that no magic alone could accomplish. And so, once again, we see the more-than-magical effectiveness of the human mind at work in even the most challenging of situations.

We need to clarify something important about the concept of logic in its most comprehensive understanding. Logic isn't just formal reasoning that employs classical rules for the sake of discovering truth and pleasing fastidious college professors. It's possible to use the term in a broader sense that is sometimes employed by philosophers and other careful analysts of the human condition. In this sense, we could say that there is "a logic of the brain" and "a logic of the gut"—to take up Harry's distinctive way of talking. But I suspect that Harry's mention of "guts" in the passage quoted earlier is just his way of referring to some deep part of the inner self distinct from and beneath the level of conscious reasoning that many philosophers have alluded to differently, and more traditionally, as "the heart." With this different anatomical metaphor, the phrase "the logic of the heart" has long stood for the direct, dynamic, and structured formation of belief, attitude, and especially action at the core of human personality. But to drill down a bit more in the current context, it's interesting to note that the most important virtue traditionally associated with the metaphor of the heart is courage. With that in mind, we can say more specifically that in addition to a logic of the intellect there is a logic of courage in human life. The logic of courage involves the five steps to courageous conduct revealed by Harry and covered in our chapter on his bravery. There is a logic, or dynamic, rationally structured shape, to courageous living. And it is the pattern displayed by those five steps. The logic of the mind or intellect is the ability to use both perceptual knowledge and intuition, filtered through memory and linked with the testimony of others, to draw reasonable conclusions about what might otherwise be unknown. This is a skill that is crucial for success in life and absolutely necessary for dealing well with any difficulties along the way. It is an ability displayed by all the characters in the Harry Potter stories whenever they succeed. And it's much more important in life than luck.

In fact, many wise and subtle thinkers would suggest that the vast realm of what we colloquially call "luck" is a blended domain consisting of perhaps some real randomness, along with patterns and plans too complex and hidden to be discerned by the casual glance. There are forces in the world, both for good and for ill, that impinge on our lives in ways that we do not and cannot always recognize. We might never be able to tame these forces fully, but we can enhance the good and resist the ill most effectively when we use the logic of our minds and our hearts to pursue worthy goals and support proper values in every situation.

Both luck and logic are involved in the living of a good life. We position ourselves to make the most of our luck when we use logic the best we can in all of its forms. As Harry Potter ultimately realizes, when problems need to be solved and people need to be saved, both logic and luck can play a proper role in the unfolding of events. Each helps the other along. But the end of the stick that we have in our hands is logic. Therefore we should cultivate it, master it, and through working smart as well as courageously hard, we should take care to use the best of logic in every situation we confront.

There is an old saying that has some currency among the highly educated, a sort of commentary on life in this world first coined by A. E. Housman in his well-named poem "Terence, This Is Stupid Stuff," a simple rhyme that playfully alludes to the relative strengths of brains and beer when it comes to understanding life: "Malt does more than Milton can, to justify God's ways to man." This is funny, to some extent true, and, in addition, quite memorable. To play on it just a bit, we can make our distinctive point very simply: Wise work does more than worry can to reconcile luck to man. It takes rationally planned and determined work to make the best use of the good luck that comes our way and to overcome the bad luck that sometimes crosses our path. The logic of good work is the coming together of intellect and courage through practical reason. This is a lesson of the wisest wizards that every leader should embrace and live.

DELIGHT AND DISASTER

The Wisdom Insight: *Delight and disaster come into every life.*

As the Bible says, it rains on the just and the unjust alike. The sun also shines on both. We get some good breaks and we get some bad breaks. Certain days can seem amazingly good. Others can seem astonishingly bad. Not a single person encounters only positive experiences or only negative ones in this life, despite how it may sometimes seem. Headmaster Dumbledore has a wonderful job and some great colleagues. He has had much success in his life and is famous for his extraordinary deeds. He also puts up with a lot of difficult negative situations and is falsely accused of all sorts of things. He is revered by the good and despised by the evil. He has great satisfactions. And he labors under terrible responsibilities.

The Weasley family is also a good example of delight and disaster coming into the same lives. They are quite poor in material things but rich in spirit. They have a wonderful family life, one of true communion and delight. Then one son, influenced by corrupt officials in the Ministry of Magic, basically leaves them all and denounces both his parents for their affiliation with Dumbledore. In the life of a close, happy, and supportive family, this is a real disaster. Of course, like many families, the Weasleys suffer small disappointments and larger calamities all along the way. Their other boys are always getting into trouble, and young Ginny even gets captured by Tom Riddle—the true identity of Voldemort—and has to be saved from the brink of death by her older friend Harry. Taken all together, it's enough to make any parent go gray. The magical powers of the members in this family can't guarantee any sort of reliable delight or ward off any real threat of disaster. But their inner wisdom can help them deal with both appropriately, granting them a resilient capacity to savor the good that delights them and endure the bad that deepens them.

Ron Weasley finds real delight in his friendship with Harry. They are best mates. They have fun together and support each other in a great many ways. And yet, because of this friendship, Ron lives each day in the shadow of his immensely talented and famous pal. Their relationship is a great boon to Ron, and yet there are ways in which it brings difficulty and even disaster into his life year after year. A highly illuminating ancient curse says, "May you live in interesting times." Ron is both blessed and cursed to live in extraordinarily interesting times and to have the lightning rod of the times as his very best friend.

Harry is blessed and cursed as well. He is marked out as special. He possesses great powers and a unique destiny. And because of this, he has to face great challenges. But this is true for all of us in different ways. We're all somehow special. Each of us comes into the world marked with a combination of talents and potential not duplicated in anyone else. That allows for some of our greatest blessings. And it also sets us up for many of our most distinctive challenges. This is one of the reasons so many kids identify with Harry. His special attributes were not appreciated around the Dursley house. He grew up being made to feel that he was a misfit. He had to get out into the broader world to discover what he was capable of doing. And so, to some extent, do we all. No one who is around us when we are children, and sometimes even as we grow into adulthood, really knows what we're capable of doing and how our distinctive talents can benefit the world. At least at some points in our lives, we all feel special, somewhere deep inside, and we very often feel unrecognized for our true potential. We know it's there, but we frequently experience frustration over the difficulties and challenges we so often have to face as we work on becoming what we're capable of being—just like Harry.

Our inner resilience allows us to enjoy the good and endure the bad, while learning from both. It is a never ending process.

Harry initially arrived at school as a wizard celebrity. But he was resented by one of his professors precisely for that fact. Most of the students, however, tended to like Harry—until the day he got caught by a teacher for breaking curfew while he was trying to help a friend and, as a result of the infraction, managed to get his entire house punished with a huge loss of house points, putting them suddenly in last place for the annual school house competition. Rowling tells us that he underwent an instant transformation from being one of the most popular kids at school to being one of the most disliked (SS 244). Fortunately, this bit of disaster was also soon to be overcome. But the reversals of fortune that Harry and all the rest of us can experience are very often difficult to deal with at the time things take their turn for the worse. The fickleness of fortune, and public sentiment in particular, can sometimes be astonishing.

Harry experiences some pretty spectacular reversals of fortune. It's not often that a person can win an important sporting event for his team almost single-handedly, with extraordinary individual effort, gain the roaring accolades of the crowd, and then get banned for life from that sport on the very same day, by a thoroughly corrupt administrator (OP 411–416). Fortunately for Harry, this announced lifetime deprivation was to be as temporary as the tenure of the official who pronounced it. But at the time, it was almost devastating for our hero, who had long found his greatest moments of satisfaction in the sport that was seemingly being taken from him. It's tough to go from glory to misery in a matter of minutes. But Harry once more endured.

Life isn't all difficulty and frustration, even for the often aggravated and disappointed Harry Potter. Harry, in fact, frequently feels delight. He experiences great surges of happiness when he's staying at Ron's house and often when he's in school, flying on his broom or hanging out in some companionship of activity with his friends. He can enjoy immensely a game of wizard chess with Ron or just having a snack with his buddies. This same young man of course also experiences sadness and depression, fear and anxiety, frustration and irritation—the whole range of human emotions, both positive and negative. For that matter, nearly every sympathetic character in these stories is shown in moments of triumph and tragedy, joy and disappointment, pleasure and grief. Careful readers can't easily avoid the conclusion that Rowling is conveying well the ups and downs that life has in store for all of us. One of the lessons we come away with in a fresh form is that we should never take for granted the good in our lives, and that we should always do our best to see past the bad. The wheel will turn, and what we're experiencing now will not always be what we'll encounter in the future. We must learn to deal with the lows and the highs, the opportunities and the difficulties, and be understanding with others when they're doing the same.

During many of my years teaching at Notre Dame, our head football coach, Lou Holtz, had on his desk a little sign that said, "This too shall pass." It had nothing intrinsically to do with football. This particular coach liked to run the ball and actually hated to pass. His sign was a comment on life. And it was one we should all keep in mind. Harry's happy days at Ron's house—"the Burrow"—came and went. The incredibly difficult days at Hogwarts under the corrupt power of the very temporary headmistress Dolores Umbridge came and went. It may often seem to us that the good things pass away too quickly and that the bad take their time, but the wheel of fortune does continue to spin, and we should never forget that fact. If we work hard to keep the right attitude and take the right action in any situation, however good or bad it may seem, we can step up and give that cosmic wheel a spin ourselves.

The right wisdom about the vicissitudes of life can help us all to deal better with whatever the day might bring us. If you like what's going on in your life right now, don't take it for granted. You should really enjoy it. If you're frustrated or suffering at this moment in time, don't give up hope. You can endure it. Just understanding the changing nature of our world can help us to keep our bearings and do the right thing in any set of circumstances. And if we keep this in mind, nothing has the power to throw us.

This piece of wisdom is equally needed in business and in life. No journey of success is smooth and trouble free. We all encounter troubles, disappointments, and unpleasant surprises, as well as good and wonderful times. We have to be able to make it through the array of ups and downs that life can throw our way. The most insightful philosophers in history have counseled us to keep our heads throughout these changes, enjoying the good and learning from the bad, but never losing our overall sense of who we are and where we're going.

I fully believe that we can't read the Harry Potter stories thoughtfully without emerging a little more in love with the magic of our everyday world and a little better prepared to live in it. That's the transformative experience of reading Rowling, and that's a good part of what has made her books such runaway bestsellers. We sense beneath the captivating story line a great deal of wisdom about life, and it strikes us deeply—we are touched and altered in a very positive way. We put down these books a bit more fully prepared for the difficulties we may face and even better able to enjoy the good things that we have each day. And this is a state of heightened wisdom that can benefit us both in business and in life, thanks to the wizards.

APPEARANCE AND REALITY

The Wisdom Insight: *Things are not always what they seem.*

There are times when something seems great, and it's really terrible. A turkey sandwich I once ate at a beautiful new restaurant seemed wonderful, but by the time I got home, I had a serious case of salmonella food poisoning that kept me in bed, in terrible pain and absolute misery, for a week. Worse yet, years later while on a book tour, I enjoyed a very expensive, wonderful looking, and delicious meal at a famous resort. The grouper was extremely tasty, but a couple of days later it began to show its true colors—with two trips to the emergency room, six weeks in bed, a total workup at the Mayo Clinic, and five years of serious neurological symptoms. There are many things in our lives that are like this, but fortunately, they are most often much more subtle. Of course, there is no way for a wise person to discern the toxins lurking in beautiful food at a highly regarded restaurant and prudently refrain from the repast. But the eyes of wisdom can more easily identify the poisons that may be hidden in many other areas of life.

Those who have never tasted fame may often dream of it. People who aren't rich crave wealth. Others seek power, believing that it will bring them the solution to all their problems and the source of the personal nobility they ache to experience. Sometimes, it's an object—a piece of jewelry, a car, a house—or a particular sort of companion or spouse that we think will change our lives and elevate us to a new level of existence. The wise person sees through such false promises. Unfortunately, this wisdom most often has to arise out of firsthand disappointment. The veil is lifted and we see the light, never to be fooled again—not, at least, by this particular illusion. But there is always another illusion out there. A life of wisdom is an ongoing quest to peel away appearances and connect up with the deeper realities around us.

True wisdom sees beyond mere appearances.

Long ago, the great philosopher Plato distinguished clearly between appearance and reality. Too many of us live lives of illusion, are misled by appearances, and stumble through our days never fully in touch with the realities that alone would give us what we truly need. The young characters in the Harry Potter stories learn throughout their years at Hogwarts that not everything in life is what it seems, to put the point very mildly indeed. In fact, it often appears that in a world of witchcraft and wizardry, very little is actually what it appears at first to be.

To the Dursley family, appearances are everything, and the realities of their family life are quite opposite from the image they seek to portray. Throughout all the books about Harry Potter, we see his uncle Vernon and aunt Petunia desperately trying to manage appearances for the sake of their own desired and pretended social status in the community. And we are put in a privileged position to know the harsh realities behind those false fronts. What is perhaps one of the most unexpected little surprises, at least to many readers, involving a divergence between appearance and reality crops up in book six, when Dumbledore pays a visit to the Dursley home, sits with all of them, and calmly chastises Harry's aunt and uncle for their mistreatment of Harry over the years. He tells them that they haven't done as he had asked. They haven't treated Harry as a son should be treated. They have been cruel to him. They have been abusive. But he then surprises and baffles them both by expressing his relief that, at least, they haven't inflicted the terrible damage on Harry that their real son, Dudley, has suffered at their hands (HB 55). This remark leaves them completely speechless and utterly confused. And it takes most readers at least a second to realize what's being revealed here. The appearance has always been that Harry is the one in the house who is neglected, mistreated, and harmed while, by contrast, his cousin Dudley is treated by his parents like royalty. He is indulged, placated, catered to, and spoiled in every possible way. How, then, can Dudley be the one who has been terribly damaged?

Rowling cleverly uses our illusions to impart an important lesson here about parenting and life. Dumbledore sees the situation more deeply than many readers might. Dudley is not treated well at all by being spoiled rotten. He has been given everything he ever wanted, treated like a prince and heir to a royal throne, and coddled beyond belief, and all that has had disastrous consequences for his character, as it always does. The Dursleys have not prepared their son for the realities of life. They have not formed and molded his character in strong and positive ways. They have not mentored him in preparation for the real world at all. They have, rather, surrounded him with illusions concerning who he is, what life is like, and how he needs to act in order to take his proper place in the grand scheme of things. He has been misled for nearly two decades and has become habituated to all the wrong things. Far from what superficial appearances might suggest, it is he, not Harry, who has been the most abused and damaged in that house. To convey this is to impart an important lesson about life.

Leaders who are keen to do what is best for their organizations and their people need to be careful students of human nature. Otherwise, with even the best of intentions, they can do damage of which they're completely unaware. People need truth, they need reasonable goals to strive for, they need sufficient resources and various forms of help along the way, but they also need to be trusted to work out their own solutions to many of the problems they face. Of course, no corporate paternalism will ever take on a form that mirrors how Vernon and Petunia Dursley treat their son, Dudley. But mistakes can be made with consequences that are just as great when people lead without the benefit of genuine wisdom and a capacity to see the difference between how things seem and how they really are.

The difference between appearance and reality is manifested in many ways throughout the Harry Potter stories. Near the beginning of book one, Rubeus Hagrid first appears to Harry like a frightening force of nature, tearing a large heavy door off its hinges to get to the young wizard and rescue him from the Dursleys. He's huge, with long shaggy hair and a wild, tangled beard (SS 46). His appearance is fierce, but we soon learn that he is the quintessentially gentle giant, a person of great kindness and tremendous sensitivity.

When Professor Quirrell enters the story in *The Sorcerer's Stone*, he seems to be an utterly innocuous and fragile little man with delicate sensibilities. He is extremely pleased and overly excited to meet the famous Harry Potter and later appears to faint from fear when a dangerous troll enters the school building. He comes across as very kind and helpful to all. He offers his assistance to Ron and Harry early in the school year when they get lost in the halls. But he is very different from what he appears to be, and his true intentions are not revealed until a culminating battle at the end of the book.

Gilderoy Lockhart seems to be one of the most accomplished wizards in their world. He has written many books on his amazing exploits and his extensive knowledge that are used as texts in various subjects at Hogwarts. Lockhart is the handsome celebrity author of his day, loved by all the women and admired by many of the men, at least those who can overcome a natural resentment of his apparently multifaceted greatness and his very carefully cultivated impact on the ladies around them. What we come to discover is that he's all hype and fake, living a lie and selling it to anyone who would be so gullible as to buy it. He is the worst possible sham celebrity, and because of this he endangers all those around him who are naïve enough to believe his act.

Professor Snape is perhaps the most interesting and frustrating example of a divergence between appearance and reality to be found in all the stories. He often looks like a secret confederate of evil, siding with the haughty, cynical, ambitious Slytherin students, constantly disparaging Harry, and acting quite suspiciously in many ways, and yet, mysteriously, Dumbledore trusts him. In *The Sorcerer's Stone*, Harry and his friends come to believe something bad about him that ends up being completely false. He is later revealed to be a former follower of the Dark Lord who has publicly disavowed his evil master and returned to the side of good. But the authenticity of his repudiation of evil is always in doubt for Harry, as it is in most readers' minds. Yet, Dumbledore—a man not easily misled—continues to rely on him for sensitive and important matters in the fight against Voldemort. As soon as we decide that Snape is really an unreformed spy still in league with evil, he does something to shake our confidence in that conclusion. And then, when we begin to be convinced that, perhaps after all, he is a genuinely though imperfectly reformed man, he does something to pull that rug out from under us completely. This happens at the end of *The Half-Blood Prince*, where what looks to be as decisive an answer about Snape's true allegiance as we could possibly have can still leave a residual doubt, carried along by a hope against appearances that many readers can't easily abandon. The case of Professor Snape shows, more clearly than most anything else, how difficult it can sometimes be to distinguish between appearance and reality in the lives and actions of people around us.

The student Luna Lovegood, first introduced in *The Order of the Phoenix*, initially seems like a total flake, and yet she ends up being a source of great hope and balance for anyone who gets close enough to her. The new teacher introduced to Harry as Mad-Eye Moody isn't at all what he seems to be. A vivid and terrifying vision that Harry has during his fifth year at Hogwarts isn't what it appears—and very bad consequences follow. Most of the world is wrong about Sirius Black. He is widely regarded as a mass murderer by almost everyone, and for quite a long time. But the real truth about him is very different. People disbelieve Harry when he's telling the truth and ridicule Dumbledore as crazy when he's working hard to save their lives and their world.

Very often, the things that happen around Hogwarts, and in its general environs, aren't in any way what they seem. That's of course to be expected in any mystery story, and Rowling is a good mystery writer. We are surprised left and right to find out the truth about a person or an event. And so are the characters in the stories. As attentive readers, we can begin to form the impression that the author wants to remind us of the simple but powerful truth that things in this world are often not what they seem, and neither are people. We must be cautious as we form our opinions and grant our trust to others. Taking things at face value can get us into deep trouble. Caution beats correction, and it's much easier to be careful about our beliefs early on than to try later to reverse the damage caused by a false assessment of appearances. Some damage that can arise out of false belief is, after all, irreversible.

The importance of truth can be seen by the damage falsehood can cause.

One of the most interesting cautionary tales in these stories involving belief and appearances, and one that is extremely relevant to the present day, comes in book two, *The Chamber of Secrets.* It's a small part of the book that easily can be read and forgotten. But it contains great wisdom. One day, Ginny Weasley finds a magical diary and begins to write in it. She starts to tell it her most intimate secrets— her feelings, thoughts, worries, and hopes. When she makes entries, new words mysteriously appear in response to her from a young man she's never met. He replies in kind, understanding ways, asking about her, sympathizing with her, and making her feel better about revealing even more details concerning her life. What she sees appear on the page in reply to her thoughts is mesmerizing and seems to be just what she needs. She has no idea that the person she is dealing with is not at all who he appears to be, and that he's somehow magically living in the book and writing to deceive her, actually sucking out her life force as she reveals herself more and more to him. In a very short time, she is in terrible trouble and imminent danger of death without a dramatic rescue by Harry Potter.

Harry finds Ginny in miserable shape and almost dead. As he is about to save her, he asks the man who is responsible for her plight how it all had happened. He replies quite candidly:

> "I suppose the real reason Ginny Weasley's like this is because she opened her heart and spilled all her secrets to an invisible stranger." (CS 309)

As I write these words, the local news has just reported that an area teenager has disappeared because of an online predator. Rowling's magic diary is, of course, an obvious metaphor for the Internet-connected computer. By confiding in someone she has never actually met or seen, Ginny sets herself up for serious trouble. In everyday life, things are often not what they seem, but in the land of Internet chat-room conversations with strangers, it's safe to say that things are hardly ever what they seem. Ginny's mystery correspondent appeared to be a caring friend, but he was in reality an evil fiend.

When Harry manages to save Ginny, he and Ron take her to Professor McGonagall's office, where her mother sits crying and her father is anxiously waiting for news of her, alongside Headmaster Dumbledore. After Mr. and Mrs. Weasley hear the whole story about the magical diary and what happened because of it, her father Arthur Weasley responds instantly:

> "*Ginny!*" said Mr. Weasley, flabbergasted. "Haven't I taught you *anything*? What have I always told you? Never trust anything that can think for itself *if you can't see where it keeps its brain.*" (CS 329)

As cleverly and strangely stated as this is, it is wonderful wisdom for life. It is, in fact, a piece of wisdom just as needed by adults in our time as by young people. You can find it hard enough to distinguish between appearances and realities when you have full access to a person or situation. If someone is hiding behind a screen name and communicating through instant messages, e-mails, or postings in a chat room, there is no way to tell what is real and what is false. Bad people always take advantage of good disguises. Ginny got herself into such horrible trouble by trusting someone unseen in circumstances where no such trust is ever well advised.

Of course, the business world is full of various analogues to this situation. Business proposals, corporate entities, rumors about a merger, and things you hear the competition might be doing aren't always what they seem. We have to develop the skill of discernment, an ability valued by the ancients at a time when hard data was much more difficult to obtain than it is now. But it's just as important now as it has ever been, because deceptive people take advantage of all the smoke screens they can construct, and so, even in our era, we have to be very discerning about how we interpret the information that comes our way on any new opportunity, any new challenge, or any aspect of our business environment.

Ginny's rescue by Harry is one of many instances in these stories where a situation seems so bad as to be irredeemable, or unsalvageable, and yet somehow gets turned around by the use of intelligence, courage, and heart. The ancient Stoic philosophers believed that hardly anything in this world is either as good as it seems or as bad as it seems, and so we should all, for the most part, just calm down. In the Potter books, circumstances often come to seem impossibly terrible, and yet good still somehow manages to overcome evil in the end. We should not panic when things seem bad, and we should not lose our heads by being overly confident or even careless when things seem great. An ever-changing and complex world has a way of surprising us on a frequent basis, and we should always be ready for the changes that may come our way.

Perhaps one of the most striking tales in the books concerning things not being what they seem involves the beautiful "veela," first spotted at the Quidditch World Cup Match in *The Goblet of Fire*. The

Bulgarian national team arrives in the stadium with their mascots, exotic creatures known as veela. They are the most beautiful visions Harry has ever seen. They are very much like astonishingly attractive women, but they are also somehow more. Their skin positively glows and their long, white-blonde hair shines and fans out behind them as if lifted by a breeze, even when there is no wind. Seeing them, Harry's brain seems to stop working. He is completely transfixed (GF 103).

The veela, with their tremendous beauty and captivating movements, are utterly mesmerizing. Their effect on men is to make them lose all common sense and want very badly to do incredibly stupid things in a ridiculously juvenile effort to impress them. On this particular occasion, only Hermione is able to call Harry and Ron back from an utterly irrational, senseless, desperate attempt to gain the attention of such lovely beings.

What the boys learn very quickly is that beauty can sometimes indeed be only skin-deep. Later in the day, something happens on the Quidditch field to make the veela angry. They completely lose control of themselves and become enraged. In the process, their physical appearance is shockingly transformed. Suddenly, they don't look beautiful at all but develop extremely frightening features. Mr. Weasley immediately makes the most of the opportunity and reminds the boys that this is why you should never make your relationship choices in life based on looks alone (GF 11–112).

This is, of course, a new insight for many young people, as well as for quite a few forgetful older men and women who ought to know better. It's a lesson in basic wisdom that is by itself worth the full price of these books, in hardcover. Appearances aren't always the best guides to the realities that lurk beneath. We sometimes have to fight to avoid believing what we want to believe, whether it's accurate or not, and struggle to seek the real truth in a situation. There are many forms of infatuation that can dislodge common sense, and they don't always involve long flowing hair and glowing skin. We sometimes need our friends and trusted elders to shake us out of a trance into which an apparently wonderful person, thing, or opportunity has pulled us.

I can't resist pointing out before moving on here how interesting it is that the rage-prone veela are described as having long, flowing blonde hair. The wicked young Draco Malfoy is blonde, and so are his evil father and mother. The good Hermione Granger, by contrast, has very dark hair, as of course does Harry. Their closest friends in the Weasley family are described as all being redheads. At a certain point, it can begin to look as if the good people here are all non-blonde. In book one, *The Sorcerer's Stone*, on page one, Rowling describes Harry's unpleasant aunt Petunia as being both thin and blonde. But a bit later, when Rowling herself began to become immensely wealthy from the sales of these wonderful books, her promotional photos started to show her looking both attractively thin and beautifully blonde. Interestingly, her descriptions of Petunia Dursley correspondingly began to change. By book two, this unsympathetic character is no longer characterized as "thin and blonde," but rather as merely "horse-faced and boney" (CS 4). I had to smile when I first noticed the change. Rowling is right to show us that classic beauty is no guarantee of classic virtue—that good looks aren't always a sign of good hearts—but we just as properly should avoid assuming that anyone "thin and blonde" is someone to watch out for—whether or not they are simply enjoyable to watch. This is a lesson we all learn in a striking way about the extraordinarily beautiful and very blonde Fleur Delacour, through a quite unexpected turn of events at the end of *The Half-Blood Prince*. There are no reliable correlations, either positive or negative, between a certain form of appearance and a certain state of soul, and there are even fewer connections between hair color and virtue. Most of us know that, but the best of us can sometimes forget, and then we need friends to point out the error of our ways.

The wise counsel of friends can safeguard us from mistakes that would otherwise derail our progress in life.

Harry, Ron, and Hermione—sometimes with the assistance of a well-disposed adult—often help each other to see behind and beneath appearances. They don't always like hearing a contrary opinion, but it often benefits them in the end. They give us a model for why two heads, or three, or more, are quite often much better than one. Their friendship allows the three of them to augment one another's perspectives and correct one another's misimpressions about a particular situation or person. And we all can learn from that. It's very hard to steer our lives forward with accuracy and perceptiveness if we never listen to and absorb the perspectives of other people we can trust.

Some of the best business books in recent years, like Larry Bossidy and Ram Charan's fine book *Execution,* focus on the importance of interrogating reality, never being satisfied with superficial information, and finding ways of getting to the real truth in any situation. Too many business ventures and enterprises fail because people have been too casual about the truth. They haven't sought it earnestly, and they haven't shared it freely with one another. The competitiveness of our century will not allow that attitude and approach to succeed. The more perspectives we can gather on any situation of importance to us, the better. We need to be investigators, detectives, analysts, and then teachers of truth in everything we do.

The truth is too crucial for long-term business success for us ever to allow it to be eclipsed and shrouded by illusion. And it has been known since ancient times that people in any position of authority often lack full access to the truth. Those who report to them are generally more inclined to tell them what they think they want to hear than what they really need to know. That can isolate a top executive from the very reality whose contours he must understand in order to move forward effectively. Like Harry and Ron, every manager, every executive, and all of us in our own careers and lives need the counsel of friends we can trust, friends who will talk straight to us and correct us in love whenever it's necessary. We all need people around us who will help free us from false appearances and keep us in touch with reality.

All of us who are in any sort of business should think of ourselves as being in the reality business. There is really no such thing as building a successful business on nothing but illusions. Even people who believe it's their job to sell wonderful dreams and beautiful illusions to those who want them need to be firmly in touch with realities themselves. If the top Las Vegas magicians and the most creative advertising designers of New York, Chicago, and L.A. weren't students of human nature firmly grounded in the realities of business, they could not flourish, and they would not have gotten to be where they are today. The rest of us need to live by the reality principle as well.

We fail to secure our own deepest interests when we surround ourselves with people who think just like us. Friends and family members are to be cherished in their differences. So are associates at work and colleagues in other walks of life. We can't benefit in all possible ways from being around someone who is exactly like us in every conceivable respect, who sees things just as we do, and who agrees with us on absolutely everything. A friend who views situations and people a bit differently can help us to escape illusions that may grip us and miss him. Likewise, we can perhaps do the same favor for him. But we can be helpful in this way to our friends only if we speak the truth as we see it, and only if we are genuinely open to the same from them. It takes a good measure of humility to recognize that things aren't always as they appear to us, and that others can sometimes help peel back the surface illusions that are misleading and confounding us. We need to be humbly open to other perspectives, and this means that we have to be prepared on occasion to be wrong. That's not easy for most of us, and it's not always easy for Harry, Ron, and Hermione.

COMPANIONS AND GOOD FRIENDS

The Wisdom Insight: *It's important to have good friends.*

This may be one of the most crucial pieces of wisdom running through all the Harry Potter books. Friendship is portrayed throughout these stories in all its many facets. Friends talk, share, fight, disagree, help each other, delight each other, support each other, correct each other, irritate each other, save each other from the brink of disaster when necessary, and generally adorn life, making it a much more interesting experience overall. The great philosopher Aristotle said that he couldn't imagine a happy life without the presence of friends. I believe J. K. Rowling can't either. And this is further testimony to her wisdom.

Friends help to magnify the good in our lives and to diminish the bad. They celebrate with us when things go well and commiserate and encourage us when things go wrong. They give us trustworthy sounding boards for our ideas, and they provide us with new and interesting perspectives of their own. They offer us help, and then they give us the chance to be helpful in turn. There are many things that just can't be accomplished without the collaboration of friends. And no celebration is complete without them. Just being around a friend can be relaxing, or energizing, or both.

The great thinkers in every world culture have realized something very important about solitude and society. Goodness is never just an individual quality. It is realized and enhanced most fully in some form of community. And real community begins in friendship. When Headmaster Dumbledore speaks to his own student body, and to the visiting students from two other wizard schools at the end of year four, he states his firm belief that they are all only as strong as they are united and as weak as they are divided. He explains that the evil Voldemort has a knack for spreading discord and antagonism, and he tells the students that they will be able to fight him and his effects only by showing an equally strong unity of friendship and trust (GF 723).

I've come to believe that there are four fundamental dimensions of human experience in the world, and correspondingly four foundations of happiness and sustainable excellence in any enterprise or relationship. I've written at length on these before, and over the years I've become increasingly convinced of their vital importance for any positive human endeavor:

The Intellectual Dimension that aims at Truth
The Aesthetic Dimension that aims at Beauty
The Moral Dimension that aims at Goodness
The Spiritual Dimension that aims at Unity

Dumbledore is a deeply spiritual man. In his words to the visiting students, he appeals to them to understand the importance of unity, the goal of the spiritual dimension of our experience, and contrasts that with the "discord and enmity" sown by evil people. Truth, beauty, goodness, and unity in this life are a bit like a package deal. Violate one and you violate more than one. Ignore or neglect any of these dimensions, and you inevitably suffer in many ways. The great Dumbledore is always calling his students back to the path of truth, beauty, goodness, and unity. You can look at the entirety of his headmastership over Hogwarts and see the intellectual, aesthetic, moral, and spiritual dimensions of life respected and nurtured. And this has tremendous consequences. These four dimensions, and their related four foundations, make positive community, true friendship, and real collaboration possible.

Friends can do together what they never could have accomplished separately. Without the teamwork provided by Ron and Hermione, as well as a last-second intervention by Dumbledore, Harry would never have been able to keep the Sorcerer's Stone out of Voldemort's grasp at the end of his first year at Hogwarts. Harry and his schoolmate Cedric Diggory join forces at one point to stop a dangerous giant spider—something we are told that neither could have done alone—and they succeed in their partnership (GF 632). Ron and Hermione help Harry prepare for the Triwizard Tournament tasks. Hermione helps the boys with their schoolwork all the time. Even Neville Longbottom surprises us now and then with the contributions he can make to a collaborative effort.

Of course, the support and collaboration of colleagues and friends are just as important in the business world as they are in any war against evil wizards. We need the talents of others and their distinctive perspectives. In his book *Winning*, Jack Welch says that "any organization—or unit or team—that brings more people and their minds into the conversation has an immediate advantage." We benefit from really listening to the opinions of other well-informed people, and we derive even more benefit from the counsel of true friends.

Any time we can involve more good people in our enterprises, and especially draw on the talents of our friends, we position ourselves much better to get the best outcomes possible.

Before Harry was rescued from what basically amounted to his protective custody at the Dursley house, before he was allowed to go out and make any real friends, he was a very sad little boy. Once he arrived at Hogwarts and began making friends, his whole world came alive. He finally had a support system, a collaboration of comrades that helped him face any new situation and any difficulty with greater strength and a sense of higher purpose. One of the most common mistakes made by high achievers in our day is focusing so much on their individual careers and personal goals that they neglect their crucial human need of friendship. Ironically, it's only when we take our eyes off our careers and goals long enough to build great friendships that we provide ourselves with the firm foundation necessary to attain those goals that are genuinely worth reaching and build careers that are truly worth having. Friendship is not peripheral to the good life, but is at its core. As Dumbledore says so wisely to his star student:

"You need your friends, Harry." (HB 78)

To emphasize the deep importance of friendship in our lives, Rowling has Dumbledore describe to Harry what Tom Riddle was like as a boy and how he developed into the villainous adult Voldemort. Riddle had a desperate need to believe that he was different from other people in a special way, and he distanced himself from anything that would connect him with his peers or anyone else, ultimately even refusing to use his birth name. Dumbledore described him as "different, separate, and notorious" as well as having had "contempt for anything that tied him to other people" (HB 277). He always sought independence, autonomy, and what he perceived would be in his narrow self-interest. To him, other people were just objects of no particular interest, to be stolen from, tortured, or killed as it might suit him. The headmaster sums it all up by saying:

"Lord Voldemort has never had a friend, nor do I believe that he has ever wanted one." (HB 277)

Evil arises out of alienation and enmity with others. The person who cannot respect others enough to accept them as friends, and who cannot humble himself enough to give himself to others as a friend, has cut himself off from one of the richest sources in this life of happiness, satisfaction, and good. The results can be appalling. Proper relationships can mitigate our weaknesses and enrich our lives. Without them, we are more vulnerable to the worst impulses and can never enjoy the best experiences.

Friendships are the foundations of a flourishing life.

There are many different kinds of relationships represented in the Potter stories. Some are true friendships and others are not. I suspect that Albus Dumbledore and Minerva McGonagall have long been true friends, however formal their relationship at times might seem to be. Ron's parents aren't just spouses but are also real friends to each other. George and Fred aren't merely brothers but are also fast friends and collaborators. More examples could be given, but it's just as important at this juncture to mention an example of a personal relationship, or set of relationships, that does not offer us an exemplary case of true or complete friendship by any stretch of the imagination.

Draco Malfoy, Vincent Crabbe, and Gregory Goyle hang out with one another all the time. They are constant companions, but they are not friends in the deepest and truest sense. Malfoy is the leader, the mastermind of nearly criminal intent, and clearly the only real brains in the outfit. Crabbe and Goyle are his followers and lackeys. Rowling says that these other boys seemed to exist just to do his dirty work (PA 79). These two are presented as being a bit like brainless bodyguards, sticking with the malevolent young wizard out of habit and because of their greed for the mischief that he's able to create. There is also a suspicion that the three of them are together largely because of the relationship of their fathers, who are all secret but committed devotees of the Dark Lord. They are using each other. Malfoy uses his large friends for protection. They use him for excitement and a sense of power over others greater than what their undirected brawn alone could bring them. Their relationship stands in stark contrast with the rich, rewarding friendship to be found among Harry, Ron, and Hermione, a positive network that branches out farther through Neville, Ginny, Fred, George, Luna, Hagrid, and many others at Hogwarts and beyond its borders.

Aristotle believed that there are, loosely speaking, three distinct varieties of friendship: friendships of utility, friendships of pleasure, and what we can call complete friendships, or virtue friendships. Friendships of utility, the lowest kind, are created when two or more people come together in a bond of mutual usefulness. Each believes the other can help him or her to achieve certain goals. The friendship lasts as long as the benefits are believed to continue. These friendships are common in the world of business and in many other organizational settings. They can also be found in all types of schools. What holds the friends together is some form of mutual utility. Draco Malfoy and his henchmen may perhaps rise to this lowest level of friendship. Harry, Ron, and Hermione often help one another out, but there seems to be so much more to their friendship than just this. And there is.

The second level of friendship is one of pleasure. This is perhaps the most common form of friendship to be found among children and adolescents. They are not using one another to attain independent goals, but are doing things together because they enjoy one another's company. A pleasure friendship is all about enjoyment. Pleasure friends hang out together because it's fun, and not for any other extrinsic reason. Draco and his buddies may even enjoy one another's company. They laugh a lot together when making fun of others. Like is attracted to like, and despite their many differences of intellect, the Slytherin gang seem to be of similarly corrupt character. Harry, Ron, and Hermione are very clearly friends of the pleasure sort. They enjoy hanging out together and doing things with one another. And their enjoyable friendship is of such a nature that, unlike

Malfoy and company, they also may be well along the path to what Aristotle viewed as the highest form of friendship possible.

In each case of a complete friendship, Aristotle poetically stated, there is one soul sharing two bodies. Complete friends are not together for the sake of mutual usefulness or even for the purpose of shared enjoyment. They may indeed be extremely helpful to each other, and they certainly enjoy each other's company, but neither of these facts is the sole source and baseline of the friendship. These are, rather, positive side effects of a complete commitment of care and value that the friends share in common.

Complete friends are true friends in the deepest sense. They share the most fundamental and total unity that different people can attain. The biblical phrase "closer than a brother" comes to mind. Aristotle believed that this complete, or virtue, friendship is an important ingredient for a full and happy life. In a great marriage, spouses attain this elusive state. In a wonderful family, all the family members can share in it. It may happen with good neighbors or lifelong acquaintances. And it can come about in the workplace. But it is as rare as it is valuable.

Aristotle thought of this form of friendship as a virtue friendship because he held that people are incapable of it if they aren't virtuous individuals first. In his view, only the classic virtues allow a friend to focus on all the right things, and do all the right things, for a friendship to truly flourish. People without virtue are users and are always manipulating others for their own narrowly perceived self-interest. Only real virtue provides the possibility of the highest friendship. Because of this alone, it's clear that Malfoy, Crabbe, and Goyle could not, in their present state of character, possibly experience complete and true friendship of this deepest sort, either among themselves or with any other people outside their small circle. Harry, Ron, and Hermione, however, may be well on their way to this wonderful state of being and may already be developing by fits and starts these ties that Aristotle believed to be crucial for true human flourishing.

Friendships of utility can be good. Friendships of pleasure can enhance our lives greatly. But they should always be understood in the light of this ideal sort of relationship that Aristotle believed we could become capable of enjoying with the right inner development and the right outer actions. I am convinced that we all have an innate desire for such friendships, and that it's this, among other things, that sets us up to enjoy so much reading about and watching the relationships we see building between Harry and his closest friends. We cheer them on, and we enjoy their companionship vicariously, as if we ourselves were a part of their circle. We sense in their friendship the magic that is so often missing from our own busy lives. And I think that this is exactly what Rowling wants us to feel.

For decades, serious people have talked about not mixing business and pleasure. But it's crucial to do so in the right ways. The more pleasure we take in our work, and the more enjoyment that we experience partnering up with our colleagues, the better work we are able to do and the more reliably successful our results will be. Friendship is a foundation for excellence and an ingredient in it. The better we know our coworkers and our clients, the better positioned we are to genuinely team up with them in new and powerfully collaborative ways.

Rowling doesn't ever discuss what friendship is, and she doesn't represent any of her characters as waxing philosophical about its nature and role in our lives, but she shows us the importance of it in many ways throughout the stories of every book. As the influential twentieth-century philosopher Ludwig Wittgenstein liked to point out, there are some things in life that are better shown than said. The deep value of friendship is clearly an insight that our philosophical novelist Rowling wants us to see in these stories, enjoy, and put into action in our own lives.

GETTING WORSE AND GETTING BETTER

The Wisdom Insight: *Things often get worse before they get better.*

Have you ever decided to clean up a room in your house, or a very messy office, finally gotten started, and after hours of work suddenly realized that everything now looks worse than before? That's the way it often is with problems. From the moment you realize you have a problem to the time you get it fixed, it can often begin to look worse and worse until it finally gets resolved. That's why we have the old saying "It's always darkest before the dawn."

Friends sometimes have problems creep into their relationship and, rather than dealing with them right away, let them grow and get worse. Often, it's because each person involved is embarrassed to bring up the topic of the problem and silently hopes it will eventually just go away. At other times, it's because each person is really hoping that he's simply misunderstanding the situation, or that the cause of the apparent trouble is temporary and will resolve itself on its own. Married people can make the same mistake. While they each recognize that they have a problem but put off doing anything about it, the difficulty can get worse and worse until it becomes nearly disastrous.

Bold conversations, even on things you prefer to avoid, can help to identify and solve the most difficult problems.

Ancient philosophers had an interesting observation about this. When a problem is hard to see, it's easy to solve. When it's easy to see, it's hard to solve. Take cancer as an example. When it's just starting to grow, it's very hard to detect but typically easy to cure. When it's easy to spot because it has grown or spread a great deal, it's often very difficult to cure. In business, or in life generally, when anything is just beginning to go wrong, it's usually fairly easy to correct. A small adjustment is all that's needed. But it's sometimes hard at first to spot that there is a problem at all, and if you have some inkling of one, it's typically tough at such an early stage to define well what it is. The situation often has to get much worse before we can see clearly what is wrong and what needs to be done to change it.

Sometimes things get worse before they get better because we can tolerate amazingly bad situations, but if they get terrible enough, and literally intolerable, we're finally motivated to do something and make a change. Bad is not good enough—terrible is what it takes to motivate most people into action. We dither as things decay and situations deteriorate, and then at the last possible moment, we intervene to turn things around. This is not very beneficial as a general life strategy. But, of course, it usually beats never doing anything at all.

Occasionally, it seems that things get worse and worse in our lives just to test us and strengthen us as people. Like a refiner's fire, the difficulties we face burn away the dross from our attitudes and personalities, impurities that don't serve us at all and actually get in the way of our true good. We are hammered on the anvil of frustration and suffering, and are as a result sharpened in our insights and our abilities to prevail. Whatever the purpose and whatever the result of this common phenomenon of things getting worse before they get better, it helps us to make it through such a situation just to remember that this is often how the world works, and that we should hang in there and not give up hope as the darkness descends. The sun will rise again.

Harry and his friends see this happen over and over. Ron seems to get worse and worse at Quidditch—to a horribly depressing extent—before he finally turns it around and prevails. For Harry, living at the Dursley house always seems to go from bad to worse, and often gets to the very brink of being utterly intolerable each summer before he is somehow finally rescued. The fact that Dolores Umbridge comes to Hogwarts as a Defense Against the Dark Arts teacher in their fifth year at the school is just something awful in the minds of Harry and all his friends. She is an ugly old witch with a hypocritically forced smile and a deeply perverse temperament. But then she decides not to teach the students what they really want to learn—the practical side of the subject—preferring instead to prepare them in a minimally bookish and completely boring way for their written exams. As if all that isn't bad enough, she begins punishing Harry for the slightest infractions with a particularly sadistic and cruel procedure. She finally even becomes the new headmaster of Hogwarts for a time, changing the school dramatically and turning it into a place where no regular student would ever want to be. She completely bans Harry from his beloved sport of Quidditch for life. And then things get really bad—before there is even the hint of a new dawn.

Every confrontation with evil throughout the books seems to take this same path. Things look bad. Then they get much worse. Finally, the situation seems hopeless. Something horrible happens. Then someone or something completely unexpected intervenes and all the good people—or at least most of them—are saved. So when we ourselves see problems develop in real life, and then watch them worsen even as we try to solve them, we should not panic, but realize the wisdom of the wizards that, in this world as well as in theirs, things often get worse before they get better. That's the way it has always been, and that's the way it is. If we can stay calm with this realization, we give ourselves the chance to continue to work our hardest and turn things around. The darker things get, the closer we are to the new dawn. And merely remembering this can be very reassuring. When Harry is having increasingly frequent and intense pain in his lightning-shaped head scar, which is usually a sign of Voldemort's physical proximity or dramatic activity, and he is also undergoing a series of troubling dreams, Hermione tries to console him, and also herself, with precisely this sort of insight. His problem could just be a little bit like an illness that has to get worse before it can get better (OP 554). Sometimes, just calling this to mind can take the edge off a situation. Increasing deterioration or incremental worsening is not always an indication of an unending downward spiral toward doom. Often, improvement and restoration will follow. Just knowing this general fact about the way things work can help us to keep our heads and move forward with a measure of confidence in even a very bad situation.

LOVE AND LIFE

The Wisdom Insight: *Love is the greatest power in the world.*

This bit of wisdom is, paradoxically, the simplest, the deepest, and the most important insight in all the Harry Potter books, and it takes us right into the topic of our final chapter. Let me say here that, with all the powerful magic on display in the fight of good against evil, the most powerful and the most magical force of all is presented as love. And the love Rowling has in mind is no superficial enjoyment, emotional craving, or romantic attachment. It's the deepest, most self-sacrificial, and yet most fulfilling form of commitment possible. In our time, we live in danger of completely forgetting the real nature and depth of love, understanding it instead in a variety of superficial ways. It isn't an inherently sentimental, old-fashioned feeling, and it isn't simply a socially acceptable camouflage for a more primitive form of desire. It is, rather, our deepest connection with what is perhaps the most fundamental power in the universe.

Love is one of the most important things imaginable for great business, and it's almost never thought of in connection with our business lives. It's also crucial for great leadership of any kind. We unfortunately tend to compartmentalize our existence into the personal and the professional, with love and family and friends embraced as important parts of our personal sphere of life, but, oddly, not even on the radar screen for the world of work. However, the deepest of our human emotions and attitudes are not, or at least should not be, foreign to the realm of our business and organizational endeavors. To the extent that we cut work off from the deeper parts of our lives, we make it more likely that we'll never be as good at it as we could be, and that it will never mean as much to us and others as it should. Business is a genuinely human endeavor, a place where the whole panoply of human dimensions and positive attributes is meant to come into play. Great business requires great virtue, and the greatest business demands the greatest array of virtues. We've often heard enthusiasm and passion praised by motivational speakers and highly successful people. But the deepest enthusiasms and the most productive passions are always just manifestations of love.

Of course, in ordinary language, we colloquially use the word "love" in many different ways and to refer to many different attitudes, connections, and feelings. You may say that you love great wine, dark chocolate, German cars, Swiss watches, golf, tennis, or beautiful sunsets at the beach. You might even say that you love your new office. You certainly may indeed like such things very much, and there may even be a sense in which you actually do love them. But you probably experience very different attachments and levels of enjoyment, concern, and care, for which you can use the same word. You might also say, for example, perhaps expressing an interestingly different connection, that you love the old dog who has been your pet and companion for many years. You love your neighbors on the street where you've lived for so long, and that's one of the reasons you've never moved. You love your close friends. You love your wife, or husband, and your children. You may even say that you love life. And I hope you do. But when you reflect on these many affirmations of love, it's clear that they represent a wide variety of enjoyments, affections, connections, commitments, values, and levels of personal investment.

It may be that our use of the word "love," for all its variety, is consistent enough that everything we express with it is somehow directly connected to the deep force and power that Rowling wants to bring to our attention. When she speaks of love, or, in particular, when she has her wise mouthpiece Dumbledore speak of it, she means to refer to that deepest level of experience and value—an openness, compassionate acceptance, and unconditional commitment that goes beyond, and underlies, everything else positive that we ever experience or do. To the extent that we are in touch with this sort of love, to the degree that it directs us, motivates us, and gives us a touchstone for all our actions, we can flourish in our noblest endeavors and serve as leaders of the highest sort. When we are connected with this power, we can experience success in all the best ways, but when we are cut off from it by our own choices and confusions, we drift and ultimately fail.

Love is simply the most important key to proper success, authentic happiness, and genuine meaning in life that there is, despite any appearances to the contrary in our world. But to see how that's so, we'll have to jump right into the full exploration of all these topics in our next chapter.

7

HAPPINESS AND MEANING

Happiness is the activity of a good spirit.
—Aristotle

hat are the Harry Potter books really all about? They are certainly about good and evil. They are about the classic virtues. They are about many more forms of magic than initially meet the eye. They are about adventure. They are about friendship. And they are about growing up in a dangerous world. But they are also about happiness and meaning in life. And they are about love. To see these themes, we have to look a bit deeper. But when we do, we discover that some very important ideas emerge.

MONEY, POWER, FAME, AND STATUS

In Harry's world, as in ours, many people tend to waste their lives chasing the wrong things. Too many of us seem to think that the path to happiness and meaning in life is paved with money, power, fame, and status. But Harry sees through most of this. He is famous before he understands why. He is a celebrity of the wizard world, and that just brings him a lot of unwanted attention, trouble, and unhappiness. On his very first day of school at Hogwarts, the other students are lining up to get a look at him, and whispers follow him everywhere he goes (SS 131). In one of his first classes, Professor Snape snarls over the new student, his words dripping with disdain:

"Ah, yes," he said softly, "Harry Potter. Our new celebrity." (SS 136)

Professor Gilderoy Lockhart is almost equally famous and is a completely superficial fake. He has allowed his monomaniacal quest for fame to replace the acquisition of any real virtues or merits in life. And as a result, he ends up totally exposed, thoroughly shamed, and barely existing in miserable shape on the mental ward of the central wizard hospital. So fame again is no guarantee of happiness. It can even be a serious obstacle to the happy life, whether or not you have to tussle with paparazzi outside your house every day and hear from friends all the slanderous lies about you that are being printed by the tabloids each week.

And then there's power. Lord Voldemort has tremendous power and is in quest of even more, but he is a paradigm of desperate misery. He provides us with a concrete example of Lord Acton's well-known adage that power tends to corrupt, and absolute power corrupts absolutely. For it's the absolute power over life and death that Voldemort has long been intent on pursuing, and it's this desperate pursuit that turns him into an increasingly despicable creature. One of life's extreme ironies is that a total fixation on extending one's existence can drain that existence of its meaning.

Money, fame, power, and status can be great burdens or powerful tools. One of our chief challenges is to develop the discipline of using them well.

Other wizards also display the negative consequences of an unbridled quest for power. Barty Crouch wanted to be both powerful and admired. He was consumed by unfettered personal ambition, thinking that position, power, and status would make his life meaningful and happy. He climbed the ladder of success as he defined it. Then his son was arrested for collaborating with known forces of evil. In telling the whole sad story to Harry, his godfather and friend, Sirius Black, muses that this entire turn of events must have been a real shock for Crouch. He adds that Crouch would have been much better off spending more time with his family, leaving work early every now and then, and getting to know his son (GF 528).

After the events narrated by Sirius up to that point, it gets even worse for Crouch. His son is tried, convicted, and sent away to Azkaban, the terrible wizard prison, his wife dies, and his son escapes, later to return and kill him. In short, everything falls apart in the worst possible ways. Rowling knows this will strike home for many of her adult readers, who far too often sacrifice family and personal time to a relentless quest for power, status, and public recognition. Further elaborating on the story, with all its terrible outcomes, and describing how Crouch had sought power without ethics and as a result had eventually tasted the inevitable consequences of such a trajectory, Black adds:

> "So old Crouch lost it all, just when he thought he had it made . . ."
> (GF 529)

Fame, status, and power are no guarantees of happiness at all. What, then, of money—the great quarry and fixation of modern life, the contemporary fallback measure of all things? Ron's family is described in *The Prisoner of Azkaban* as "very nice and extremely poor" (PA 9). Their poverty does not diminish their happiness. On the contrary, their home environment is one of the two places where Harry ever experiences real happiness. Toward the end of one summer-vacation stay that Harry had enjoyed in Ron's humble home, known as "the Burrow," we are told that:

> He was looking forward to getting back to Hogwarts, but his month at the Burrow had been the happiest of his life. (CS 65)

A lack of funds does not necessarily impede the possibility of happiness. In fact, simple living often seems to facilitate happiness. Now, it's certainly undeniable that money means possibility. Those who have more of the former usually have more of the latter. Money provides options. And those who live in dire poverty are typically faced with a distinct lack of options. But above the line of abject poverty and desperation for life's basic needs, there doesn't seem to be any firm correlation between fortune and fulfillment. I've personally known very wealthy people who were tremendously unhappy, and moderately impoverished people who lived with great contentment and even an enviable measure of bliss.

In the very first book of the Harry Potter adventures, the Dark Lord has been in pursuit of an item, known in the American edition of the book as "the Sorcerer's Stone" but in the original British edition as "the Philosopher's Stone," a priceless thing that will turn any metal into gold and give its possessor complete power over aging and death. Dumbledore explains to Harry that the rightful owner of the Stone has turned it over for destruction so that it will never fall into the wrong hands, and that this man has accepted, as a result, the consequences that he will give up all his potentially endless wealth, as well as the deathless and ageless life that he and his wife have enjoyed for hundreds of years because of its powers. Harry is astonished that anyone could ever do such a thing. It seems like too much of a sacrifice to understand. Dumbledore explains to him that the Stone wasn't such a great thing after all, and that even though most people seem to think that unlimited money and endless life on earth would be better than anything else imaginable, they are just wrong about this. Those two things might actually just be the worst things we could ever have (SS 297).

Money, according to the wise Albus Dumbledore, is not a key to the happy life. Neither is having power over death and in that way attaining a humanly contrived everlasting existence. He even says that these things are bad for human beings. Why? I suspect that it is at least in large part because of their diversionary power. Financial wealth and physical security are the ultimate distractions, keeping us from thinking hard about the most important things in life and beyond.

Comfort and superficiality often go together. When we live under no known threats, we normally skim the surface of existence, indulging ourselves in artificial pleasures and pursuing the most unnecessary things, while missing out on some of the truly important experiences that life has to offer. By contrast, people who face the abyss in some way can be goaded by their limits to be more reflective, more philosophical, and much deeper in their experience of each moment, while at the same time seeking more of an understanding of it all.

People with lots of money are very strongly tempted to think they can buy their way to contentment, fulfillment, and happiness. They can easily imagine that money holds the secret to meaning in life. They believe that they've played the main game of human existence and won. And because of this, they feel they can now play any game they want. The problem is that life isn't really a game at all. All of the world is a stage, as Shakespeare reminded us, and life is a drama we enact upon it. Too much money makes us think that what we own or can buy is more important than what we do or can be. Too much security makes us think that we can put off the truly important issues until later. The individual who never thinks of death with any sense of its inevitability rarely thinks of anything truly important, with any sense of its value. A life of seemingly endless entertainments and opportunities would never challenge a person to think deeply and focus on what really matters. It's not that money and security are in themselves bad for us, but if we don't have a proper foundation of values, either of these things can divert us from and tempt us to ignore what really matters.

People who suppose that money, power, fame, or status hold the secret to happiness and meaning in life are always disappointed with the results of their quest. Either they fail to get as much of these things as they desire, in which case they're tremendously disappointed at that fact, or they do get exactly as much as they want and discover to their surprise that real happiness and meaning are just as elusive, in which case they're often distraught. Those who have little of such things can still dream that in them lie the secrets. They can still hope to win a lottery or get plucked from obscurity to star on a reality television show, with book deals, commercials, and movie roles to follow. Those who have experienced great levels of fame, power, and money, and have had the chance to see through the illusions of our world, and yet don't know where else to look, are disillusioned and desperate indeed. Fortunately, we can pick up many hints in Harry's world for exactly where we should search for the things that will indeed satisfy.

THE MIRROR OF ERISED

In his first year as a student at Hogwarts, Harry discovers a magical mirror. It's late at night, and he has been sneaking around in the restricted section of the school library after hours doing some important research. The school custodian, Filch, comes close by looking for intruders, and Harry tries to get away and hide. He sees an open door to a room he's never been in, and he quickly slips inside. In what appears to be an unused classroom, he finds a huge and beautifully ornate mirror (SS 207). Harry looks into the mirror and is shocked by what he sees looking back. He gazes on himself surrounded by ten or more people—but there is no one actually in the room where he is standing. Two of the people in the mirror seem to share some of his physical features. A woman waving at him has his green eyes, and a man has his black, unruly hair. He realizes that they are his mother and father, surrounded by other relatives. They're all waving and smiling at him. This is his extended family, which he's seeing for the very first time ever (SS 209). Harry stands there, just staring, with his hands pressed against the glass, and feels an ache of joy and at the same time a sadness deep in his soul. Suddenly, there is a noise nearby, and he has to leave and get back to his dorm, in accordance with school rules. He promises himself that he'll come back the next day.

The following night, Harry and Ron find the room again together, and Harry shows Ron the mirror. Harry sees his parents once more, right away, but Ron can see only Harry in the mirror, not Harry's family. When Harry steps away so that Ron can get a better look, Ron sees only himself, in his pajamas. But suddenly he looks surprised, and he tells Harry that he sees himself in the mirror as older and as wearing the badge of Hogwarts Head Boy, an honor he had long secretly hoped to receive one day. He also sees himself as Quidditch team captain, and he's holding the Quidditch Cup. Ron wonders whether the mirror shows the future, but Harry points out that this can't be what it does, because he saw his family and they are all dead. Before the boys can figure out what the mirror really reveals, they have to tear themselves away from it and leave the room quickly to avoid getting into trouble.

The third night, Harry goes back to visit the mirror again alone, although Ron had warned him against it. Ron had told Harry that he just had a bad feeling about it. However, Harry can't resist the chance to see his family one more time. He finds the room, arranges himself in front of the mirror, and is greeted by a familiar adult voice behind him. Surprised, he turns to see Headmaster Dumbledore in the room with him. Dumbledore asks Harry if he realizes what the mirror is doing. He calls it "the Mirror of Erised"—which we soon learn is "desire" spelled backward. Harry indicates that he doesn't yet really understand it. The great wizard at first enigmatically remarks that a completely happy person would be able to use it like a regular mirror, seeing himself as he actually is. He then explains more fully that it shows anyone who gazes into it the deepest, most desperate desires of his heart. Harry's deepest desire is to know his family. Ron's deepest desire is, by contrast, to stand out and be accomplished on his own. That's why, when Ron looks into the mirror, he sees himself festooned with awards and dressed as Head Boy of the School.

After explaining all this, Dumbledore warns Harry that the mirror is actually quite dangerous, and that people have wasted away staring into it, not knowing whether what it showed was really possible or not. He concludes by telling Harry that it will soon be moved to a safer location and asks him kindly but firmly not to go looking for it again.

Harry can't help but ask the great Dumbledore what he sees when he looks into it. He replies, to Harry's surprise, that he sees himself holding a pair of nice, thick socks (SS 213–214). Our young wizard is deeply impressed by the entire experience, and yet he is a bit perplexed by this answer to his question. But he lets the matter drop, agrees to what Dumbledore has asked of him, and never goes looking for the mirror again.

Now let's review for a moment how the mirror is supposed to work. Dumbledore has first explained how it functions by saying that a completely happy person would be able to use it like a normal mirror, looking into it and seeing himself exactly as he is. Anyone else will see in it the deepest desire of his heart—he will see what he desperately wants rather than what is. Harry's deepest, most desperate desire is for the family he has never known, and Ron's is to be independent and to excel beyond his high-achieving brothers. Dumbledore claims he sees himself holding a pair of socks. Rowling tells us that when Harry got back to his room and into bed, he began to wonder whether this remark about socks could actually be true. Perhaps the great man was just joking. But even if he was, the joke was very telling. The wise man becomes a happy man by diminishing the gap between his heart's desires and their satisfactions. If only a pair of nice, thick socks stands between you and contentment, you're probably close enough to be considered truly happy already.

The happy man sees himself in the mirror just as he is because he doesn't have unrealized, desperate desires deep in his heart. How does anyone get to such a point? There are, of course, two ways to arrive at this state of being. One is to work hard to satisfy all our deepest desires. The other strategy is to work just as hard to reduce the number of those desires that we have. Most truly happy people attain that ideal state of mind by the use of both these strategies together. They distinguish clearly between genuine, proper desires of the heart and those more fleeting cravings we all have that are much less important. Through a process of gaining increasing self-knowledge and self-discipline, they work to uproot any desires they might have that they know aren't right for them, however strong those cravings might feel. And then they work hard to clarify, refine, and satisfy the remaining desires that they believe are proper and healthy for them to have.

Uprooting improper, useless, or self-destructive desires isn't easy. It requires controlling our imagination, refusing to allow ourselves to dwell on mental pictures of the thing we want that we don't really need or that would be bad for us to have. Sometimes, in order to conquer inappropriate desire, we have to talk it over with a good friend or a close family member. We have to reason things through and remind ourselves what's really in our long-term best interest. One of the most forgotten insights in the modern world is that self-discipline is necessary for self-fulfillment. Happiness is endlessly elusive for the utterly undisciplined mind.

Not every desire should be pursued. The challenge is to sort through them wisely.

We need to notice a couple of things here about our magical mirror. First, the Mirror of Erised does not show a person standing in front of it all of his or her current desires. Ron doesn't see himself surrounded by new, flashy broomsticks and bags of his favorite candy. There are many things Harry wants that don't show up in the mirror when he gazes into it. If it did show all a person's desires, even the happiest individual in the world would see in it all sorts of things other than his or her own image. We all have desires, and properly so. Desires are the seeds of goals, and without goals we cannot live a distinctively human existence. Even the happiest person in the world will have at any given moment some unsatisfied desires. Otherwise, there would be nothing to hope for, aspire to, or look forward to experiencing tomorrow or the day after that. Unsatisfied desire is not in itself a bad thing. It's the foundation and preparation for many good things. It inspires our creativity, goads us into action, and motivates us to persist when the road is tough. Desires are the fuel of life. How we use them and how they affect us are always ultimately up to us. As our great headmaster would say, it all comes down to the choices we make.

The wise person does four things with desires. He works to satisfy good ones. He works just as hard to resist and uproot bad ones. He seeks to keep unimportant desires from taking root at too deep a level in his soul, like weeds that can choke out the beautiful plants that he really wants to have there. And he cultivates, refines, and clarifies the right desires day to day.

Wrong desire comes in three forms. Sometimes, we desire the wrong things, things that would just be harmful or bad for us to have. Harmful desires are wants whose satisfaction would inflict damage on us or on other people around us who don't deserve that harm. Wants and needs are often very different things, and a failure to see the difference can cause havoc in any life. One sort of example would be that of desiring an inappropriate relationship with a coworker. Another example that is quite common in the business world might be a wild and creative entrepreneur's desire to run a large company, when his talents aren't at all organizational or managerial, and the demands of steering such a ship of commerce every day would frustrate him immensely and wreck his family life.

But not all inappropriate forms of desire are a result of wanting the wrong things. At times, we just desire things too strongly—with a fervor or intensity that is simply inappropriate to the particular object of desire. When the felt intensity of our desire is out of step with the true importance of its object, we can be led to do things we really shouldn't do in pursuit of that desire. Young, ambitious people in a new job or career sometimes want promotions and new responsibilities, along with the perks of a higher organizational status, with too much intensity. Beyond a certain point, such intensity can alienate the very people whose support might be necessary for the desired result. Or it can alienate a person from others in his life whose love and support he needs for reasons far greater than professional concerns. Ron's brother Percy Weasley may be an example of a person suffering from such an intense degree of ambition out of control. He has let his ambitions take over his life and turn him against anyone he perceived as standing in his way. And the price that he and his family have had to pay for this is a high one.

Related to this is the third mode of wrong desire. We frequently desire things in too much of a hurry. We want something with too much impatience. We feel like we have to have it now. We're in a huge rush for what might be a good thing at its proper time, but our own sense of timing is very different from what the world is making possible. If a desire you're feeling is too strong or urgent to be patiently pursued, and if its lack of immediate satisfaction is leaving you absolutely unhinged, it's definitely time to reevaluate the way that this desire is functioning in your life. You can take control of it and make it conform to what you know deep down is right. This is always within your power. Choice is destiny, as Dumbledore has taught us. Regardless of how intense our desires might be, we always have some degree of choice over whether and how we might pursue them. Strong desires can feel quite insistent. But we should never allow ourselves to be bullied by them. Wisdom understands all this and seeks to keep its house in order by guiding proper desire and helping us to avoid all these mistakes.

The Mirror of Erised shows only a subcategory of desires—as Dumbledore says, it reveals "the deepest, most desperate desire of our hearts." That can be one thing or many. But whatever is desired at this level stands between a person and a full experience of happiness. That's because, at this level, desire touches love. An object of love is an interesting thing—when you have it you embrace it, and when you lack it you pursue it. A desire at the deepest level in any human soul is just a fundamental need to pursue some particular object of love. This need is born of absence. It is a cry from a vacuum, from a form of inner emptiness, a lack, or a hole that must be filled. It's not the sort of need that allows a sense of contentment, fulfillment, or complete happiness in a person's heart as long as it's unsatisfied. Lesser desires, when they are unsatisfied, need not at all detract from our overall sense of satisfaction or happiness.

I've just used the words "happiness," "contentment," and "fulfillment" in roughly the same ways, along with the concept of satisfaction, but I need to say a few words and draw some quick distinctions among them, for the sake of accuracy in our thinking on these important issues. We often use these terms as if they were just roughly synonymous, but I think they differ in their meaning in some very interesting and insightful ways. By appreciating those differences, we can fine-tune our own understanding of what it will take in our own lives to experience each of them.

Contentment is an emotional acceptance of the present as being what it is. It's fully compatible with a desire for the future to be different. But it's essentially an emotional or attitudinal state of being okay with the present moment. A content person isn't enslaved and bullied by the negative emotions of frustration, irritation, anger, envy, resentment, despair, or regret. Contentment is a form of inner peace. And as such, it's a precondition of free-flowing power. It frees us from the emotional turmoil that often blocks people from moving forward productively. When we understand this, we can see that true contentment isn't the same thing as complacently giving up, acquiescing, or settling for less than the best. It's a strong inner state of harmonious readiness for whatever needs to be done next.

Fulfillment in this world isn't primarily an inner state of mind at all but, by contrast, is both an objective and a subjective process—it is the progressive realization of your potential. To say that a person is fulfilled or that she is experiencing fulfillment in her work is just to say that she is experiencing a progressive realization of her potential for proper self-development and creative contribution. And this is, of course, a very good thing. Related to the objective process of fulfillment is an inner awareness, the feeling of fulfillment, which is also a very good thing. But fulfillment isn't primarily a feeling. It's a dynamic reality first that gives rise to a pleasant subjective experience, or to a baseline of positive feeling, as an important psychological side effect.

Satisfaction can be understood in two senses. In the narrow sense, we can talk about the satisfaction of a particular desire, meaning only that the thing desired comes about or is attained. In the broader sense, we can speak of a person being satisfied or experiencing satisfaction. I think that what this is best understood as meaning involves the coming together of contentment and fulfillment. A satisfied person is content and fulfilled. He accepts the present as being what it is and is also undergoing a progressive realization of his potential. And that involves the ongoing attainment of his best and most important desires.

Happiness can also be understood as a combination of things. It is simply satisfaction plus enjoyment. And enjoyment at the deepest level requires love. It encompasses the delightful sensations of ordinary pleasures as well. But enjoyment at its greatest depth is always tinged and entangled with love. By defining happiness in this way, we can understand it as a comprehensive positive state of human existence. It isn't perfection, but it is what Aristotle believed all of us seek.

Interestingly, it can even be said that happiness is not just a state of being—it's also a state of doing. Aristotle understood it as action in accordance with excellence, or action in harmony with virtue. The happy person is engaged in life as a participant, not just as a spectator. The happy person's life balances doing and being. And there are many things we can never do alone. So the happy person finds some of his greatest fulfillment in doing things with others. That's what friends are for. As I've pointed out earlier, Harry's happiest times are at the Weasley house, engaged in all sorts of antics with Ron and the others (CS 65), as well as on the Quidditch field practicing and playing with his schoolmates, using his talents, and enjoying the process with every fiber of his being. We are given a glimpse into an incredible surge in Harry's feelings when we are told:

It felt wonderful to be back on the Quidditch field. (CS 109)

Harry is often so beset with difficult problems that very few things strike him as feeling wonderful when he is in the process of experiencing them. But this active engagement of talent, energy, and focus on the playing field, with the wind whipping around him and his mates shouting encouragement, touches his heart in that deep place where happiness can gush forth.

If you want to be happy, find something you love and do it with people you love. That seems to be a nearly universal prescription for happiness. Nothing short of this will give us what we really need in this world.

Real happiness is not a feeling, but a way of being and doing that's tied to full life success.

Let's review for just a moment. Based on what we've said so far, we can lay out something like an informal mathematics of happiness, in the broadest and most general sense. With each term understood in the way just explained, we have:

Contentment = An emotional acceptance of the present
Fulfillment = A progressive realization of our potential
Satisfaction = Contentment + Fulfillment
Enjoyment = Pleasure + Love
Happiness = Satisfaction + Enjoyment

Contentment is a passive state of mind that often takes a great deal of activity to achieve, and fulfillment is clearly active in its participatory engagement. Pleasure is a receptive and often transient state of mind, however important it is, while love is by contrast a much deeper commitment. The happiness that we all seek magically encompasses all these things. That's why I've tried to stress in previous books, like *The Art of Achievement* and *True Success,* that achievement or success in something that we love is so deeply relevant to happiness. When Harry wins an important Quidditch match in his first year at Hogwarts, he experiences contentment, fulfillment, enjoyment, love, comradeship, and the distinctive feeling of a job well done. We are told that:

He couldn't ever remember feeling happier. He'd really done something to be proud of now . . . (SS 225)

The endlessly insightful philosopher Aristotle was to my knowledge the first great diagnostician of the human condition to realize that happiness is indeed a kind of activity in accordance with virtue or excellence. We each have our own distinctive forms of potential excellence, and so there are different activities that will give us the sense of happiness that Harry so enjoyed. The key to a happy life is discovering the proper activity, or range of activities, that will allow each of us to find that sweet spot and hit it.

The Mirror of Erised, as explained by Dumbledore, teaches us that it isn't possible to be completely happy while having deep, desperate, unsatisfied desires of the heart. The wise person who finds himself in this condition will work to satisfy those desires of the heart that he can satisfy properly, and then alter or remove any that he can't. This will involve different things for different people, and the contours of happiness will be as varied as those who experience it, but the main formula and the main ingredients will always remain the same.

It's probably true that Dumbledore was kidding about the socks. But when it comes to the headmaster, like Harry, we're never really sure what's afoot.

THE MEANING OF LIFE

What is the meaning of life? That's a question human beings have asked for a very long time. Philosophy professors debate it in their academic journals, theologians ruminate over it in their books, and ordinary people worry about it now and then. Everyone wants a good life. And it's hard to see how anything can be good if it's meaningless. So the question gets raised again and again. It will not go away.

I've suggested in two previous books—*If Aristotle Ran General Motors* and the immensely fun project *Philosophy for Dummies*—that the one answer to the question of meaning in life that runs through all the greatest philosophies and religious traditions in our world, and that happens in my opinion to be the best answer ever arrived at, is that the meaning of life is as simple to state as it is hard to achieve. The meaning of life is creative love, or loving creativity. We're here in the world to make a positive difference for the other people around us, as well as in our own lives. We're here to discover our talents, develop those talents, and deploy them into the world for the good of others as well as ourselves. A life not centered on creative love, or loving creativity, can never be a fully meaningful existence. One guided by love can embody and experience the deepest meanings that this existence holds for us.

At the end of his first year at Hogwarts, Harry has an important conversation with Headmaster Dumbledore. The wise old wizard is trying to explain some of what has just happened to Harry, who has suffered through a frightening confrontation with evil, as embodied in the nefarious Professor Quirrell, a secret cohort of Voldemort, and has somehow emerged victorious. Dumbledore harkens back to Harry's infancy for a full perspective on the present and reflects on the fact that his mother had sacrificed her life to save his. He explains that this sort of love leaves a mark on a person, a form of lasting protection that people driven by shallow ambition, greed, and hatred can never understand. That love blindsided Quirrell and Voldemort and blocked their attempt to kill Harry (SS 299).

Toward the end of book five, *The Order of the Phoenix*, and year five, Dumbledore has another conversation with Harry, where he reveals many extremely important things to the young wizard. Harry has just expressed very serious doubts about whether he has sufficient power to face Voldemort again in the future and survive. It seems to him clear that the Dark Lord wields spectacular powers he will never have. Dumbledore tells his young friend that he has a power Voldemort can't even understand. The evil wizard had most recently attempted to enter Harry's mind and fully possess him and had failed. In one of the most intriguing and enigmatic passages of all the books, Harry's mentor and guide explains to the young man that he made it though this ordeal because of his heart—not the anatomical organ, of course, but the metaphorical site and conduit of that greatest power of all, love (OP 843–844).

The most amazing magical power in Harry's heart—in Harry's life—is the power of love. His mother's love for him defeated evil and saved his life long ago, and his love for others can continue to overcome evil now and in the future. Dumbledore makes it clear that once having been on the receiving end of this force in its full measure is often enough to provide a key for unlocking it and using it yourself.

Ultimately, the deepest truth is simple. The choice to love is itself the most effective key to the power of love. So again we come back to the importance of choice.

For Christmas during their fifth year as classmates, Hermione gives Harry a book that's like a daily diary but is also enchanted to speak clever little motivational slogans every time he opens it (OP 501, 541). She clearly thinks her talented friend could use some help with motivation. But, fortunately, the single greatest motivator in the world is love. As we've seen, Harry does extraordinarily brave things when motivated by love. Whenever he realizes what's at stake in a dangerous situation and understands that someone or something he loves greatly is being threatened with destruction or even harm, he leaps into action, regardless of danger, and despite all the odds. Dumbledore has assured Harry that he has some sort of special and deeply significant access to this power of love. It's both a practical power and a mystical one, according to the headmaster. Fortunately, we all have access to it. And it's the one power that gives our lives meaning.

It's also the power that contemporary business needs the most. When we remember love, we recall the real needs of the people we serve, or that we could serve. Current General Electric CEO Jeff Immelt has sketched out a new path for this great company that involves in many ways a return to its roots. What do people need? What would improve the lives of everyone around us? Clean energy, environmentally friendly products, advanced nanotechnology, and cures for many diseases that have resisted our efforts thus far and that consequently have bedeviled the human condition—these things and others like them should be our focus as we move forward. How can we help others? How can we leave the planet a better place for our having been here?

You don't need to run a huge corporation like GE in order to be in a position to ask such questions and do something about them. You can do this wherever you are positioned in life. If you're a financial advisor, a retailer, a manager in a small business, someone in sales, a frontline worker in a larger enterprise, someone's assistant, or a stay-at-home parent doing volunteer work in the community, you can make your proper mark each day if you guide your steps by love. Rather than being a "soft value" inappropriate for the rough and tumble of business, love is and always has been the driving force behind the best, most sustainable achievements in business and in life. More business leaders need to be asking these questions about real service, grounded in the highest form of love, and encouraging all their associates to think in these terms as well.

When we can experience at least some small measure of the love and compassion shown by Jesus, Gandhi, the Buddha, and other shining lights of humanity redeemed and triumphant, in our work roles as well

---

Love is the deepest force for change; when embraced fully, it shapes all that we're able to do.

---

as in our private lives, then we will move forward to the proper greatness of which we are capable and to which life calls us. Anything less is a waste of our time and a real tragedy on a cosmic scale. Love is the key to a meaningful life, and it's the only path to a truly great business career. Any pseudosophisticated, allegedly pragmatic, "worldly-wise" cynicism that resists this insight or denigrates its value should be recognized as an insidious obstacle to real happiness and humanly appropriate success. It's time for us in the world of business to escape the posturing and illicit constraints of the dominantly militant imagery that keeps us so far away from the proper roots and ends of business. Yes, we may at times have to fight evil and all the negative forces it spawns, and, like Harry, we may face that more often than we'd like. But the only way to do that properly is to be guided by ethics grounded in love. Love is the great liberator, our deepest source of strength, and the only reliable directive force on earth. Properly understood and consistently lived, a deeply wise, rational, and creative love is an amazing, nearly magical guide for the business future, as well as for each of us as human beings.

Dumbledore lives a life guided and thoroughly ordered by love. And because of that, he is an embodiment of the ancient insight that "perfect love casts out fear." He is fearless in any situation because he is thoroughly motivated and supported by the extraordinary power of love. This is a force and a support that the wicked Voldemort can never have. Love is all about truth, beauty, goodness, and unity. It's a form of caring and commitment that honors all these things. And it holds other human beings in the highest respect, always remembering their intrinsic value and potential dignity. Evil, by contrast, is about greed, hate, and the negation of these transcendental virtues and attitudes—whether the evil person ever recognizes that fact or not. The real story behind all the Harry Potter stories is simply, and profoundly, a story about the power of love. Understanding and living that power every day will help us to find the real magic all around us, in business and in life.

There are many times in Harry's experience when the power of love flows through him and helps him to fight and conquer evil. The most surprising example of this might be found at the beginning of *The Goblet of Fire*, when the dreaded dementors attack Dudley Dursley and Harry. Harry saves Dudley's life—not because of any particular fondness he has for the boy who has made his existence so difficult, but because of the general love he has for what is good and right, and so for protecting any person around him who is unjustly attacked by the forces of evil. The fundamental power of love that's motivating Harry is sufficiently strong to help him overcome deep resentments and personal dislikes when it's really necessary. But, despite such a striking example, Harry's overall character at that time is not yet sufficiently ordered by wisdom, virtue, and love that he is able to live as well as, and respond to all things as appropriately and consistently as, his great mentor, Dumbledore.

As long as Harry is buffeted about frequently by contrary emotions like quick anger, frustration, fear, irritation, hostility, and resentment, his life can't serve as a perfect conduit for love, and he ends up at cross-purposes with himself, engaging in various forms of self-defeating behavior. After one outburst of his in Dolores Umbridge's class, Professor McGonagall confronts him and sharply commands him to get control of himself (OP 319). Even Professor Snape, who on Dumbledore's orders is at one point training Harry to resist the mind control that is often being attempted over him by Voldemort, explains that the young man needs greater self-discipline in his life. He tells Harry that people who are weak and can't control their emotions will never be able to stand up to and resist this strong a form of evil. He then orders Harry to master himself, control his anger, and discipline his mind (OP 536).

In the end, Snape cannot succeed in teaching self-discipline to Harry, perhaps because he doesn't seem to practice it consistently himself. A history of bad relations between Snape and Harry's father long ago still apparently infects the professor's emotions and attitudes and prevents him from ever treating Harry fairly or with any measure of kindness. As far as Harry can see, Snape may claim intellectually to understand the importance of self-discipline, he may preach it to Harry, and he even may practice it in many other departments of his life, but his apparent inability to display it in his dealings with Harry can easily make all his words about it ring hollow to his reluctant student. The biggest part of what we say is always what we do. And we should never allow ourselves to forget that.

The professor is attempting to stress to Harry the vital importance of the quality of self-discipline because of the fact that, without it, he will continue to be vulnerable to his evil opponent. It is precisely this sort of self-discipline—the virtue often forgotten in the modern world—that allows the power of real love to flow uninhibitedly through a person's feelings, attitudes, and actions. The passions that would derail us, the negative emotions that would deceive us and defeat us, must be controlled. And this is the sort of control that is pervasively neglected in recent times. It's a skill to which Rowling wants to recall us.

It certainly seems to the casual reader of these stories that if Snape could just come to practice what he is preaching, the old hurts and resentments from his boyhood would be rendered powerless to keep him from displaying a full allegiance to good and a full manifestation of the power of love in his own life. Of course, it could be that all the hostility, anger, and resentment that Snape shows toward Harry, as well as all the insults and apparent cruelty that he directs at the young man, are all part of an elaborate ruse, meant to deceive the forces of evil into thinking that he is secretly still one of them. And if this turns out to be the ultimate story about the snarling professor, then he will have demonstrated an extraordinary degree of self-discipline and consistency in playing his role convincingly. But, even if it's true, this is not a self-discipline and consistency that Harry or his friends are in a position to see, or even suspect, as they end their sixth year at Hogwarts. So from Harry's point of view, Snape is the worst possible person to preach and teach self-discipline. He is consequently unable to learn from him. If Harry nonetheless can manage somehow to attain a greater measure of self-discipline in his own emotions, thoughts, and actions, the unusually powerful force of love flowing through his life because of the sacrifice of his mother will be even more formidable and unconquerable by the evil represented by his nemesis.

Love, it turns out, is the most fundamental source of the great good that each of us can do in this world. It is the reason for our existence and is the meaning of our lives. We each build particular meanings throughout our lives, in accordance with our response to this primordial force, but we are born into a world where the power of love is already present as a foundation for meaningful living. Rowling wants to give us some sense of that, but without ever fully explaining it. But then, this should be no surprise. Who can fully explain it? It is one of the great mysteries of life. And it is more powerful than any other form of magic. A discovery of this power, and a deeper appreciation for it, will increasingly strengthen Harry in the classic virtues, prepare him for his distinctive mission, further enrich his already strong relationships, and bring him the most meaningful life possible. It can do the same for each of us as well.

If a mature, grown-up Harry Potter ran General Electric, or any other organization in the worlds of business, government, community affairs, or the nonprofit sector, I believe that we'd see a form of leadership grounded in the classic virtues, ethically courageous in its actions, and both motivated and directed by love. The results, I suspect, would be magical indeed.

I don't know how the Muggles manage without magic.
—*Rubeus Hagrid, Keeper of Grounds and Keys*

INDEX